International Political Economy Series

General Editor: **Timothy M. Shaw**, Professor of Political Science and International Development Studies, Dalhousie University, Halifax, Nova Scotia

Titles include:

Francis Adams, Satya Dev Gupta and Kidane Mengisteab (*editors*)
GLOBALIZATION AND THE DILEMMAS OF THE STATE IN THE SOUTH

Preet S. Aulakh and Michael G. Schechter (*editors*)
RETHINKING GLOBALIZATION(S)
From Corporate Transnationalism to Local Interventions

Elizabeth De Boer-Ashworth
THE GLOBAL POLITICAL ECONOMY AND POST-1989 CHANGE
The Place of the Central European Transition

Edward A. Comor (*editor*)
THE GLOBAL POLITICAL ECONOMY OF COMMUNICATION

Helen A. Garten
US FINANCIAL REGULATION AND THE LEVEL PLAYING FIELD

Randall D. Germain (*editor*)
GLOBALIZATION AND ITS CRITICS
Perspectives from Political Economy

Barry K. Gills (*editor*)
GLOBALIZATION AND THE POLITICS OF RESISTANCE

Takashi Inoguchi
GLOBAL CHANGE
A Japanese Perspective

Jomo K.S. and Shyamala Nagaraj (*editors*)
GLOBALIZATION VERSUS DEVELOPMENT

Stephen D. McDowell
GLOBALIZATION, LIBERALIZATION AND POLICY CHANGE
A Political Economy of India's Communications Sector

Ronaldo Munck and Peter Waterman (*editors*)
LABOUR WORLDWIDE IN THE ERA OF GLOBALIZATION
Alternative Union Models in the New World Order

Craig N. Murphy (*editor*)
EGALITARIAN POLITICS IN THE AGE OF GLOBALIZATION

Michael Niemann
A SPATIAL APPROACH TO REGIONALISM IN THE GLOBAL ECONOMY

Ted Schrecker (*editor*)
SURVIVING GLOBALISM
The Social and Environmental Challenges

Leonard Seabrooke
US POWER IN INTERNATIONAL FINANCE
The Victory of Dividends

Timothy J. Sinclair and Kenneth P. Thomas (*editors*)
STRUCTURE AND AGENCY IN INTERNATIONAL CAPITAL MOBILITY

Kendall Stiles (*editor*)
GLOBAL INSTITUTIONS AND LOCAL EMPOWERMENT
Competing Theoretical Perspectives

Caroline Thomas and Peter Wilkin (*editors*)
GLOBALIZATION AND THE SOUTH

Kenneth P. Thomas
CAPITAL BEYOND BORDERS
States and Firms in the Auto Industry, 1960–94

Geoffrey R. D. Underhill (*editor*)
THE NEW WORLD ORDER IN INTERNATIONAL FINANCE

Amy Verdun
EUROPEAN RESPONSES TO GLOBALIZATION AND FINANCIAL MARKET INTEGRATION
Perceptions of Economic and Monetary Union in Britain, France and Germany

Robert Wolfe
FARM WARS
The Political Economy of Agriculture and the International Trade Regime

International Political Economy Series
Series Standing Order ISBN 0–333–71708–2 hardcover
Series Standing Order ISBN 0–333–71110–6 paperback
(*outside North America only*)

You can receive future titles in this series as they are published by placing a standing order. Please contact your bookseller or, in case of difficulty, write to us at the address below with your name and address, the title of the series and one of the ISBNs quoted above.

Customer Services Department, Macmillan Distribution Ltd, Houndmills, Basingstoke, Hampshire RG21 6XS, England

Structure and Agency in International Capital Mobility

Edited by

Timothy J. Sinclair
University of Warwick and Harvard University

and

Kenneth P. Thomas
University of Missouri – St Louis

palgrave

First published 2001 by
PALGRAVE
Houndmills, Basingstoke, Hampshire RG21 6XS and
175 Fifth Avenue, New York, N.Y. 10010
Companies and representatives throughout the world

PALGRAVE is the new global academic imprint of St. Martin's Press LLC Scholarly and Reference Division and Palgrave Publishers Ltd (formerly Macmillan Press Ltd).

ISBN 0–333–72553–0 hardback
ISBN 0–333–72554–9 paperback

This book is printed on paper suitable for recycling and made from fully managed and sustained forest sources.

A catalogue record for this book is available from the British Library.

Library of Congress Cataloging-in-Publication Data
Structure and agency in international capital mobility / edited by Timothy J. Sinclair and Kenneth P. Thomas.
p. cm. — (International political economy series)
Includes bibliographical references and index.
ISBN 0–333–72553–0
1. Capital movements. 2. International relations. 3. International finance. I. Sinclair, Timothy J. II. Thomas, Kenneth P. III. Series.

HG3891 .S77 2001
332'.042—dc21

2001021748

10 9 8 7 6 5 4 3 2 1
10 09 08 07 06 05 04 03 02 01

Printed in Great Britain by Antony Rowe Ltd, Chippenham, Wiltshire

Contents

Part III Responses to International Capital Mobility

List of Figures and Tables

Figures

Tables

Acknowledgements

The editors and publishers would like to thank the following for permission to use their copyright material in this volume. Chapter 3 by Kathleen R. McNamara is reprinted from Kathleen R. McNamara, *The Currency of Ideas*, Copyright (©) 1998 by Cornell University. Used by permission of the publisher, Cornell University Press. A longer version of Chapter 9 by Eric Helleiner was published previously as 'Globalization and Haute Finance: Deja Vu?' in K. McRobbie and Kari Polanyi Levitt (eds), *Karl Polanyi in Vienna: The Contemporary Significance of the Great Transformation* (Montreal: Black Rose Books, 2000), pp. 12–31. Reprinted with the kind permission of Black Rose Books, Montreal, *http://www.web.net/blackrosebooks*, from one of a series of books published by the Karl Polanyi Institute of Political Economy (Concordia University, Montreal) which also grants permission. Some portions of Chapter 9 also appeared in *Studies in Political Economy* (Helleiner, 1995a).

Notes on the Contributors

David M. Andrews is Associate Professor of Politics and International Relations at Scripps College, Claremont, California, and Director of the European Union Centre of California at the Claremont Colleges. His research into the implications of international capital mobility has been published in *International Organization, International Studies Quarterly, Policy Sciences,* and elsewhere.

Eric Helleiner is Associate Professor in the Department of Political Studies, Trent University, Peterborough, Canada. He is co-editor of *Nation-States and Money: The Past, Present and Future of National Currencies* (Routledge, 1999), editor of *The World of Money: The Political Economy of International Capital Mobility* (special issue of *Policy Sciences*, 1994) and author of *States and the Reemergence of Global Finance: From Bretton Woods to the 1990s* (Cornell University Press, 1994) as well as various articles on global finance and international political economy. He is currently completing a book on the historical origins and future of national currencies.

Jennifer Holt-Dwyer is Assistant Professor in the Department of Political Science at Hunter College, City University of New York. Her previous work has focused on the feedback between structure and agency in explaining the changing dynamics of financial market reform in Japan in the postwar period. She is currently part of a team of Japanese and American scholars examining US–Japan relations in the post-Cold War era.

Kathleen R. McNamara is Assistant Professor of Politics and International Affairs at Princeton University. Dr McNamara is the author of *The Currency of Ideas: Monetary Politics in the European Union* (Cornell University Press, 1998) and articles on Germany's role in Europe and the politics of exchange rates.

Jonathon W. Moses received his PhD in 1995 from the Department of Political Science, University of California, Los Angeles (UCLA). Since 1993 he has been employed in the University of Trondheim's (NTNU) Department of Sociology and Political Science, where he is currently an associate professor. Jonathon has publications in several international journals, including *Politics and Society, Review of International Political*

Economy, and the *Journal of European Public Policy*, in addition to several book chapters. His forthcoming books include *Open States in the Global Economy: The Political Economy of Small-State Macroeconomic Management* and *The End of Scandinavian Social Democracy?* (co-edited with Robert Geyer and Christine Ingebritsen).

Tony Porter is Associate Professor of Political Science at McMaster University, Hamilton, Ontario, Canada. He is the author of *States, Markets and Regimes in Global Finance* (Basingstoke: Macmillan – now Palgrave, 1993) and the coeditor, with A. Claire Cutler and Virginia Haufler, of *Private Authority and International Affairs* (Albany, NY: SUNY Press, 1999).

Timothy J. Sinclair received his PhD in 1995 from York University, Toronto. He is Lecturer in International Political Economy at the University of Warwick in England, and External Associate at the Centre for International and Security Studies, York University, Toronto. His publications include (with Robert W. Cox) *Approaches to World Order* (Cambridge University Press, 1996), book chapters, and articles in *Environment and Planning C: Government and Policy, Policy Sciences*, and *Review of International Political Economy*. He is the editor (with Martin Hewson) of *Approaches to Global Governance Theory* (Albany, NY: SUNY Press, 1999). A former New Zealand Department of the Treasury official, Dr Sinclair's research interests are focused on governance issues in global finance, digital capitalism, and international relations theory. He is currently completing a book on bond rating and the global economy.

Kenneth P. Thomas is Associate Professor of Political Science, and Fellow in the Centre for International Studies, at the University of Missouri–St Louis. His work focuses on capital mobility and its consequences. He is the author of *Capital Beyond Borders: States and Firms in the Automobile Industry, 1960–1994*, an editor of the *International Political Economy Yearbook*, and recently completed *Competing for Capital: Europe and North America in a Global Era* (Georgetown University Press).

Michael C. Webb is Associate Professor of Political Science at the University of Victoria, Victoria, B.C., Canada. His research focuses on the implications of capital mobility and the globalization of financial markets for national economic policy and international cooperation. He is the author of *The Political Economy of Policy Coordination: International Adjustment Since 1945* (Cornell University Press).

List of Abbreviations

APA	advance pricing agreement
AMUE	Association for Monetary Union in Europe
BIS	Bank for International Settlements
BOJ	Bank of Japan
CPI	comparable profit interval
CUP	comparable uncontrolled prices
CWI	commensurate with income attributable to the intangible
EMS	European Monetary System
ERM	exchange rate mechanism (Europe)
EU	European Union
FCC	foreign-controlled corporations
FDI	foreign direct investment
GAAP	generally accepted accounting principles
GAO	General Accounting Office (US)
GATT	General Agreement on Tariffs and Trade
GDP	gross domestic product
ICM	international capital mobility
IMF	International Monetary Fund
IPE	international political economy
IR	international relations
IRS	Internal Revenue Service (US)
JGB	Japanese Government Bond
KWS	Keynesian welfare state
LDC	less-developed country
LBO	Leveraged Buyout
MNC	multinational corporation
MOF	Ministry of Finance (Japan)
NAFTA	North American Free Trade Agreement
NIC	newly industrializing country
OECD	Organization for Economic Cooperation and Development
S&P	Standard & Poor's
SEA	Single European Act
SEC	Securities and Exchange Commission (US)
TNC	transnational corporation
TRA	Tax Reform Act of 1986 (US)

UK	United Kingdom
US	United States
USCC	United States-controlled corporations

Structure and Agency in International Capital Mobility: An Introduction

Kenneth P. Thomas and Timothy J. Sinclair

A sea change is happening in front of our eyes. From a world concerned with strategic weapons and the risks of mutual annihilation, a new world is emerging in which quite different forces loom large in the communal consciousness. In this order, resources and the jobs and prosperity they produce have for the most part – at least in the West – pushed security matters firmly into second place. Like the bombs and missiles of the Cold War, these resources and how they behave produce anxiety and competitiveness amongst the nations of the world and their peoples. Unlike the weapons of the past, though, these economic and productive resources involve a much wider field of actors – not just states, but businesses, banks, stockmarkets – about which comparatively little is known in an international relations context.[1]

This volume is intended to increase our knowledge of the constraints posed by mobile resources over our political choices and expand our understanding of the agents involved in those constraints. Specifically, the group of younger scholars who have contributed to this volume wanted to establish a more realistic understanding of what the world is up against today and, as a consequence, destroy the myth that the constraint of international capital mobility is so complete that no options are available other than the surrender of any democratic ambitions to the dictates of global capital.

In this introduction, we discuss globalization and explain why the issue of capital mobility is the more focused and politically consequential issue upon which to focus analysis. International capital mobility is then tentatively defined and some of the major concerns it raises are identified. The issue of structure and how it relates to agency are subsequently discussed. The purpose of this introduction is to undermine the idea that the structure of international capital mobility is always necessarily determining of outcomes.

Decomposing globalization

'Globalization' was the buzzword of the 1990s, and it is a fair bet it will continue to be a hot topic well into the twenty-first century. Like 'interdependence' before it, however, it suffers from a great deal of imprecision and its true meaning is highly contested (Jones, 1995, p. 3).

Depending on one's view of what globalization *is*, certain evaluations tend to follow. At an economic level, it combines promises of increased economic efficiency with likely problematic distributional consequences. At a cultural level, Benjamin Barber (1995) has written of its homogenizing effects (Hollywood, McDonald's, and so forth) and the resistance to even national governance in the name of smaller communities. One element of this homogenization may be more desirable in terms of the wider, if not yet global, acceptance of norms of democracy and respect for human rights.

Because of the great diversity of definitions, we argue that the notion of globalization should be unpacked. Of the many factors thrown into its definition, we suggest that increasing capital mobility is by far the most significant and causes the most change. While the growth of international trade is clearly important already, and convergence in global values may become so in the future, we believe that the far more explosive and innovative growth of capital mobility has the most impact on governments' policy options and the relative bargaining strength of labour and capital (for one application of the latter, see Kurzer, 1993).

Another reason we focus on capital mobility is that it makes it possible to cut the Gordian knot of 'globalization *vs* regionalization'. Whether we are moving towards a world of three (competing? hostile?) blocs or a truly globalized economy, it is clear that both types of economic integration are characterized by the growth of capital mobility. While it is often debated whether regional economic integration is a stepping-stone to global free trade, or is trade-diverting and an obstacle to the GATT/WTO process, the removal of tariff barriers that characterizes both globalization and regionalization in itself increases capital mobility (Thomas, 1997, and this volume).

Moreover, once such secondary debates are swept away by focusing on capital mobility, it becomes possible, indeed necessary, to see the distributional consequences of the patterns associated with increased capital mobility. We are no longer dealing with a diffuse notion ('globalization'), but with a concept that applies to both global and regional economic integration and which, moreover, has a well-defined meaning and developed theory explaining its distributional consequences. Since these consequences are generally inegalitarian, keeping them in the foreground via a discussion of capital mobility rather than globalization makes it impossible to sweep this problem under the rug, as it were.

Capital mobility and its consequences

What is capital mobility? It is the capacity to move resources between different (not necessarily national) territories as determined by owners or controllers of that capital. The greater the number of alternative locations which can be regarded as substitutes for each other, the higher the degree of capital mobility. This refers not to actual capital flows between states, which are only a symptom of capital mobility, but to the *capacity* for resources to move (Andrews, 1994; Thomas, 1997). Even in the absence of actual movements of capital, the ability of capital to move may be anticipated and action taken by governments to meet any perceived policy expectations on the part of the owners and controllers of capital. Capital movements can, therefore, be linked to relational or direct power of the 'A gets B to do what B would not have otherwise done' formula, whereas capital mobility implies the much more subtle and important form of power that has come to be known as structural power, in which the expectations of the resource-rich are anticipated by the resource-poor.

What are the consequences of (renewed?)[2] capital mobility? The contributors to this volume have different answers to this question. Other studies have hotly contested the idea that international capital mobility is as important as some of the popular accounts have proclaimed (Hirst and Thompson, 1996). At the minimum, we can say that few pressures impinge on the policy choices of national states to the extent that capital mobility does. Crises like the Mexican peso devaluation of 1994/95 and the more recent financial crises in East Asia, Russia and Brazil have made office-holders, officials and their constituents aware that their competence is under scrutinty beyond the confines of conventional political interests. But how far does this go and in what circumstances is international capital mobility crucial? These are questions for research and the chapters in this volume are an effort at addressing these.

Capital mobility does cause major problems for the established basis of political decision-making. As things stand, for most of this century and certainly since the 1930s, national policy autonomy has been the preserve of territorial states. With this potentially compromised and with macro and microeconomic policy open to the effects of the structural power of capital, the legitimacy of states as decision-making and deal-making institutions seems open to question. If this is so, major problems of direction and control are likely in the future for states, and we are likely to witness considerable institutional innovation in the legitimacy vacuum. Those who will lose out from this state of affairs are the skilled and semi-skilled workers who benefitted from the postwar settlement. It is their security which is now vulnerable as direct investment decisions are made with a much greater set of locations in mind, and as portfolio investment becomes increasingly volatile and aware of its capacity to exit as financial markets become more liquid around the world.

Structure and agency

A characteristic of much of the contemporary writing on globalization is that it tends to assume that structure, such as the capacity of capital to exit, is overwhelming and prohibits any effective response. We think this ignores the empirical evidence. The competencies of agents certainly vary and perfect information about policy and economic conditions does not exist. And agents, including states, do look for ways to control their own fates (Garrett, 1998; Watson, 1999). Rather than an equilibrium in which structure seems to determine all individual actions, and agency simply follows structure, we have tended to assume that structures such as international capital mobility are constituted by the practices and self-understanding of agents themselves, who have in turn been created by structures (Wendt, 1987, p. 359). We are interested in understanding both how capital mobility affects states and how states respond to it, but also in how capital mobility (the structure) was recreated by states and how the role of particular agents makes the structure more (or less) effective as a constraint. All this implies a desire to understand the origins of capital mobility and its inner relations, as well as the potential it contains for its own transformation. The constraint of structure on agency is but one step in our investigation and one we consider has been undertaken elsewhere.

Plan of the book

The chapters which follow can be grouped into three broad themes. David Andrews, Jennifer Holt-Dwyer and Kathleen McNamara consider the effect of capital mobility as a cause of convergence among economies. The contributions of Jonathon Moses, Timothy Sinclair and Kenneth Thomas focus on expanding the agenda of studies of capital mobility. Michael Webb, Tony Porter and Eric Helleiner examine the responses to the increasing mobility of capital, in particular the possibilities for re-regulation.

Andrews brings Wendt's (1987) agent–structure analysis to bear on the co-evolution of states (agents) and international financial markets (structure) in the area of Economic and Monetary Union in the EU. He shows how the constraining effects of increasing capital mobility led European states, particularly France, to conceive of monetary union as a way to augment *effective* policy autonomy. Holt-Dwyer argues that financial regulatory changes in Japan are a product of a *competitive* dynamic in response to increasing capital mobility. This contrasts with the downward harmonization of tariffs in the postwar period which, she suggests, were the result of *cooperation* among states. McNamara approaches the European case from a different tack than Andrews (and especially in contrast with Frieden, 1991b), suggesting that capital mobility is by no means sufficient to explain the preferences of European multinational firms, or of governments. She argues that we need to pay greater attention to the uncertainty surrounding economic policy, as well as to the ideas that shape actors' understanding of their stake in capital mobility.

Moses argues that increasing capital mobility has both reduced monetary policy autonomy and hurt tax bases through the threat of capital flight. This has forced governments to rely more heavily on debt to finance the welfare state, as Moses shows for Sweden. He argues this approach will have inegalitarian distributional consequences favouring holders of mobile assets in the long run. Sinclair contends that understanding international capital mobility requires an appreciation of it as a social process or institution, rather than as a spontaneous occurrence, emphasizing the key enforcement institutions that make capital mobility possible. He illustrates the social construction of capital mobility and its implications by reference to his research on the role of debt-rating agencies in the global capital markets. Thomas argues that discussions of capital mobility have disproportionately focused on the mobility of financial capital, and not enough on foreign direct investment. His contribution seeks to bring both forms of capital mobility under a single rubric, while at the same time specifying the differences between the two forms.

Webb's contribution demonstrates the difficulties the United States had in trying to introduce new rules to reduce transfer pricing abuse by transnational corporations. He shows that, while the USA was not constrained directly by threats to disinvest, it was ultimately deterred from making major changes by its desire to maintain the structure of international capital mobility it had done so much to establish. Porter sees the US transfer pricing changes as more successful than does Webb, and also sees banking regulators as successful in strengthening international bank supervision (capital adequacy standards, and so on). Since this stands in contrast to the lack of success in controlling foreign-exchange transactions through a Tobin tax or similar mechanism, he argues that we should not see a single structure of capital mobility, in sharp contrast especially to Andrews. Helleiner argues that Karl Polanyi's analysis of 'countermovements' to *laissez-faire* economics is just as relevant today as when Polanyi wrote. He suggests that a multi-layered reaction may eventually lead to the imposition of the Tobin tax, perhaps catalyzed by major currency instability.

Together, these contributions enhance our understanding of the phenomona associated with increasing capital mobility. We hope this volume will encourage more work on these issues of great practical as well as theoretical significance.

We would like to thank the International Studies Association and the Council on European Studies for their financial support of the workshop at Princeton University that led to this book. Kathleen McNamara took the lead role in organizing that conference, for which we are eternally grateful. We would also like to thank IPE Series Editor Tim Shaw for helping us through this process.

Notes

1 Two recent volumes which address these issues are Cutler *et al.* (eds) (1999) and Hewson and Sinclair (eds) (1999).

2 While some argue that contemporary 'globalization' is only a return to pre-1914 patterns (notably Hirst and Thompson, 1996), others contend that growth rates of capital movements (as distinct from capital mobility; on this distinction see Andrews, 1994, and Thomas, 1997) are far higher in the post-1973 period than the pre-1914 era (Pollins, 1993).

Part I

International Capital Mobility and Convergence

1

Financial Deregulation and the Origins of EMU: The French Policy Reversal of 1983

David M. Andrews

As this chapter was being written in July 1998, the governments of the member states of the European Union officially formed a European Central Bank to oversee the planned introduction of a single European currency. The creation of this supranational institution is among the final steps prior to the introduction of Economic and Monetary Union (EMU), a project that has been well over thirty years in the making.[1] These developments are nothing less than extraordinary. If successful, this exceedingly ambitious policy experiment will have defied very widespread skepticism from official and academic circles alike.

While it is true that some other regions of the world are deepening economic and, to a lesser extent, political linkages (Mansfield and Milner, 1997), no other group of states – and certainly no other group of advanced industrialized nations – is seriously contemplating a transfer of national policy-making authority on a scale even remotely approaching monetary unification. Of course, national monetary independence is not an intrinsically necessary property of statehood; indeed, the trappings and powers associated with sovereignty have evolved considerably since the emergence of the concept, traditionally associated with the Peace of Westphalia (Thomson and Krasner, 1989; Cohen, 1998). Nevertheless, jurisdictional authority over monetary policy has been a major source of both practical and symbolic power among the sovereign states of Europe, especially since the rise of central banking in the late eighteenth and nineteenth centuries (see, for example Goodman, 1992, chapters 1 and 2, and Helleiner, 1995c). In short, EMU is at odds with the standard array of economic policy choices normally thought to engage political leaders.

This chapter seeks to address these developments from the perspective of a structural theory of international monetary relations; at the same time, careful examination of the emergence of EMU provides an opportunity to assess the strengths and weaknesses of the structural approach. Limitations of space will not permit either of these projects to be comprehensive; the chapter therefore focuses on one episode that was critical to the recent consolidation of plans to seek Europe's monetary unification, namely the reversal of French economic policies beginning in 1983. An explanation of this choice of cases follows, together with a survey of essential features of the structural approach. The French case is then examined in more detail, before turning at last to an assessment of the explanatory value of structural theory. The chapter concludes that while helpful – perhaps even essential – to an understanding of this episode, structural theory is as yet too underdeveloped to provide a comprehensive explanation. Indeed, skepticism is justified as to whether structural theory (in isolation) can be fully adequate to the task of historical explanation.

Financial deregulation and the emergence of EMU

The existence of a connection between the emergence of EMU and changes in the financial regime of the European Union is widely recognized. Standard accounts of these developments suggest that European financial deregulation during the late 1980s increased official interest in monetary union as an alternative to exchange-rate management under the European Monetary System or EMS (Padoa-Schioppa, 1987; Eichengreen, 1996). In particular, implementation of the Single European Act's provisions for the progressive development of a unified European financial area increased pressure on national monetary authorities in many member states within the Community to abandon, at least on a *de facto* basis, monetary independence in order to maintain pegged exchange rates within the EMS. By doing so, the Single Market concentrated minds on the attractiveness of what would otherwise be regarded as a radical alternative to national monetary sovereignty.

The Single European Act (SEA) certainly revitalized the multilateral liberalization of finance within the European Community, a process that had been mostly dormant since the late 1960s (Bakker, 1996). Nevertheless, to a substantial extent the SEA simply ratified decisions that had already been made in Bonn, London and Paris to liberalize their financial markets. West German authorities had returned to a liberal financial regime in the early 1970s, after a brief hiatus during which they engaged in a half-hearted experiment with capital controls. In the

United Kingdom, controls were abolished at the end of the decade, with Margaret Thatcher's accession to power. Even in France, financial liberalization efforts had begun in earnest in 1984 – all well before passage or even negotiation of the SEA. Most observers would agree with Moravcsik (1991, p. 21) that these events were among the preconditions for the successful negotiation and passage of the SEA, and especially plans for substantial financial deregulation within the new Single Market.

Accounting for the decisions to liberalize in Germany and the United Kingdom is relatively straightforward: authorities in the Federal Republic had a pronounced preference for liberalization dating back at least to the 1950s, whereas the British decision can be dated to the 1979 election, when a new Conservative prime minister, committed to finding market solutions to a variety of economic, social and political problems, immediately reversed the previous Labour Party policy of financial segregation. The French case, however, is more intriguing. Indeed, among the many changes in European politics of the past thirty years that made the introduction of EMU imaginable, few are more remarkable than the decision of the Mitterrand government to undertake a programme of fiscal and monetary *rigeur* in conjunction with a liberal reform of French financial markets. After less than two years in office, the first Socialist government in the history of the Fifth Republic completely reversed the direction of its economic policies and ultimately embarked on a far bolder experiment in market liberalization than any right-wing predecessor had previously dared – a reversal that was all the more shocking because it had been explicitly ruled out in the Socialist election platform, and by Mitterrand himself before coming to power (Halimi, 1990).

The French decisions of the early 1980s proved to be critical for the future development of European monetary relations. To appreciate this, consider for a moment the likely trajectory of developments in the *absence* of suddenly orthodox French economic policies, and of French financial reforms in particular. Passage of the SEA would have been unthinkable; revitalization of the European integration process under the Commission presidency of Jacques Delors would either have been stillborn or else have had to manifest itself in some other way. The young and largely untested European Monetary System would probably have suffered the defection of the French franc (as the Paris government actively contemplated in March 1983) and, in all likelihood, the Italian lira as well (authorities in Rome would have been loath to permit rival French exports to benefit from a competitive devaluation). As was the case in the 1970s, then, European exchange-rate stabilization would be increasingly divorced from the full membership and formal institutions of the European Community – hardly promising circumstances for the multilateral negotiation of European monetary unification.[2]

Given the significance of the French policy reversal, how can it be explained? Attention to the changing financial environment in which French authorities found themselves provides some important insights.

Financial integration and monetary policy I: the capital mobility hypothesis

Unfortunately, a great deal of the popular literature has drawn loose (and sometimes insupportable) conclusions about the policy implications of international financial integration.[3] Together with press accounts and statements by private bankers, some of this literature has overstated the problems involved, made careless inferences, and generally drawn implausible conclusions.[4] It is not uncommon, for example, to hear that states have completely lost control over national macroeconomic policies – in effect, that they no longer exercise sovereignty with respect to these matters.[5] Sometimes these contentions are supported by unrealistic assessments of the practical autonomy exercised by states in past generations, sometimes by conflating capital mobility and capital flows, and sometimes by maintaining that capital is now perfectly mobile across borders. Not surprisingly, the uneven quality of these assertions has engendered skepticism regarding the effects of capital mobility, especially among theorists who take seriously the importance of political choices with respect to the past and future development of the international system.[6]

Genuine insights into developments as complex as the emergence of EMU require a more discriminating approach. For example, careful theorizing about the nature and policy consequences of international financial integration depends in the first place upon a clear conceptual distinction between capital mobility and capital flows.[7] While leading international monetary economists have routinely discriminated between these phenomena for a generation (for example Machlup, 1965), others have been less careful, especially since the measurement problems associated with capital mobility provide a powerful incentive to substitute data about financial flows instead.[8]

Capital mobility refers to the capacity of financial assets to move, especially across jurisdictional boundaries. Put differently, capital mobility refers to the relative absence of friction on financial flows across different jurisdictions. At the international level, the relevant jurisdictions are states, most of which possess their own currencies. As a consequence, capital mobility can have important implications for individual states' balance-of-payments positions. But changes in net capital flows at any given point cannot be taken *prima facie* as evidence of changes in mobility: it may be the case that the profit motives for international capital transfers have been altered without any change in the ease of such transfers.

A great deal of economics literature has focused on the appropriate measurement of capital mobility[9] and, while analysts generally agree that capital mobility has increased, there is no consensus on how best to quantify this development. One practical solution to this quandary is to consider the difficulties faced by central bankers attempting to enforce exchange-rate pegs for their currencies. Building on a suggestion by Williamson (1977, pp. 46–51), Figure 1.1 depicts (on a logarithmic scale) average and maximum weekly changes in the foreign-exchange holdings of the German central bank between 1949 and the collapse of fixed exchange rates in March 1973.[10] The accelerating costs of maintaining the D-mark's peg within the Bretton Woods system are evident, as intervention increased by approximately one-hundred fold during this 24-year period. As Williamson notes, 'the increase must be a reflection of the increase in capital mobility, coupled with the commitment to prompt adjustment of par values in the later period, which provided an obvious incentive for the market to react faster than was previously necessary' (Williamson, 1997, pp. 48–9).

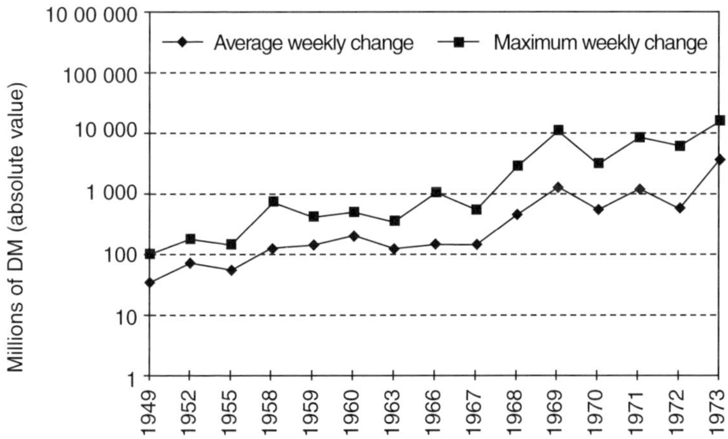

Figure 1.1 Weekly changes in Bundesbank holdings of foreign exchange

These observations suggest that capital mobility is better understood as a structural condition than as an activity or a behaviour. Like most other structural conditions, it defies direct measurement; however – again, like other structural phenomena – capital mobility influences behaviour.[11] Analysts wishing to assess changes in capital mobility must therefore identify circumstances where such adaptive behavior can be clearly observed.

And, indeed, many have done so. Recognition of the medium- term incompatibility of exchange-rate stability, private capital mobility, and domestic monetary independence has been variously referred to as the Mundell–Fleming approach (owing to the early contributions of Mundell, 1968, and Fleming, 1962), the Inconsistent Quartet (Padoa-Schioppa, 1985, 1987), and the Unholy Trinity (Cohen, 1993).[12] A number of political scientists have recently incorporated recognition of this phenomenon into their studies, including Frieden (1991a,b), Goodman and Pauly (1993), Henning (1994), Webb (1995), Keohane and Milner (1996) and Thomas (1997). These theorists share the common supposition that international financial integration has raised the exchange-rate costs associated with pursuing national policies at odds with regional or international trends, a view sometimes termed the capital mobility hypothesis (Andrews, 1994).[13]

Financial integration and monetary policy II: two dimensions of political choice

Politics, here meaning the authoritative choices of political authorities, immediately enters into this equation in at least two fundamental ways. First, authorities choose how to respond to their environments – in this case, to the policy dilemmas created by increased capital mobility. Second, and at a more fundamental level, political authorities can attempt to shape (or reshape) the environment in which they function.

Consider the nature of these different choices. First, responses to the financial environment are not predetermined. Instead, the consequences of increased capital mobility can usefully be characterized in public-choice terms (Andrews, 1994).[14] As national capital markets become more integrated, the foreign-exchange pressures associated with the pursuit of independently chosen monetary objectives increase; consequently, the choice set available to states between the pursuit of their domestic policy preferences and stabilizing their mutual exchange rates narrows. States are generally less autonomous in the sense that monetary independence has become more costly, either in terms of undesired changes in their exchange rates or their foreign-exchange reserves.

This formulation emphasizes the role of political agency by stressing the continuing importance of policy choices within a context of shifting structural constraints, or costs. Of course, political authorities vary substantially in the degree of their aversion to these costs. For example, the smaller states of western Europe (for example the Netherlands and Belgium) have consistently displayed more active concerns about exchange-rate stability than have monetary authorities in the larger states (such as France and Germany), while at the same time western European states as a group have evinced a much stronger preference for exchange-rate stability than have monetary authorities in the United States. The extensive literature on optimum currency area theory (see for example Tower and Willett, 1976) is devoted to understanding the bases of these differences; for present purposes, however, it is sufficient to note that European states are not indifferent to movements in their mutual exchange rates, and that the intensity of this preference is partly explained by differences in state size.

In addition, the public-choice formulation draws attention to the role of bargaining power in international monetary relations (Andrews, 1994, pp. 211–14). Given a preference for mutually stable exchange rates, the pursuit of differing national policy preferences can result in costly (undesired) exchange-rate movements; but the adjustment of policy to avoid exchange-rate movements is costly as well, and there are good reasons to believe that these costs are unlikely to be shared equally among states (Andrews, 1997). For example, there is substantial evidence that Germany's European partners have unilaterally altered their policies in order to limit movement of their exchange rates against the D-mark (see for example Giavazzi and Giovannini, 1989); such behaviour was initially evident with respect to the small states that directly neighbour Germany, but has since become more widespread.[15] Among the many reasons why this pattern has spread is that international financial integration has made the pursuit of independent policies more costly, even for relatively large states like France, Italy and Spain.[16] Nor are the consequences of financial integration limited to pressure on domestic interest- rate policies. By altering the circumstances under which key national and international economic negotiations take place, changes in capital mobility have influenced a broad range of interstate relations.[17]

Governments' choices are not limited to tactical responses to a changing international financial environment, however. As mentioned above, a second and more fundamental decision available to political authorities consists of efforts to shape, or to reshape, the nature of the environment in which they function. While rarely an easy task, successful reorganizations of the financial environment are possible (as was the case, for example, with the restrictive order initially associated with the Bretton Woods system).[18] Conversely, political authorities have at various times been at the very least complicit in the deepening of financial market integration, despite the fact that this process has resulted in a steady reduction in governments' macroeconomic policy autonomy (Helleiner, 1994).

French policy authorities have expended great energies, especially during the period 1968–83, to erect capital controls on a national basis and to develop a more restrictive multilateral financial regime in Europe. These latter efforts met with only a modicum of support by France's Community partners, and were largely abandoned with the switch to monetary and financial orthodoxy in the mid-1980s. The next section attempts to place these efforts into historical perspective, before turning to a more detailed examination of the policy reversal of 1983. The chapter's concluding remarks return to the issue of reinventing the financial environment.

Money and finance in postwar France

For states around the world, there necessarily exists an intimate relationship between the national financial system and the general orientation and mechanisms of monetary policy (see for example Zysman, 1983). In postwar France, financial policy has generally been subordinate to the aims of monetary policy: changes in the financial regime have typically been preceded by, and have been intended to be supportive of, changes in monetary policy. A brief historical survey should suffice to demonstrate this point.

As was true in the other states of western Europe after the end of the Second World War, authorities in France developed comprehensive capital and exchange controls in order to limit the balance-of-payments crises that accompanied reconstruction efforts.[19] Such measures were permitted on a temporary basis under the terms of the Bretton Woods agreement, which had been negotiated near the war's conclusion; it was not generally recognized, however, just how long this 'temporary' state of affairs would prevail. Eventually the remarkable recovery of the French and other European economies that began in the early 1950s allowed monetary authorities in these states to husband sufficient foreign-exchange reserves to permit partial liberalization of these regulations, especially with respect to current account transactions, and to prepare for an eventual return to full currency convertibility.[20]

By the time of the negotiation of the Treaty of Rome and the founding of the European Economic Community, however, the French franc (like other European currencies) was still not fully convertible, and indeed the French external situation was quite weak.[21] This state of affairs influenced the French negotiating position on the proposed treaty, since the agreement (like the Spaak Report on which the treaty text was based) called for the liberalization of capital movements, conditional upon progress in other dimensions of integration. French negotiators insisted on the inclusion of various safeguard clauses in the treaty, aimed at protecting *dirigiste* national policies from being undermined by currency speculation. Only when these conditions were satisfied did French authorities agree to the 1 January 1958 inauguration of the European Economic Community (EEC).

Almost immediately thereafter, the collapse of the Fourth Republic, the creation of the Fifth Republic, and the election of Charles de Gaulle raised serious doubts about future French involvement in the project of European integration, including financial integration. The eventual development of De Gaulle's relationship with Konrad Adenauer, however, reduced uncertainties about a high-level political commitment by France to the EEC; meanwhile, a substantial monetary reform, in conjunction with two devaluations (in June and December 1958) in anticipation of the franc's return to convertibility at the end of that year, positioned French authorities to undertake limited economic and, later, financial liberalization.

The evolution of the French position allowed the Commission to press successfully for early multilateral financial deregulation in its Directives of 1960 and 1962.[22] At the same time, the French (still wary of potential external weakness) insisted that further capital market liberalization at the Community level would have to be dependent upon improved monetary coordination among member states. This position did not preclude French authorities from undertaking deregulation unilaterally, which they did in 1963 (with the abolition of the *divises-titres* market) and, more radically, in 1966. At that point the finance minister, Michel Debré, announced before Parliament that the franc had developed into a strong currency, that Paris was in a position to emerge as a major financial centre, and that the bases of the French financial system would be reformed accordingly. In a thorough reversal of policy, all financial transactions (including international transactions) would be permitted unless expressly prohibited; at the same time, plans were underway for the adoption of market- oriented mechanisms for the conduct of monetary policy.[23]

Shortly thereafter, *'les evenements'* of May 1968 persuaded French authorities to abandon these efforts, first on a temporary and later an ongoing basis. The budgetary promises which helped to defuse the crisis were highly inflationary, and entailed a substantial loosening of monetary policy; this led to serial runs on the franc throughout the remainder of 1968 and 1969. Old financial restrictions returned, accompanied by new instruments aimed at protecting the national currency; but even with these in place, the government felt obliged to devalue the franc in August 1969, followed by a further revaluation of the D-mark just months later.

The exchange-rate crises of 1968–69 portended the later collapse of the Bretton Woods system; for French authorities, however, the shadow cast by the events of May 1968 reached far beyond the traumas of the early 1970s. Indeed, for the next 15 years fears of (maximally) social unrest and (minimally) electoral failure compelled one French government after another to accept inflationary budgetary agreements accommodated by periodic expansions of the money supply; these typically led to speculative pressures on the franc, which was in turn protected (without great success) by restrictive financial measures.[24] Already by the end of the 1960s these speculative pressures could be quite substantial (see again Figure 1.1); the further integration of global capital markets only increased the exchange-rate costs associated with pursuing policies out of step with France's major trading partners, and especially Germany.

Just such speculative pressures obliged authorities in Paris to abandon the Community exchange-rate system of the 1970s on two occasions, in 1974 and 1976.[25] Meanwhile, on the domestic front, the more austere economic policies pursued by the government of Raymond Barre during the late 1970s were rejected at the polls in 1981, first with the defeat of fellow conservative Giscard d'Estaing and then with the election of a Socialist majority in the National Assembly. It was left to François Mitterrand and his associates to develop a solution to the perennial French problem of external pressure and internal weakness.

The policy reversal of 1983

The incoming Socialist government was rapidly faced with a deteriorating balance-of-payments situation which, at least initially, had less to do with French trade or competitiveness problems than with policy developments in Germany. In the wake of expansive macroeconomic policies undertaken after the Bonn summit of 1978, the Federal Republic had been ill-prepared for the second oil shock; consequently, during the first several years of the EMS the D-mark was (quite unexpectedly) under consistent downward pressure (Henning, 1994, pp. 189–93). As a result, there was very little exchange-rate pressure on the Italian lira and none whatsoever on the French franc from shortly after the inception of the EMS in 1979 until the Bundesbank decided in February 1981 – three months before Mitterrand's presidential victory, and for reasons entirely unrelated to developments in France – to tighten policy rather considerably.

The consequences of German tightening began to be felt as early as the summer of 1981 as, for the first time in two years, the D-mark began to reach the upper limits of its bands within the exchange-rate mechanism of the EMS. These pressures were temporarily relieved by the realignments of October 1981 and June 1982; but by the time of the March 1983 speculative crisis against the franc, the political situation had changed somewhat. Rather than bargaining with representatives of Helmut Schmidt, himself a co-founder of the EMS, Mitterrand's leftist government was met across the bargaining table by members of the new conservative German government headed by Helmut Kohl. No warm bonds of friendship existed yet between these two national leaders, and the German negotiating team was much less willing to accommodate periodic devaluations of the French currency than in previous years. Given these circumstances, it is hardly surprising that the March 1983 realignment negotiations proved to be a major turning point, both for French monetary policy and for the informal workings of the EMS (Andrews and Willett, 1997, p. 495).

It is interesting to consider the different retrospective analyses of French policy that have emerged over the past 15 years. There has been considerable soul-searching amongst the government leaders who launched the French state on a policy of austerity following the *rélance* of 1981–82;[26] these policy-makers have tended to explain the eventual reversal of macroeconomic policies primarily in terms of a learning curve, both for themselves and for the country, about the current-account effects of pursuing 'Keynesianism in one country'.[27] Indeed, Mitterrand himself later represented the early period of his presidency in almost Machiavellian terms.[28]

These retrospective accounts should not be taken at face value. Despite later renditions, the earliest accounts provided by the major participants in the French government's decision to adopt a strong currency policy within the EMS was instead largely driven by concerns about capital-account movements. The determining factor appears to have been a calculated assessment of the economic and especially financial costs of allowing the franc to float;[29] similar concerns motivated the non-devaluation decision of 1981.[30] It was only afterward that a trade-based (and hence pro-European) slant was offered as a justification for these decisions.[31] By focusing on the trade imbalances generated by the *rélance* (an angle readily adopted by most external commentators as well[32]), French policy-makers were able to emphasize the solidaristic consequences of the 1983 policy reversal for the European integration process. The resulting narrative greatly facilitated Mitterrand's successful efforts to retain centre-left support while assembling a centrist coalition in support of his bid for reelection in the 1988 presidential contest.

These machinations were not without consequence at the European level. The policy reversal of 1983, and the successful blame-management strategy that allowed it to be sustained,[33] substantially improved the prospects for an eventual accord on EMU. French macroeconomic policy was subsequently adjusted to validate the new strong-currency regime, followed by a series of reform measures aimed at liberalizing national financial markets – reforms which, as previously noted, constituted necessary preconditions for the later negotiation and ratification of the Single European Act. These internal changes were aimed at improving the competitiveness of national industry while demonstrating France's commitment to a strong-currency policy; but government negotiators also recognized that the elimination of barriers to international capital flows would ultimately undermine the effectiveness of exchange-rate stabilization within the EMS.[34]

Few people were as conscious of these concerns as Jacques Delors, who as France's finance minister had personally conducted the negotiations leading to the 1983 realignment. In his new capacity as president of the European Commission, Delors (along with authorities from Belgium) introduced proposals for the SEA to include language calling for the eventual realization of monetary union (Louis, 1988; compare also Bakker, 1996, pp. 163–5). Despite initial resistance from Germany, these proposals – backed by the French government – resulted in the insertion into the treaty's preamble of a clause devoted to EMU, the first time that monetary union had gained such status.

Immediately upon ratification of the Single Act, the Commission launched its programme for further liberalization of capital movements within the Community. Less than two years later, in January 1988,

France's latest finance minister, Edouard Balladur, publicly reintroduced EMU as a topic of high-profile negotiations, a gambit which ultimately led to the negotiation of the Maastricht Treaty (Andrews, 1993).

Structural theory and the French policy reversal

Careful examination of this sequence of events highlights some of the merits as well as the deficiencies of a structural approach to the study of monetary relations. This approach includes both a public-choice dimension and a structural dimension, each of which deserves attention.

First, changes in capital mobility lead to changes in the exchange-rate implications of pursuing macroeconomic policies at odds with one's major trading partners. To the extent that such exchange-rate movements run counter to the wishes of national authorities, they have incentives to modify policies accordingly. National monetary policy choices are not determined by international financial markets, nor are policy-makers compelled to make particular choices; nevertheless, unless authorities' policy preferences are highly inelastic, their choices will tend to reflect changed circumstances. Arguably, the French government's 1983 decision to reverse the direction of macroeconomy policy reflected just such an adjustment to changes in the international economic environment: associated changes in the French financial system, while improving the microeconomic competitiveness of French industry, further constrained national monetary policy.

Second, as noted earlier, purposeful actors are capable of successfully reorganizing their financial environments. For the purposes of theory construction, however, the ease of such reorganizations is a central concern. Generally speaking, efforts to liberalize policy and to enhance capital mobility over the past generation have met with considerable success.[35] Conversely, efforts to restrict capital movements – for whatever intended purpose – have generally proved costly and have, in many instances, ultimately been abandoned.[36]

While explanations of this pattern vary (see for example the survey by Cohen, 1996), it is important to note that changes in governments' financial policies have not occurred in a vacuum; rather, they have taken place in tandem with changes in technology and in market practice that have independently reduced the friction of transnational capital transactions.[37] There are, in other words, a multiplicity of sources of increased capital mobility, with two important consequences. First, while the degree of policy liberalization has varied greatly across states, no advanced industrialized state has been able to evade the effects of heightened international financial integration altogether. Second, the difficulties associated with reversing this state of affairs, whether for individual states or for the international community as a whole, are substantial. In conjunction, these two facts underpin the argument that the resulting constraints on policy can be regarded as structural in nature (Webb, 1991, p. 313).[38]

The French case is exemplary in this regard. Unlike the situation in the United States, Germany and Britain, French authorities in the mid-1980s were not predisposed to a liberal financial regime, and indeed initially resisted its development. It is precisely for this reason that the Socialists' eventual policy reversal produced such a powerful demonstration effect for other monetary authorities elsewhere (see for example Helleiner, 1994, pp. 143, 162).

At the same time, the significance of the French case should not be overstated. Capital market integration is not irreversible, despite the abandonment of the Socialists' *autre politique*. For various reasons, however, reversal of this trend is unlikely. In effect, a kind of hysteresis in international financial markets has taken place: a new equilibrium has been achieved that is no longer dependent on the forces which originally produced it. A glass of water, once overturned, is unlikely to return to its previous equilibrium state without the expenditure of a great deal of energy; it is likewise with the international integration of financial markets.

Examples of circumstances that might nevertheless produce a reversal of current trends towards further financial integration include systemic financial crisis (see, for example Helleiner, 1994, p. 118; Pauly, 1995, p. 385). However, as long as 'rollback' cannot be achieved easily or unilaterally, and as long as at least some of the effects of increased capital mobility are experienced on a system-wide basis, characterizing the effects of capital mobility as structural remains broadly justifiable. Indeed, from the standpoint of theory development, even if some system-wide crisis did return the degree of international capital mobility to levels like those prevailing in the 1950s and 1960s, the effects on international monetary relations would still be systemic and could still usefully be described as structural in nature: the resulting external constraints on governments' policies would simply be more relaxed than they are currently.

But the utility of the structural approach (especially in isolation) should not be exaggerated, particularly in its present underdeveloped form.[39] While providing helpful insights, the structural approach to international monetary relations leaves many important questions about the French policy reversal, as well as other important developments associated with EMU, unanswered. Of course, it would be surprising indeed if attention to a single variable could wholly account for *any* policy decision, much less the collective agreement of a dozen states to abolish national monetary sovereignty. Indeed, the very peculiarity of EMU as a regional solution to the challenges posed by financial integration suggests the limitations of the approach.[40] More bluntly, while abstract observations about the implications of increased capital mobility can inform a theory of international monetary relations, they cannot constitute an adequate explanation of particular international monetary policies.[41]

The structural approach provides insights into key problems in international political economy without offering definitive explanations of particular developments therein. As a consequence, the value of a structural theory of international monetary relations remains largely heuristic; satisfactory explanation of such complex phenomena as the emergence of EMU requires recourse to other perspectives as well.

Notes

1 Monetary unification had been proposed by the European Commission in the early 1960s, and was adopted as a medium-term goal by the member states in 1969.

2 In addition, the collapse of the Soviet empire in eastern Europe at the end of the decade would have been extremely unlikely to have coincided with the publication of a report outlining a detailed framework for the realization of monetary union by stages, as in fact happened. German unification would have therefore loomed as an imminent possibility without the counterbalancing prospect of anchoring the new German superstate to the west through the medium of EMU; compare the actual sequence of events as related in Andrews (1993).

3 Cohen (1996, p. 269, footnote 1), provides an extensive compilation of such instances.

4 For an analysis of this phenomenon, see Pauly (1995 and 1997).

5 For example, McKenzie and Lee (1991, p. xi): 'Governments at all levels... have lost the vestiges of unchecked economic sovereignty.' An earlier and more sober study of the effects of financial integration on policy was provided by Aronson (1977).

6 'Analysts should therefore be cautious when interpreting the current dimensions of international capital flows as constituting... an exogenous structure that irrevocably binds societies or their states' Pauly (1995, p. 385). See also Cerny (1994), Kapstein (1994a) and Helleiner (1994).

7 Limitations of space prevent consideration of additional distinctions – e.g., between perfect and imperfect capital mobility, between the mobility of different types of capital, between the constraints imposed by capital mobility on various types of policy, and between formal and practical monetary autonomy.

8 Some rather straightforward measures of capital and foreign exchange market volumes are available, including the growth in volume of Euro-currency markets, international lending, and foreign-exchange market activity. For example, total stocks of international financing (net of double accounting) approached $6 trillion by the mid-1990s, a substantial proportion of which consisted of bank credit denominated in foreign currencies. See the *Annual Report of the Bank for International Settlements*, various issues.

9 For example, Frankel (1990, p. 4), assesses the relative usefulness of four alternative operational definitions of capital mobility, describing covered interest rate differentials as 'an unalloyed criterion for [measuring] capital mobility in the sense of the degree of financial market integration across national boundaries;' Willett and Wihlborg (1990, pp. 61–5), however, remain skeptical.

10 I have expanded Williamson's data set by including all years from 1949 to 1973 (inclusive). Following his practice, the data for 1959 exclude the weekly increase for the week ending 31 March, in which unique factors operated; likewise, the data for 1971 and 1973 refer to the weeks prior to the (in the first case temporary, in the second permanent) floating of the D-mark. Note that Williamson does not include year-end changes.

11 Or, as Williamson (1977, p. 48), puts it, behaviour is reflective of this condition. Compare Waltz (1979, p. 73), who argues that 'structure acts as a selector, but it cannot be seen, examined, and observed at work.'

12 Padoa-Schioppa's 1987 formulation explicitly includes international trade as an additional variable.

13 The capital mobility hypothesis should not be confused with the so-called convergence thesis of the 1950s and 1960s; on the revival of the convergence thesis, see Berger and Dore (1996). More generally, the distinctions enumerated in endnote 7 are essential to the study of the policy implications of financial integration, and if ignored risk caricaturing the capital mobility hypothesis.

14 Some authors have recast the capital mobility hypothesis in more deterministic form; see, e.g., Oatley (1997, pp. 77–8, 99–100).

15 Kurzer (1993), provides an excellent study of the effects of financial integration on western Europe's smaller states.

16 Other reasons include the changing causal beliefs of European monetary authorities; see Verdun (1996), and McNamara (1998), for analyses.

17 For example, international financial market integration greatly helped the United States externalize the costs of its exploding public debt during the 1980s; see Willett and Wihlborg (1990).

18 Tobin (e.g. 1978) perennially champions efforts to reduce the mobility of short-term capital assets, thereby mitigating debilitating effects on national policy autonomy.

19 The best single source on these developments is Bakker (1996), from which the following four paragraphs draw; see also Zysman (1983), Petit (1989) and Loriaux (1991).

20 French authorities were aided in this respect by their participation in the European Payments Union, whose arrangements allowed member states to

minimize demands on foreign-exchange reserves in support of intra-European transactions.

21 During 1957, France experienced substantial deficits on both the budget and current account.

22 First Council Directive of 11 May 1960 for the Implementation of Article 67 of the Treaty, amended by the Second Directive of 18 December 1962.

23 The Banque de France, together with other elements of the French state, was not enthusiastic about these developments; officials there argued that Debré's proposals were being undertaken too rapidly and were dangerous, given the underdeveloped nature of cooperation between European monetary authorities. See the citations in Bakker (1996, p. 108, endnotes 39 and 40).

24 For an overview of these years, see Goodman (1992, chapter 4).

25 The Common Margins Agreement, typically referred to as the European currency 'snake,' was initially intended as a prelude to EMU; the collapse of the global system of fixed exchange rates caused the proposed transition schedule to be abandoned.

26 Halimi (1990), provides an excellent summary of these accounts, although my analysis differs from his.

27 For example, in 1986 Pierre Bérégovoy, then France's finance minister, explained that the French reflation had been intended to coincide with the worldwide economic recovery expected to follow the election of Ronald Reagan; the absence of this recovery, he argued, fully accounted for the external deficit of 1982–83. Interview in *Les Temps Modernes*, March 1986.

28 See, e.g., his statement in *Le Monde*, 17 March 1988, in which he suggests that the French people (rather than his government) had been mistaken about the benefits of a reflationary policy.

29 At the critical 16 March meeting, treasury chief Michel Camdessus reported to Mitterrand that French foreign reserves could prop up the franc for several days at best; a report from the finance ministry, already leaked to the press, concluded that the resulting plunge in the value of the franc would probably exceed 20 per cent. See Bauchard (1986, pp. 142–5) and Goodman (1992, p. 136, especially footnote 127).

30 Early eye-witness accounts generally explained the 1981 decision in terms of the government's fear of capital flight (e.g., Mauroy, 1982, pp. 17–19, 25–28).

31 For example, Pfister (1985, p. 242), who was Mauroy's political advisor, retrospectively offered a trade-based, European slant to the 1981 non-devaluation decision (compare endnote 30).

32 See, e.g., Hall (1987, p. 62), Bauchard (1986, p. 34), Halimi (1990, chapter 6).

33 Beginning with Andrews (1992), I have argued that the European Monetary System provides opportunities for authorities to manage the political costs of austerity policies, an idea later explored by Moravcsik (1994) and Oatley (1997), ch. 5.

34 Such fears were realized little more than a year later, when speculative pressures forced a January 1987 realignment of central rates within the EMS that central bank governors did not regard as justified by economic fundamentals.

35 By 'success,' I mean here only that liberalization policies have been imposed and sustained; no evaluation of their economic merits is intended.

36 See the discussions and references in Goodman and Pauly (1993) and Andrews and Willett (1997, pp. 483–4).

37 Of these multiple causes, I suggested in Andrews (1994, pp. 197–9), but did not argue as strongly as does, for example, Cerny (1994, pp. 325 and 332), that technological changes took causal precedence.

38 Helleiner (1994, pp. 196–8), similarly concludes that dynamics of global finance make resegregation of national financial markets extremely unlikely (absent wide-scale crisis).

39 There are several limitations to the structural approach as it currently exists. There is a lack of specificity as to the costs imposed on policy autonomy under conditions of advanced financial integration; the distribution of these costs among states remains indeterminate; and the role of mediating domestic political structures remains underexplored. Andrews (1997) represents an early attempt to address the second of these difficulties.

40 There is good reason to believe that the success of EMU negotiations owed as much to the end of the Cold War as it did to the effects of financial integration, and that variation in political responses to the postwar bipolar struggle help account for why EMU is so out of step with developments elsewhere in the advanced industrialized world (despite the presence of some similar structural incentives); see Andrews (1993).

41 Compare Waltz (1979, pp. 121–3), on the distinction between theories of international relations and theories of foreign policy.

2

Does Capital Mobility Cause Regulatory Convergence? Illustrations from Japan

Jennifer Holt-Dwyer

Introduction

Throughout the past quarter-century, many nations have undertaken substantial financial-market restructuring and regulatory reform.[1] A multitude of factors have contributed to these transformations, including technological advances, financial-market innovations, interest-group mobilization, diplomatic efforts, and changing ideas about how financial markets should be organized and supervised. This chapter focuses exclusively on the ways in which regulatory reform in Japan has been affected by increases in the mobility of financial capital since the late 1970s.[2] In particular I argue that increased capital mobility explains in large part why the Japanese government began in the mid-1980s to implement financial market reforms that reduced many of the uniquely Japanese characteristics of the domestic regulatory structure and promoted in their place regulatory arrangements that look more similar to those found in other major financial centres.

Capital mobility is a critical factor shaping contemporary financial market developments because it largely determines for both government and private actors the costs and benefits associated with any set of regulatory policies. Regulatory arrangements are tending to converge cross-nationally because capital mobility promotes competition between not only market actors, but also regulators. That is, once capital can freely exit a regulatory jurisdiction, governments face stronger incentives to provide a financial-market environment as attractive as found elsewhere in order to achieve various fundamental policy objectives, including financing government debt and simply maintaining a sound domestic financial system. In short, capital mobility promotes convergence because it injects a cross-nationally competitive dynamic into the otherwise predominantly domestic politics of financial-market reform.

Although capital mobility is an increasingly prominent factor influencing state and market actors' regulatory preferences, it does not determine specific policy choice. Accordingly, increased capital mobility is expected to promote, not a radical shift towards a predetermined 'most-competitive' regulatory arrangement, but rather a transformation in the process of regulatory reform reflecting many governments' heightened sensitivity to the preferences of those actors managing internationally mobile financial-market assets,[3] and including more focused attention to the regulatory arrangements that have proven attractive to them elsewhere.

Illustrating this change in the politics of reform, this chapter details how in the mid- to late-1980s, increased capital mobility skewed financial-market reforms in Japan towards those that effectively promoted a degree of cross-national regulatory convergence not seen earlier. The following section introduces the dependent variable, the tendency towards cross-national convergence of regulatory environments; discusses the independent variable, capital mobility; and outlines the logic of competitive regulatory reform. The third section offers case-study illustrations, contrasting the financial reform process and policies adopted before and after capital mobility increased significantly in Japan. The following part discusses limits to competition and convergence, drawing further illustration from developments in Japan in the 1990s.

Convergence and capital mobility: explaining the causal link

The pressures for and against policy convergence have been examined fairly extensively with regard to monetary policy, and research is expanding into numerous other issue areas as well. The question addressed in this chapter is why nations with very different domestic political economies have implemented over the past two decades financial-market reforms that reveal a clear tendency towards greater cross-national convergence of regulatory environments and associated financial-market policies. The tendency towards greater cross-national convergence means simply that a nation's regulatory policies are more similar rather than equally or more divergent from those in other countries compared to twenty years ago. Looking back over the past two decades this tendency is readily apparent.

At the beginning of the 1970s the regulatory structures in the USA, the UK and Japan, as well as in most other countries, were quite different from one another. Interest-rate structures were shaped by a variety of factors, the regulations determining types of financial institutions and allowable business activities were often nation-specific, and the ways in which actors entered and exited national markets varied as well (Kemp, 1984). Each arrangement reflected a unique historical path of financial- market development that ran largely independently from those in other countries. Not surprisingly, the means through which governments sought to influence domestic economic development through their financial markets also varied accordingly (Zysman, 1983).

From our vantage point at the end of the century, however, it is clear that financial-market reforms have brought about a rapid diminution of the previous cross-national differences in financial-market regulations and promoted greater commonality of market prices, products, practices and participants. Moreover, when government officials intervene in these markets in pursuit of their various objectives, they face increasingly similar constraints on macroeconomic policy options and use an increasingly common set of standards, rules and intervention tools. This is the tendency towards convergence we observe.

This convergence tendency in regulatory environments is not simply an extension of economic liberalization. Under conditions of limited capital mobility the pace and pattern, as well as the timing and the scope, of reform efforts are determined predominantly by the specific regulatory conflicts, organization of interest groups and mediating political institutions found in each domestic market. Therefore, except when approaching the extreme of completely unregulated markets, concurrent programmes of financial liberalization under conditions of restricted capital mobility are not expected to promote significant convergence of regulatory environments. Rather, it is in the incompleteness of deregulation and convergence that we clearly see the impact of capital mobility and the competitive dynamics of reform. There is greater convergence where high levels of capital mobility fosters the most regulatory competition, and less convergence where there is little or none. Accordingly, regulations concerning market participants who can move their capital easily (for example large corporations and institutional investors), are much more similar cross-nationally than are regulations concerning those who are more constrained (such as small savers and local finance companies). In short, it is not simply the general tendency towards convergence, but rather the particular pattern of convergence that points to the critical role played by capital mobility and regulatory competition in explaining this outcome.

This revealed tendency towards convergence does not presume or foretell market uniformity. There are still significant cross-national differences in regulatory politics and policies, and these are neither uninteresting nor trivial.[4] Regardless of the relative weight of the similarities and differences, however, attention to convergence leads us towards aspects of the financial reform process and future state–market relations that focusing on remaining differences simply cannot. Specifically, convergence points us towards newly-evolving political-economy dynamics rather than towards a reiteration of traditional or national patterns in policy-making. Moreover, convergence provides us a unique lens through which to view the interaction between domestic and international politics. Financial-market policies are changed predominantly through domestic politics, yet the unique cumulative effect of these seemingly independent national policies arises because of the competitive relationship between states imposed by the structure of international capital mobility.

Finally, given the well-recognized importance of domestic institutions in buffering or distorting the impact of seemingly powerful international variables, cross-national divergence is the anticipated outcome and convergence is not. This is certainly true concerning Japan, which has so often been portrayed as fundamentally different compared to the other major financial-centre states, whether described in terms of the strong state, weak state spectrum; the developmental state, *laissez-faire* state distinction; or the hegemonic, declining hegemonic and supporter state perspective. Still, despite the notable differences in traditional financial-market structures and the wide variety of political institutions through which each nation's regulatory policies are changed, the overall trend in financial-market developments is clearly towards greater convergence rather than towards either greater divergence or a simple perpetuation of unique national regulatory politics and structures. Most tellingly, this degree of convergence of regulatory environments far exceeds any convergence of the institutional arrangements, political mobilization patterns, or other domestic political economy variables that have traditionally explained national regulatory policies. We turn now to explore why and how changes in the level of international capital mobility affects the domestic process and product of regulatory reform in individual countries such that the cumulative effect of multiple reforms is this tendency towards greater cross-national convergence of regulatory environments.

Since consideration of capital mobility as a structural constraint on domestic policy is relatively well-known in the IPE literature[5] and discussed in greater detail elsewhere in this volume, I will simply reiterate that the logic of this constraint is derived largely from the structural dependence of states on capital. This dependence exists because the benefits capital brings to an economy are so critical to the continued political success of any incumbent administration that no government can run the risk of inducing a capital strike or capital flight (Przeworski and Wallerstein, 1988). As a result, those who control capital enjoy a 'privileged' position such that government policy generally accommodates their interests (Lindblom, 1977). Although this privileged position is in part a function of financial executives' advantaged access to the political élite, here I am concerned with their ability to influence government policy through market behaviour, even without overt political participation. Fundamentally, the preferences of actors managing internationally mobile financial-market assets take on greater political salience in the domestic politics of financial-market reform because newly emerging and more liberal market structures result in their actions having greater influence on domestic economic outcomes. This economic impact is what gives their preferences greater weight.

In this chapter, I focus on financial-market regulations as a key link between capital mobility and government efforts to manage domestic economic developments. In industrialized capitalist democracies, governments' claims to political authority depend to a large extent on their ability to influence domestic economic outcomes and thereby provide to their constituency some politically acceptable distribution of social and economic values. Yet, in no contemporary case would unfettered economic exchange produce the specifically desired outcome (Polanyi, 1970). Accordingly, governments establish regularized means of economic intervention with which to pursue these outcomes.

Regulations most concretely exemplify these regulated entities' perspectives. Regulations are a set of constraints on behaviour, enforced by the political authority of the state, which can impose burdens or provide benefits (Kane, 1987; Spulber, 1989). From the government's perspective, however, regulations are one of the main tools facilitating pursuit of the various economic and political outcomes, such as economic growth, market stability and resource redistribution on which their claims to political authority are based. It is for this reason that changes in regulatory structure often affect not only the economic opportunities afforded market actors, but also the effectiveness of government policies. Although regulations are certainly not the only means available, to the extent a government pursues its objectives using regulatory intervention, it must first establish or maintain jurisdiction over the economic actors and activities that, with regulatory intervention, can produce the desired policy ends.

The implication of this relationship between regulatory effectiveness and jurisdiction for this study of financial-market reform is that governments want to maintain financial-market activities within their jurisdiction, not simply because these activities provide general economic benefits such as employment, related business investments and tax revenues. Rather, maintaining adequate jurisdiction over financial-market activities is deemed essential because the financial system serves as both the foundation for all other domestic economic activity and the channel through which the government pursues so many of its goals.

Under conditions of restricted capital mobility, governments can respond to diminished regulatory effectiveness or pursue alternative objectives by introducing new binding regulations (re-regulation) because they maintain a jurisdictional monopoly over the financial-market activities influencing the success of these endeavours. Under conditions of significant capital mobility, however, this becomes problematic. By definition, capital mobility provides market actors the potential to cross jurisdictions, and thereby challenges regulatory powers. For example, capital mobility reduces the effectiveness of coercive or burdensome regulations if it enables actors to maneuver around them. Even subsidies and inducements provided through anti-competitive regulations are more difficult to sustain given increased mobility because they are effective only to the extent all relevant competitors are similarly constrained. In addition, capital mobility hinders policy effectiveness if it reduces the government's control over the quality and quantity of financial-market activity taking place within its jurisdiction. That is, policy-driven economic or regulatory interventions simply will not be effectively transmitted through the financial system to the broader economy if the target market is inadequate in size or quality due to capital mobility.[6] Therefore, under increased capital mobility the effectiveness of government intervention becomes dependent on the government's maintaining within its jurisdiction not just any financial market, but one of sufficient size and quality to ensure that exercising its political authority through regulations or other means produces the desired result.

In sum, governments are dependent on both capital for investment and adequate financial markets for their role in transmitting policies throughout the economy. This dependence implies that under conditions of increased capital mobility a government's success in maintaining adequate jurisdictional market share becomes a prior condition to achieving any number of policy objectives. Governments are thus compelled to produce, through regulatory reform if necessary, a financial-market environment as attractive as can be found elsewhere. From this perspective, financial-market reforms designed to increase the relative attractiveness of the domestic market can be understood as part of a government strategy to achieve authority-maintenance objectives under the capital-mobility constraint.

As high levels of international capital mobility creates in other nations similar incentives, the product of these individual efforts to increase the attractiveness of national financial markets through regulatory adjustments and other means creates a competitive dynamic between states (Kane, 1987, 1988). As Kane describes, 'running parallel to this competition between private financial institutions is a less-visible layer of competition for rights to produce and deliver regulatory services to financial institutions' (Kane, 1987, p. 119). Regulatory competition is a strategic endeavour in which each government's regulatory options are evaluated in terms of the expected responses of market actors as well as other nation's regulators.[7] This heightened government attention to market behaviour and alternative regulatory environments distinguishes the domestic politics of regulatory reform under high levels of capital mobility from those under more restrictive conditions.

Incentives to change national regulatory environments arise whenever economic developments alter the domestic distribution of burdens and benefits of regulation in a politically unsatisfactory way. From that point, the politics of reform are propelled by the ongoing push and pull of a multiplicity of social actors, each trying to take profitable advantage of existing market and regulatory incentives, as well as government actors trying to both serve the interests of their most important constituents and maintain their political authority through continued policy effectiveness. Accordingly, under conditions of restricted capital mobility regulatory policies in any one country arise from the policy preferences and relative political resources of domestic market and state actors mediated through domestic political institutions. Thus, as suggested above, it is not surprising that up through the 1970s regulatory policies and regulatory reforms varied considerably cross-nationally and tended to perpetuate recognizable national patterns of domestic regulatory politics.

Under increased levels of capital mobility, however, the domestic politics of regulatory reform change, and with it policy outcomes.

I restate two propositions suggested by the theory of the state's dependence on capital and the related capital-mobility constraint on regulatory policy options. The first concerns the politics of reform and suggests that as mobility increases the possibility that capital will leave a particular jurisdiction, the policy-shaping power of the managers of mobile capital becomes even stronger *vis-à-vis* the government and relative to other domestic interest groups. Certainly in the IPE field it is not uncommon for scholars to borrow from Hirschman (1970) to suggest that as greater mobility strengthens the credibility of any threat by capital to 'exit' the domestic market, managers of capital obtain greater political 'voice'. In this case, 'voice' must be understood as influence over policy choice rather than greater political access, because the more readily capital can 'exit' the domestic market, the less incentive those who control capital have to bear the often sizable costs of exercising their domestic political voice. Accordingly, I offer the corollary that as capital mobility increases, and the cost of 'exit' declines relative to the cost of political participation, the power wielded by financial-market participants is likely to reside less in how effectively they pressure the government through domestic political mobilization, and more in self-motivated government attention to how these powerful market actors' preferences are expressed through their economic behaviour.

This corrolary thus suggests that the policy-making process of regulatory reform is itself a function of the level of capital mobility. Specifically, when capital mobility is limited, we expect the policy-making process to involve extensive political negotiation and result in policies that reflect primarily the balance of political power among domestic interests groups, and only marginally international economic conditions. Conversely, when capital mobility is high we expect the policy-making process to involve more proactive and strategic attempts by the government to discern the preferences of mobile market actors, and then accommodate domestic political interests within this range.

The second proposition concerns policy outcomes and restates the main argument of this chapter, which is that as each government responds to the preferences of an increasingly integrated and international financial market, the policies with which they respond will tend to converge. The causal mechanism bringing about this convergence is the competitive dynamic between governments that arises once high levels of capital mobility begin to affect regulatory jurisdiction and policy effectiveness. That is, under conditions of significant capital mobility, government's are not only compelled to entice capital and financial-market activities into their jurisdiction so that they can achieve their various policy objectives and justify their claims to continued political authority,[8] they are compelled to compete against other governments seeking the same. Thus, in stark contrast to common tariffs produced through international agreements, the tendency for regulatory environments to converge is produced by regulatory competition, not cooperation. Convergence is, therefore, a somewhat unintended consequence arising from the interaction of state actors making independent and strategically rational choices about how best to achieve their respective national policy goals given high levels of capital mobility and considering the choices made by other states.

But is convergence towards greater regulatory effectiveness and/or market efficiency? Or is it towards the lowest common denominator of regulatory standards and a market free-for-all? This answer is suggested by our earlier discussion of convergence as more than an extension of the liberalization bias in economic reforms. Capital became more mobile through the concurrence of national liberalization policies (Helleiner, 1994), but the regulatory competition it provokes does not necessarily lead to further liberalization. Although this strategic restructuring is commonly called 'competitive laxity,' because *in general* financial-market activities are expected to shift to less-regulated markets, the most competitive regulatory environment is not necessarily the most liberal.

Market actors seek low prices and a wide variety of products, as well as convenience and assurances that their transactions are legally binding and fair. Accordingly, the most attractive markets are those in which high levels of competition between a variety of financial service providers is most likely to produce the lowest prices and most innovative products; and where convenience, stability and the transparency of rules and procedures, including disclosure requirements and prohibitions against unfair business practices, provide adequate assurance of financial soundness and the credibility of market actors and the government.

Detailed explication of how competition is expected to affect specific regulations is beyond the scope of this chapter. One can see from cross-national case studies, however, that in general reform has promoted both the relaxation of constraints previously used to limit competition, such as regulations concerning prices, products, access and institutional specialization, as well as some fortification of constraints designed to ensure market quality, stability and financial-system credibility, such as insider-trading laws, and disclosure requirements (see for example Moran, 1991, and Lawrence, 1996). It is, nevertheless, impossible to determine *a priori* the environment towards which regulations are converging. Capital standards deemed adequate last year may prove unsatisfactory tomorrow, and product innovations may require redefinition of adequate financial disclosure. But, the indeterminancy of where regulatory competition will lead only reinforces the argument that when capital mobility is high, governments tend towards policies that accommodate the mix of regulatory burdens and benefits preferred by dominant market players, whatever that mix may be.

There are crucial limits to both regulatory competition and cross-national convergence, which are outlined in the final section of this chapter. Before addressing those, however, I consider whether the two aforementioned propositions help us understand why financial-market reform in Japan produced a more cross-nationally convergent regulatory environment. Although not a rigorous test of these propositions, the Japanese case illustrates the contrast between the dynamics of reform under low and high levels of capital mobility, as well as Japan's promotion of a more internationally competitive regulatory environment.

Illustrations from the Japanese case[9]

Capital mobility into and out of Japan increased substantially from the late 1970s as the government eased many restrictions and market actors' devised means to avoid others. For purposes of comparison, I date the shift from low to high levels of capital mobility as occurring between 1981 and 1983.[10] Actual capital flows suggest changing levels of capital mobility, and we find, for example, that outward portfolio investment from Japan increased from less than US$100 million in 1982 to well over US$1 billion by 1986 (Nakanishi, 1991, p. 256). Since actual flows are influenced by a number of factors, however, measures of capital mobility should attend to the capacity of capital to move, without requiring its actual movement. Measures incorporating this potential include the extent to which covered interest parity holds and the correlation between domestic savings and investment (Feldstein and Horioka, 1980). McKenzie (1992) summarizes a number of studies showing that while covered interest parity between onshore yen and offshore US dollar assets did not hold for the 1970s, it has held for much of the 1980s. Similarly Feldman (1986) measures 'internationalization' using regulatory, quantity and price approaches and determines that by each of these measures Japan's capital markets have been fully internationalized since the early 1980s. Thus, we anticipate that the process and product of regulatory reform in Japan will look different before and after the early 1980s in ways that reflect different levels of capital mobility. To further simplify the comparison, the following section draws illustrations from only the 1970s and the 1980s, because reforms during these years were not influenced by the collapse of Japan's bubble economy and the financial crisis dominating the 1990s. The influence of capital mobility on regulatory reforms implemented under these more adverse and contemporary conditions are discussed in the final section of this chapter.

Meaningful reform of Japan's financial-market regulations began in the 1970s and has proceeded apace ever since. Financial- market conditions in Japan began to change considerably in the late 1960s and early 1970s due to fundamental economic adjustments taking place at the time, including a sharp reduction in Japan's rate of economic growth, severe bouts of inflations between 1969 and 1973, and the deep recession that followed the 1973 oil crisis. These developments greatly altered the flow of funds in Japan as corporations cut back investment and the government began to run considerable fiscal deficits. This change in the flow of funds created pressure on the existing regulatory structure and fostered demands for regulatory changes from a variety of actors. Of course, each interested group, including both market participants and government officials, wanted to maintain regulations that served their particular interests, and change only those regulations that no longer did so.

At that time, Japan's financial markets were heavily regulated and cross-national capital mobility was extremely limited. Financial transactions took place within an extensive web of formal and informal regulations that restricted the flow of capital both into and out of Japan, as well as the domestic activities of foreign investors and institutions. Even within the domestic market, capital mobility was constrained by regulations delimiting the allowable business activities of specialized financial institutions and the participants in any given market. Virtually all interests rates were regulated or managed in ways that not only protected financial institutions, but also enabled the government to influence the allocation of capital. Moreover, market participants regularly adhered to the guiding regulatory principle that activities not specifically approved by the government were prohibited because government officials enjoyed significant discretion and routinely employed a broad range of legal, administrative and extra-legal means of intervening in financial market affairs. Relations between the government and market actors were extremely close, and relations among financial institutions were organized around financial specializations, which promoted narrow but deeply-vested interest groups.

In short, in Japan in the 1970s, financial-market participants enjoyed only limited price-based, cross-sectoral or international competition. Regulatory restraints were high, interest groups were well-defined and capital mobility was low. Under these circumstances, regulatory politics closely reflected Japan's particular historical experience of state–market relations. Regulatory demands were routinely conveyed to and managed almost exclusively by officials at the Ministry of Finance (MOF), with intervention by politicians when bureaucrats and interest groups could not reach agreement on their own (Rosenbluth, 1989). The regulatory politics and policies emerging through this process looked little if anything like those found elsewhere, because they were designed to meet only the particular needs of the Japanese government and Japanese financial institutions.

The politics of reform during this period were manifested primarily through government intermediated conflicts between market actors. Because MOF officials were the ones routinely mediating between contending interests, however, these officials' preferences often played a considerable role in determining policy choice. Ministry officials consistently resisted dismantling their own favoured regulatory levers, and maintained relative control over the rest of the reform process by setting the pace of change, responding to market demands essentially on a case by case basis, and keeping policy outcomes within the range of options compatible with their own policy agenda. Given this pattern of domestic regulatory politics, virtually every policy change during this period reflected the area of overlap between government and market actors' interests in Japan as opposed to an emerging international standard.

As just one example, in the mid-1970s, when for the first time in the postwar period the Japanese government needed to issue massive amounts of debt, the government set up a syndicate of underwriters, issued Japanese government bonds (JGBs) at 'negotiated' below-market rates and greatly restricted secondary market sales and trading. MOF officials strongly preferred this arrangement, which was compatible with existing Japanese practices, over those found in the USA and the UK which allowed active market trading to determine rates (Horne, 1985, p.48). Despite the limitations of this arrangement, and aggressive lobbying by domestic financial institutions to change it, for many years the government steadfastly resisted adopting issuance and trading standards used elsewhere.

By the turn of the decade, however, government officials recognized that their own deficit-financing goals could not be achieved under the existing regulations governing the JGB market and its participants. In particular, Japan's top commercial banks were smothering under their obligation to absorb massive amounts of government debt. In order to avoid changing core regulations, MOF officials tried to accommodate the banking sector through accounting perks and alternative funding opportunities. Eventually, however, syndicate members began to supplement their exhausted political voice with a domestic form of 'exit' or capital strike – they repeatedly boycotted new JGB issues. This market leverage forced the MOF to negotiate more substantial reforms, including between 1979 and 1982 the issuance of JGBs at market-reflective rates and the introduction of new and very competitive products, such as negotiable certificates of deposit and medium-term government bond funds.

Another noteworthy reform agreement brokered during this period was the 1981 revision of the Banking Law. This new law gave both banks and securities firms some of what they wanted; it allowed banks to eventually trade JGBs in the secondary market and sell JGBs over the counter, and assured securities firms that the regulatory wall separating banking and securities would not otherwise be breached. Although these changes foreshadowed the eventual relaxation of boundaries defining virtually all specialized financial institutions, like the reforms above, they were adopted to overcome specific JGBs market issues and were not in any way motivated by government concerns with the international compatibility or competitiveness of the domestic market.

The Japanese government addressed market actors' demands for interest rate and access-related reforms with similar reserve and concern with maintaining as much of the traditional regulatory structure as possible. Over the next five years the government responded to demands for interest rate liberalization, not by liberalizing existing rates, but by making available to only the largest and domestically most mobile actors a variety of often uniquely Japanese new products with more market-reflective rates.[11] Concerning access, in several instances the government granted regulatory favours to a small population of foreign institutions in order to appease foreign governments, but denied these same privileges to Japanese institutions in order to avoid unsettling the domestic regulatory structure in any meaningful way. On the other side of the coin, Japanese financial institutions were gradually allowed to participate in the Eurobond market but only under restrictions, known as the Three Bureau's Agreement, devised to uphold domestic distinctions between banking and securities and minimize competition with Japan's domestic markets. Even Japan's new offshore market faltered for many years because of restrictions born of Japan's domestic financial politics, but not found in other offshore markets. In short, for at least a decade, regulatory reform under limited capital mobility brought about a generally more liberal, but still uniquely Japanese set of regulatory arrangements.

By the mid-1980s the dynamics of financial-market reform had begun to change and the motive force behind this transformation was increased capital mobility. Cross-border flows of capital were officially liberalized with the implementation of the revised Foreign Exchange and Foreign Trade Control Law (FEFTCL) in 1980, which deemed private sector external transactions 'free-in-principle,' with some exceptions, rather than 'prohibited-in-principle' as under the earlier law.[12] In addition, capital mobility increased through liberalization of yen-conversion limits, abolition of the 'real demand rule' for forward transactions and approval of a variety of new Euroyen and other Euromarket products, such as foreign-currency denominated and currency swap bonds.

Due to these changes, from the mid-1980s capital mobility became a more serious constraint on government policy options. The greater capacity for market participants to choose alternative regulatory environments intensified existing market pressure for domestic reform and increasingly dictated which policy options would prove viable. Consequently, at several points in the late-1980s, government officials sought to ensure their influence over economic developments by enticing back into their sphere of influence financial-market actors and activities that had 'exited' to other markets. Given this motivation, policies selected during this period were often directly responsive to the preferences of mobile capital and the relative attractiveness of alternative regulatory environments.

For example, in 1985 Japan introduced a uniquely structured financial futures market for only JGBs. By 1987, however, the absence of a more extensive financial futures market was retarding Japan's development as a major financial centre. At the time futures markets were already well-established in many overseas locations, including not only New York and London, but also Toronto, Hong Kong and, most importantly, Singapore, where futures of Japan's own Nikkei Index are traded. Since the government had not yet revised the laws separating specialized financial institutions, MOF officials had to orchestrate an awkward compromise between the banking and securities industries when they decided to expand the futures market. Nevertheless, unlike in the past, all participants sought a solution responsive to regulatory environments overseas.[13] The new agreement created a financial futures market providing all the instruments available overseas, and stipulated that the arrangement would be reexamined in two years in order to 'take whatever measures were necessary including legal revisions, to deal with movements in foreign futures markets and internationalize Japan's own market' (Schwartz, 1991, p. 542).

In another case, in 1988 the government changed Japan's short-term money-market regulations and the Bank of Japan (BOJ) changed its method of monetary adjustment after a substantial shift in short-term funds heightened concern about monetary policy effectiveness. BOJ officials have been among Japan's leading proponents of full interest-rate liberalization. Since open-market operations are considered the most effective way to adjust the money supply under liberalized market conditions, BOJ officials had long campaigned for an ample short-term government securities market in which to conduct these operations. Nevertheless, for years the MOF steadfastly refused large-scale issuance of short-term government securities into the market because this was expected to increase debt-financing costs and complicate foreign-exchange operations.

In late 1988, however, the interest-rate gap between open and interbank money-market rates reached close to one percentage point, causing the supply of interbank funds to contract considerably. This diminishment of the interbank market, where BOJ influence was extensive, threatened the central bank's effectiveness because at the time the BOJ did not have adequate means to conduct open-market operations. As soon as market conditions allowed, the government implemented the new monetary adjustment scheme and restructured Japan's short-term money markets. Notably, the long-standing Japanese collateral requirement in the call market was chiefly abandoned and rates for virtually all other products were liberalized to reflect market conditions through a bid–offer system. These reforms successfully enticed funds back into the interbank market and convinced the government that not only monetary policy effectiveness, but also the yen's role as an international currency and Tokyo's position as a major financial centre depended on the cultivation of a more internationally attractive domestic money market (*Kiny Zaisei Jij*, 8 July 1991, p. 25).

Japan's Financial System Reform Act (FSA) provides yet another example of how the existence of more attractive regulatory environments overseas compelled the Japanese government to reform long-standing domestic regulations in ways more convergent with overseas practices.[14] The FSA allows Japan's specialized financial institutions to gradually enter into each other's business areas. Although the government had carefully maintained the specialized financial system throughout much of the reform process, under conditions of greater capital mobility the costs specialization imposed on the domestic market became too great. As evidence, a growing number of Japanese corporations and financial institutions were choosing to conduct their financial-market transactions in overseas markets. Concern about the potential 'hollowing' of Japan's domestic corporate bond market in particular became commonplace in the mid- and late -1980s when Japanese corporations issued more bonds overseas than at home.[15] Indeed, the extent to which market participants were actively avoiding Japan's more regulated market was starkly highlighted by the fact that most of the Japanese bonds issued overseas were purchased by Japanese investors.

Meaningful liberalization of Japan's corporate bond market was complicated by the rigidity of Japan's system of specialized financial institutions. In 1985, however, the government began a systematic evaluation of Japan's specialized institutions and sought proposals for how to better accommodate liberalization trends and compete with overseas markets. The government even proposed a Japanese equivalent to London's 'Big Bang,' similarly designed to restore market competitiveness. Although the associated policy debates were long and tortuous, the government's intentions were clear throughout. As stated in the primary deliberative council's final report, Japan needed to undertake the proposed reforms because of 'the trend toward funds concentrating in more liberalized markets', and because 'the Japanese corporate bond market is experiencing a "hollowing out" due to restrictions and customs stemming from the current system' (MOF Financial System Research Council, 1991, section 2.3). Reflecting the government's concern with alternative regulatory environments and the competitive dynamic promoting regulatory convergence, the MOF's advisory groups examined other nations' markets and focused debate on five models of more liberal financial services based largely on overseas practices. They ultimately adopted the so-called 'Canadian model', which allows financial institutions to enter into other financial sectors through the establishment of subsidiaries (*ibid.*, chapter 4).

A clear and common thread running through regulatory reform in Japan as we approached the 1990s was the government's attention to securing Tokyo's place as a major financial centre by pursuing, when necessary, reforms that would bring Japan's regulatory environment closer in line to those found in the other major markets. Moreover, compared to before, government officials were giving relatively less weight to simply managing demands brought by domestic political actors, and more to systematic evaluation and proactive regulatory steps to insure the competitiveness of the Tokyo market. Thus, by 1990 the tendency for new policies to promote the cross-national convergence of regulatory arrangements could be seen in almost every financial market and sector in Japan.

As in the USA and the UK, rates in Japan's short-term money market reflected the cost of funds in open domestic and overseas markets. Moreover, the BOJ abandoned 'window guidance' as its primary means of controlling credit and increasingly manages the money supply through open-market operations. Similarly, JGBs were once issued predominantly with 10-year maturities, underwritten almost exclusively by a syndicate of Japanese financial institutions at terms set through negotiations, and traded in a very limited secondary market. Now, as is common elsewhere, JGBs are offered in a wide variety of maturities, usually issued through auctions at market-reflective rates, can be underwritten by both foreign and Japanese firms and are actively traded in secondary markets.

Along these same lines, terms in and access to Japan's corporate bond market was once extremely limited due to the restrictive practices of the Bond Issuance Committee run by Japan's leading financial institutions. Now qualification standards are clearly stipulated and refer to internationally recognized credit ratings, and issuance terms and rates are increasingly determined through the competitive proposal method prevalent in other major capital markets. Mimicking the restructuring seen in the USA and Canada among others, reforms have also lowered the walls separating specialized financial institutions, allowing a closer approximation of the universal banking opportunities found in Europe. As a result, Japanese financial institutions and investors now have greater access to most of the financial products and asset-management techniques that have proven attractive elsewhere. And finally, although still showing mixed results in Japan's domestic market, foreign financial institutions are afforded national treatment as they are in most other financial markets.

As these illustrations suggest, by the early 1990s financial-market reform in Japan had produced a domestic regulatory environment far more similar to those found in other major financial-centre states than existed before. I have argued that this is because increased capital mobility compelled the Japanese government to repeatedly address the competitiveness of Tokyo as a major international financial centre, and in these assessments pay great attention to the preferences of mobile capital. What has happened in the 1990s, however, might best be appreciated after a brief overview of some of the limits of regulatory competition and convergence.

Limits to competition and convergence

Even when capital is highly mobile, there are essential limits to regulatory competition and convergence. First we consider limits to convergence, which reflect primarily the nature of the market for regulatory services. Next we consider limits to regulatory competition, including successful international regulatory cooperation on the one hand, and cross-national differences in what constitutes politically acceptable domestic social and economic outcomes on the other.

Turning first to levels of convergence, it is clear that even extensive regulatory restructuring around the globe has not eliminated country-specific regulatory policies. Regulatory differences remain in part because not all market participants are willing or able to shop cross-nationally to find the most attractive environment. Not surprisingly, regulatory convergence is much more prominent at the wholesale level than at the retail level, and divergence is most extensive concerning financial products and services least integrated into the international markets. In short, capital mobility will not eliminate national variations so long as some actors cannot or do not take advantage of increased mobility.

The complex nature of regulatory interactions also limits convergence. To the extent regulatory environments are chosen in national jurisdiction-defined bundles of interrelated rules, as opposed to disaggregated costs and benefits, there is ample room for variation at the margins if the overall regulatory environment is competitive. Financial innovators are increasingly breaking down transactions into more discrete and independently marketable products, which are then booked in the most advantageous regulatory jurisdiction. At present, however, most market actors are still not flexible enough, and the market for regulatory services is not yet transparent and specialized enough for all participants to take advantage of these opportunities for regulatory arbitrage. Consequently, governments offering overwhelmingly competitive regulatory benefits in one important financial market sector can sometimes offer less competitive regulation in others.

Nevertheless, mobile capital is not completely indifferent between mixes of burdens and benefits across environments that seem equally competitive overall, because it is costly for market participant to learn and adhere to different sets of regulations for each jurisdiction they enter. Market actors seek not only attractive prices and trustworthy markets, but also regulatory clarity and convenience. Thus these actors prefer, and through their market behavior promote greater cross-national regulatory convergence.

The third and most significant factor inhibiting regulatory convergence it that regulations are but one element determining the competitiveness of national financial markets. Competition promotes both imitation and innovation. In the case of nations, each brings to this competition a particular set of domestic market structures. For some, the best strategy is to imitate more attractive regulatory environments. For nations hosting markets that are particularly attractive for other reasons, however, there is much less pressure to adjust. Some 'inherent' market advantages may arise from variables far removed from regulations or other politically-mandated market incentives, and include factors such as the domestic supply of financial resources, the depth of resident financial expertise and, of course, confidence in the host government. Less obvious factors include geographical location, the size and quality of the general labour force, and even language.

In the case of Japan, for example, foreign firms flocked to Tokyo in the early 1980s attracted by the tremendous domestic supply of capital, even though the regulatory environment was far from the most attractive. This non-regulatory enticement enabled the Japanese government to approach early reforms at a leisurely pace. By the early 1990s, however, it was easier to access this capital from outside Japan and many firms relocated their Japan-related business activities to the Euromarket as mentioned above, or to nearby financial centres in Hong Kong and Singapore. And currently in 1999, as the government grapples with a severe financial crisis, even Japan's long-standing status as the largest creditor nation is overshadowed by market participants' doubts about the government's ability to successfully restore Japan's financial sector. Consequently, the Japanese government is now under far greater pressure to create an internationally attractive financial-market environment than it was before the bursting of the bubble economy.

Non-regulatory factors also greatly influence which regulations become the standard towards which policies converge. I argued above that regulatory competition induces governments to adopt policies deemed attractive to major financial market players. But, these policies are not necessarily the best in any normative or even economic sense. As the oft-told story of the 'Qwerty' keyboard's popularity over supposedly superior models suggests, some regulations become standards simply because they were used first in a major market and imitated thereafter. Like most rational actors, financial-market participants often satisfice in their selection of regulatory environments, shopping primarily from among the traditionally large and attractive markets. In short, size and reputation count; cross-national competition is distorted by the oligopolistic character of the existing international financial market such that smaller or newly-established markets must compete with the regulations offered by the major financial-centre states and to which dominant financial-market actors have become accustomed.

Finally, competition itself has limits. Cross-national regulatory competition is most effectively restrained when regulators from many countries overcome their individual incentives to compete and enforce a common regulatory standard. In this respect, international regulatory cooperation represents a multi-government effort to impose regulations a fully competitive market for regulatory services would not have produced. Examination of variables promoting or inhibiting international cooperation is beyond the scope of this chapter, but it is worth noting that although international cooperation reduces the strategic and competitive elements of regulatory reform, it too promotes regulatory harmonization and strengthens the tendency toward convergence.

Competition also faces fundamental domestic political limits. As discussed, competitive reform biases policy towards accommodating the preferences of internationally mobile capital, which may or may not serve domestic interest groups. Among domestic groups, tension between those who benefit from greater international access, and those who prefer protection from more competitive markets is far from new. In this conflict of interests, however, capital mobility effectively tips the scales against those preferring protection. Moreover, because the international market for regulatory services is far from transparent, and the production costs and revenues associated with regulation are not obvious, governments can often avoid 'balancing' their so-called regulatory 'budgets' (Kane, 1987). Therefore, unrestrained regulatory competition creates incentives for government officials to provide more regulatory perks to, or shift the costs of regulation away from, actors with greater capital mobility and transfer these burdens to less mobile groups (Webb, 1996).

If the domestic costs of regulatory competition become exposed, and if a government's constituents perceive that these costs are not worth the benefits of hosting a competitive financial centre, state actors will try to ensure their own political survival before addressing continued competitiveness. They would rather manage an unattractive market than be out of a job in a competitive one. In other words, the collapse of domestic political support for regulatory reform may inhibit more aggressive regulatory competition until political authority is strengthened. But, this approach will not succeed long-term. Domestic opposition will not eliminate the underlying pressure imposed by the structure of international capital mobility. Given current levels of economic interdependence, the domestic costs of economic isolation are simply too great for most major industrialized nations to absorb. Consequently, even governments struggling to manage a domestic political crisis will have to do so within the constraints imposed by capital mobility. This is exactly where Japan, like several of its Asian neighbours, finds itself today.

The Japanese government's relatively free hand in managing Tokyo's emergence as an international financial centre became severely tied when the bursting of Japan's so-called 'bubble economy' at the end of the decade exposed to the public many of the costs involved in trying to combine internationally competitive and domestically protective elements within one integrated financial system. Within just a few short years the Japanese public's fascination with the financial revolution turned to disdain for the major financial-market participants in general, and anger at the role played by government officials in particular.

The negative political reaction was understandable, given that the stockmarket bottomed out, losing 60 per cent of its value between its peak at the end of 1989 and its nadir in August of 1992. Securities firms then fed fuel to the fire when it became known in the summer of 1991 that they had compensated their best clients for stockmarket losses while leaving their smaller clients to fend for themselves. The damage to the banking sector was even greater. The bursting of the bubble caused first a devastating drop in the value of their stockholdings, shrinking their capital base and therefore their ability to make new loans. In addition, banks lost tremendous sums as loans to finance the economic boom went bust. The perceived vulnerability of private financial institutions led investors to move their funds out of banks, as well as insurance companies and securities firms, and into the government-managed postal savings system. The Asian currency crisis in 1997 provided the straw that broke the camel's back. Quite suddenly it seemed, for the first time in the postwar period, Japanese financial institutions were failing or requiring government-assisted rescues. By the end of 1999, virtually all of Japan's financial institutions will have accepted some form of publicly-funded support.

This decade of developments has virtually eliminated the Japanese public's respect for previously venerated financial institutions and regulators. Overzealous investors and excessively competitive financial institutions are blamed for having channelled too much capital into the real-estate market, while ordinary citizens suffered under the burden of astronomical housing expenses. In addition, a seemingly endless series of financial-market-related scandals and accusations of government ineffectiveness and even complicity in these affairs, has turned public opinion firmly against Japan's financial-market regulators. Demands for reform of the MOF in particular have taken centre-stage.

Unquestionably, Japan's current financial crisis has politicized the regulatory reform process to an extent heretofore unseen. Up to this point, politicians tended to intervene in financial politics only on the rare occasion when MOF officials failed to produce an acceptable compromise, or when other scandalous financial practices, such as loan-sharking, temporarily grabbed national attention. Throughout all of the 1990s, however, politicians have faced extraordinary political pressure to step up and address the onslaught of problems associated with deteriorating financial-market conditions, including the proper role of the MOF. Disarray within Japan's major political parties during this period only exacerbated the politicization of these issues.

Since at least a year before the 1993 inauguration of the first non-Liberal Democratic Party (LDP) prime minister in over 35 years, Japan's political landscape has been in nearly continuous flux. As a result, for much of this decade, politicians' efforts to address Japan's economic woes have been complicated by the exigenciess of coalition-building and re-election. During this time, however, Diet proposals to radically reorganize the MOF and pump trillions of yen into the economy suggest they have at least resolved to play a very active role in the reform and recovery process. Given the political uncertainty of this decade and the associated re-election imperatives, one must expect their efforts to include a good deal of constituency service and the particularistic politics so well-known in Japan. Nevertheless, the existing level of international capital mobility virtually excludes from this agenda a retreat to re-regulatory protectionism. The only viable option is to pursue through further financial restructuring and regulatory reform a credible, healthy and more internationally competitive domestic financial market, and this is what the government has put forth. Although it is far from certain whether the government's 'Big Bang' package of financial system reforms will succeed, it is absolutely clear that the purpose of this plan is to make Tokyo a globally competitive financial market and that this requires greater regulatory convergence. The entire 'Big Bang' progamme is based on three principles: freely-competitive financial markets; fair trade based on transparent and consistent rules; and an institutional framework built on internationally acceptable legal, accounting and supervisory standards.

Given these specified principles, Japanese politicians and regulatory officials have very little room to maneuver. They must respond to the needs of their frustrated domestic constituents using policies deemed acceptable by major international financial-market participants. Reform and rescue efforts not embraced by mobile financial-market participants are very likely to fail; and therein lies the continuing influence of capital mobility over policy. As proposed above, under high levels of capital mobility the effective political influence of mobile financial-market participants becomes stronger *vis-à-vis* the state and relative to more constrained domestic actors, and this power need not be expressed through domestic political channels, but rather may be effectively exercised through the market behaviour; of these individuals and institutions. Accordingly, for at least the near future, exchange rates, interest rates and other market indicators are as relevant as signals of acceptable policy options as are domestic constituent polls.

Finally, as proposition two and the general argument of this chapter suggest, the policies that mobile market actors prefer, as evidenced through their behaviour, are very often policies proven effective and attractive in other leading markets. Thus, while it is natural during a crisis for governments to first consider policies that worked domestically in the past, contemporary markets players are steadfastly refusing to accept what they view as traditional Japanese solutions to the ongoing crisis. In this way, market criticism has become a powerful engine promoting further regulatory convergence. For example, the Japanese government's earliest efforts to support virtually all financial institutions using public money was roundly criticized in the market as a continuation of the Japanese 'convoy system' of protecting weak banks. Similarly, market actors expressed their displeasure with the government's initial policy of discussing bad loans only on an aggregate basis, and not bank-by-bank as is done elsewhere, by continuing to charge all Japanese banks a 'Japan premium'. By contrast, the market has responded more positively to recent proposals to establish a bridge bank, modelled after the US Resolution Trust Corp., as well as introduce some of the tax breaks and securitization techniques proven successful in managing risks elsewhere. Similarly, steps towards raising individual bank's disclosure requirements to levels imposed overseas are being hailed as absolutely necessary for reestablishing the credibility of Japanese institutions. Thus, even Japan's current crisis reveals the ways in which increased capital mobility promotes the tendency towards cross-national regulatory convergence.

As the government's past reluctance to dismantle Japanese regulatory practices amply illustrates, this tendency towards more convergent regulations obviously was not due to any Japanese ideological disposition towards international harmonization. Nor can it be explained by any increased effectiveness of US bullying. Rather, it reflects the Japanese government's efforts to manage the current political and economic crisis under conditions of significant capital mobility. This constraint effectively limits their policy options to those that more aggressively address the regulatory and government credibility issues currently undermining the international market's evaluation of Japan as an attractive financial centre. The Japanese government's policy options are limited, not because domestic political institutions have changed giving mobile capital greater political access, but because market structures have changed giving these actors greater influence over policy effectiveness, and thus policy choice.

This argument suggests two possible implications of competitive regulatory reform for Japan's political economy. First, capital mobility may in many ways free market actors from state control, but it does not free state actors from political pressure to protect domestic constituents from any ill effects brought on by this global transformation. The Japanese government's current inability to provide this protection, however, strongly suggests that further internationalization of Japan's economy most likely will invite additional domestic criticism of and further attempts to restructure Japan's regulatory institutions. In the past few years both the MOF and the BOJ have undergone significant reorganizations, and there is ample political pressure for further change in these and other institutions exemplifying the relationship between the state and economy in Japan.

Second, to the extent that Japan's political economy once afforded the government significant influence over domestic economic outcomes, financial-market reform is clearly eliminating some of Japan's distinctive qualities. Similarly, as reliance on some traditional means of influence, such as administrative guidance and personal consultations, gives way to more internationally acceptable means of administration such as greater standardization and regulatory codification, international understanding of Japan's regulatory apparatus improves, but what one sees is in some sense a little less 'Japanese'.

In conclusion, during this quarter-century the politics of financial-market reform in Japan have been shaped by government efforts to maintain policy effectiveness and political authority under changing market circumstances. Under conditions of limited capital mobility, regulatory politics were driven largely by the balance of domestic political and economic resources, and tended to perpetuate a recognizable pattern of Japanese politics and policy. Under conditions of ample capital mobility, however, regulatory competition increasingly set the parameters within which domestically palatable compromises were made, and tended to promote greater cross-national regulatory convergence. Given the current near-disastrous condition of Japan's financial sector, efforts to restore basic stability and credibility may overshadow more narrowly-strategic plans concerning the promotion of Japan as a major international financial market. As suggested above, however, even under these conditions competitive pressures remain a factor in policy decisions. Based on this evidence, international capital mobility appears to be a powerful and relatively enduring constraint on domestic regulatory politics, and its effects on financial market developments in Japan are expected to be felt far into the future.

Notes

1 Reform is used throughout as a neutral term encompassing all types of intentional change in regulatory arrangements, irrespective of the quality or desirability of these changes.

2 The definition of capital mobility is addressed by Kenneth Thomas elsewhere in this volume. Here I focus on the mobility of only financial capital. Setting aside, temporarily, issues concerning most appropriate measurements, the increase in the capacity for capital to move is readily apparent in the significant reduction in the number of regulations restricting capital flows (IMF, 1992), the approximate quintupling of cross-national flows of capital among the industrialized countries in the decade between the mid-1970s and mid-1980s (Frieden and Rogowski, 1996, p. 25), and increases in covered interest-rate parity (Frankel, 1992). Although these developments each deserve full investigation, in this chapter I treat increased capital mobility and the associated internationalization of finance as a single exogenous development.

3 Throughout the remainder of the chapter I refer to this group as mobile market actors or mobile capital. The mobility of financial capital is facilitated by low asset specificity and large-scale transactions. Consequently, large multinational corporations, institutional investors, and financial service providers tend to dominate this group.

4 Differences are found predominantly in those areas of financial-market development least responsive to market pressures, such as are imposed by physical and geographical limits or social cultural traditions, or experience/expertise-based sources of comparative advantages relating, for example, to a certain currency, product, location or client relationship. Persistent differences may also reflect intellectual disagreements such as genuine disputes about interpretations of events or the attractiveness of new alternatives. Scholars who have focused on explaining the unique aspects of Japan's financial reform

experience include Cargill and Royama (1988), Rosenbluth (1989), Vogel (1996) and Calder (1997).

5 A sense of this literature can be obtained from Andrews (1994), Cerny (1994), Helleiner (1994), Underhill (1991) and Webb (1991).

6 Capital mobility provides for three possibilities: (1) actors completely exit to alternative jurisdictions, creating financial-market 'externalization' or 'hollowing'; (2) actors straddle regulatory boundaries, passing business back and forth between jurisdictions to gain advantages through selective regulatory avoidance and arbitrage; and (3) actors remain where they are but conduct their business as if they were in a single open global marketplace, promoting market outcomes such as increased interest-rate parity. Although each of these responses has a different impact on regulatory policy and government capabilities, any one of them can significantly alter the quantity and quality of the activities taking place within a jurisdiction (Bryant, 1987).

7 To the extent reforms preferred by market actors reduce policy effectiveness, competitive pressures create a prisoner's dilemma at the international level: governments may not want more reform, especially more deregulation than is necessary, because changes in the regulatory structure inevitably affect intervention tools; accordingly each would be better off if they all agreed to stop competing; but, when capital is mobile each also faces strong incentives to compete for jurisdictional market-share because the cost of failing to maintain an attractive financial market can be great. On the other hand, to the extent that regulatory reform increases policy effectiveness, governments may find themselves collectively in a virtuous cycle. Reforms of either type that do not satisfy market actors' demands are unlikely to succeed for long or be imitated elsewhere.

8 Because capital mobility refers to the capacity of capital to move, not actual movements, high levels of capital mobility require governments to entice capital even if it is located within its jurisdiction.

9 These illustrations are drawn from more detailed case studies in Dwyer (1997).

10 Although the ease with which capital can move changes gradually over time, the following discussion treats capital mobility as if it were a dichotomous variable.

11 For descriptions, see Dwyer (1997). Interest-rate liberalization was extended to small savers only in the 1990s.

12 Although seemingly pivotal, the new law did not represent a major reform because in most respects it simply codified amendments and more liberal administrative practices introduced gradually during the previous decade (Semkow, 1985).

13 As the banking industry's report concludes, 'It is essential to create a framework that has as much as possible in common with financial futures markets overseas' (MOF Banking Bureau, 1987, p.7.) Similarly the securities industry reports, 'With futures and options trading being actively used in this way in the world's principal markets, if only Japan's market fails to provide this kind of system . . . its capital market will become less competitive' (MOF Securities Bureau, 1987, pp. 1–2).

14 Although the FSA was not formally approved by the Diet until 1992, I include it in this section because the deliberations over corporate bond market

reform took place primarily during and in response to developments in the 1980s.

15 In 1985 corporate bonds issued overseas represented 55.7% of all Japanese corporate bonds issued. Although this percentage fell to 47% during the following three years, when domestic convertible bonds were popular, by 1989 the share of bonds issued overseas once again surpassed 54%. The government's concern is evident in 'On a New Japanese Financial System', MOF Financial System Research Council Final Report (1991) Section 1.2.2.

3

Structural Indeterminacy and Sectoral Interests in European Monetary Integration*

Kathleen R. McNamara

International capital mobility is generally assumed to be a powerful structural feature of the international political economy (Andrews, 1994) which will produce relatively uniform and predictable effects on policies across all nation states. One key mechanism by which this process is assumed to occur is interest-group activity: multinational businesses and international investors are argued to play a vital role in promoting a steady liberalization in economic governance across the globe (Milner, 1988; Frieden and Rogowski, 1996). The increasing internationalization of business boosts the incentives for governments to open markets, creating a self-reinforcing circle of causation. One strand of such argumentation focuses specifically on the role of capital mobility in pushing forward Economic and Monetary Union in Europe (EMU). The level of financial integration is argued to have a powerful influence on the politics of EMU via capital mobility's effects on the policy demands of firms and sectors (Frieden, 1991b). The EMU project has been cited as an example of the process by which economic logic translates through the domestic polity, pushing cooperation among states to promote financial liberalization, monetary integration and movement towards a single European currency.

---

* This chapter draws on chapter 2 of McNamara (1998), which is used with permission of the publisher. An earlier version of the chapter was presented as 'Economic and Monetary Union in Europe: Do Domestic Politics Matter? Does Hegemony?' at the 1994 Annual Meeting of the American Political Science Association, 1–4 September 1994, New York City.

In this chapter, I challenge this argument, offering a theoretical critique and empirical evidence to support my contention that increases in capital mobility have not provoked sectoral interests into playing a central role in European monetary integration in the manner predicted in Frieden's 'modern political economy' framework (Frieden, 1991b, p. 15). The principal reason is that the sectoral-interest approach, as currently formulated, is theoretically underspecified and incomplete, relying on a single structural feature, capital mobility, to determine outcomes. In fact, I will argue, there is a high degree of uncertainty over the specific distributional costs and benefits of different monetary regimes. This uncertainty makes theoretical frameworks pitched at a very high level of temporal and spatial generalization unable to predict the interests at play in monetary integration. Country-specific institutional factors, broadly defined, are critical in determining actors' positions on the issue of European monetary cooperation. The importance of institutions means that actors' preferences will be conditioned by their historical, cultural and national political contexts (Thelen and Steinmo, 1992; Pierson, 1996; Garrett and Lange, 1996).

Accordingly, more theoretical and empirical attention needs to be paid to variations in the process by which national preferences about monetary cooperation are formed and translated into policies; that is, how agents react to and shape structural conditions, be they capital flows, or formal or informal institutions. Congruent with a rich tradition of scholarship on international monetary regimes, we conclude by suggesting that the European cases can alternatively be explained by an argument situated at the level of national governments which takes seriously the causal role of *social* institutions, namely changing ideas about economic strategy in shaping outcomes of monetary cooperation or conflict (Oye, 1985; Odell, 1986; Ruggie, 1983; McNamara, 1998).

Capital mobility, while a structural feature of the international political economy, does not by itself generate a universal and parsimonious mapping of societal interests into policy outcomes across states in the realm of international monetary politics. Agency, in the form of actors' intersubjective understandings or interpretations of the structure of capital mobility, is equally crucial and should be regarded as constitutive of that structure (Wendt, 1992). Moreover, a rich assortment of social, political and historical institutions also structure agents' interests and thus critically shape the evolution of political action (Dobbin, 1992; Vogel, 1997; Vogel, 1999; Trentmann, 1998).

The chapter begins with an overview of the EMU case, then sketches out the hypotheses of the sectoral-interests approach and assesses their theoretical and empirical validity in explaining the evolution of European monetary integration. Other cases which challenge the sectoral-interest-group approach are briefly considered, and the chapter concludes with some observations about how institutions play a critical role in the construction of actors' policy preferences.

The question of European monetary cooperation

The evolution of monetary cooperation in Europe offers students of politics two related puzzles. The first concerns the development of exchange-rate stability within the framework of the European Monetary System, the EC's fixed exchange-rate agreement established in 1979 (Ludlow, 1982). Despite being very similar in membership and institutional configuration to the Snake, an earlier, failed fixed exchange-rate regime, the new EMS confounded its many skeptics by its durability and longevity (Gros and Thygesen, 1992). The second puzzle follows on from the first: why did the EC governments decide to move forward with monetary integration, beyond the fixed rates of the EMS, to the creation of a monetary union with a single currency and European central bank?

For the Snake and the EMS, a simple comparison reveals the extent of the difference in the level of cooperation evidenced in the two regimes. In terms of national participation, for example, the Snake, established in 1972, essentially ceased to exist as a fully-fledged European Community agreement within one year of its founding (Tsoukalis, 1977).[1] The high level of discord throughout the entire Snake experience, and the inability of the EC countries to solve the problems involved in establishing a regional exchange-rate agreement, prompted a group of EC experts and policy-makers in 1975 to characterize efforts towards monetary cooperation as a 'failure,' and to state that 'national economic and monetary policies have never in 25 years been more discordant, more divergent, than they are today' (Marjolin, 1975).

In contrast, the Exchange Rate Mechanism (ERM) of the EMS did not experience any loss of membership from its founding in 1979 until 13 years later in 1992.[2] This strong record of participation throughout the 1980s was marred in September 1992 when a currency crisis caused Italy and Britain to exit the agreement, culminating in the loosening of the regime's exchange-rate bands in August 1993. That the EMS regime largely maintained its membership and quickly regained a high level of exchange-rate stability, however, is in contrast to the Snake experience when comparatively low levels of speculative pressures resulted in the early exit of the core EC states.

A second indicator of the difference in EMS and the Snake is the level of currency fluctuation, as the EC member governments' goal in both regimes was to establish a 'zone of monetary stability' by fixing their exchange rates. Here again the difference is striking: nominal variability for the ERM countries was more than cut in half on average in the EMS period (1979–95) in comparison to the Snake experience (1973–9), while for those outside the ERM regime, both within Europe and elsewhere, currency variability remained about the same (McNamara, 1998, table 1). Studies have also shown that the ERM states experienced an increase in the variability of their bilateral exchange rates in the 1979–95 period *vis-à-vis* currencies not in the EMS, making it seem unlikely that the currency stability created in the EMS would have occurred on its own, without the institutionalized cooperation of the regime (McNamara, 1998, table 2).

The agreement of the national governments at Maastricht in December 1993 to go ahead with the ambitious plan for the creation of an Economic and Monetary Union provides perhaps the most intriguing puzzle for students of both international relations and comparative politics. The Treaty on European Union constitutes a historically unprecedented experiment in governance. Never before have sovereign states agreed to set themselves on a path which starts with increasing coordination of economic and monetary policies and ends in a single currency, the euro, and a common monetary institution, the European Central Bank (ECB). For theorists concerned with the intersection of political power and market forces, the agreement at Maastricht presents a compelling case that begs explanation.

Sectoral-interest-group theories and structural determinacy

Sectoral-interest-group theories are one important source of explanation for foreign economic policy-making and cooperation and conflict among nation-states. This approach argues that national policy choices can largely be understood as a function of governments' reactions to pressures from domestic groups representing specific economic interests within society.

An early version of this approach was used to illuminate the path of European integration in the writings of neofunctionalist theorists (Haas, 1958, 1964, 1975; Lindberg and Scheingold, 1970). One of the guiding principles of this literature is a belief that interest groups play a significant role in producing integration by pushing for the building of international institutions that will bring economic gain. These institutions will entail functional linkages among issue areas and, if managed skillfully by political élites, create positive spillover effects which further the integration process. The 'stop and go' history of success and failure in the area of European monetary cooperation contradicts the general assumption of the neofunctionalist theory that the integrative process is self-sustaining through the process of spillover. However, a more explicit focus on interest-group theory and exchange-rate policy may be able to do a better job in accounting for the development of monetary cooperation in Europe.

A pioneering assessment of the role of sectoral interests in monetary integration has been undertaken by Jeffry Frieden (Frieden, 1991b). Frieden develops a framework to identify the distributional consequences of increased international capital mobility, arguing that higher levels of international financial flows produce important new sources of agreement and disagreement over the shape of national monetary policies. The main thrust of the argument is that capital mobility exacerbates cleavages between tradable-goods producers and those who produce for national markets, as well as creating divisions between internationally-oriented, diversified investors and domestically-oriented, undiversified investors. These cleavages between those with 'specific' assets and those with more fungible assets all play out in the policy arena, where the winning coalition convinces the national government to pursue those macroeconomic and exchange-rate policies that will benefit them, as will be explained in more detail below.

On first glance, Frieden's approach seems to place actors, in the form of representatives of different sectoral interests, front and centre as the source of policy outcomes. However, this approach to the dynamics of capital mobility is more fundamentally driven by international structural factors, that is, the level of financial integration or capital mobility.[3] As is the case in the broader range of such theories (Rogowski, 1989; Milner, 1988), actors' policy preferences are defined solely by their position in the international economy, and the costs and benefits of market integration for that position are assessed drawing on selected theories from the economics literature.[4] Although it is preferences themselves, not the process by which preferences are translated into political outcomes, that is the focus of this literature, the balance of political power is assumed in these writings to swing over to the sectors that are gaining the most from the opening (or closing) trend. This power translates into influence on governments, pressuring them to pursue policies congruent with those putative interests (Lindblom, 1976). Structure, that is, openness or closure to the international economy, is determinant of actors' preferences. But it is a limited conception of structure: causal weight is not given to other structural features such as variations in national setting or historical period and how they may affect actors' preferences. Nor are actors imbued with agency, as their preferences, and thus it is assumed their actions, are fixed by their position in the economy.

Sectoral interests and EMU

What are Frieden's specific predictions, and how well do they stand up to theoretical and empirical scrutiny? Frieden's framework encompasses a broad range of rich insights about the interactions between sectoral interests, capital mobility and government policies across the developed and developing world. For our purposes here, however, the key question is what the 'specific-factors approach' predicts with regard to sectoral interests in the EMS and EMU projects. Frieden draws on macroeconomic theory to identify two general, interrelated dimensions of policy choice critical to economic actors: the first concerns the degree of exchange-rate flexibility and implies a trade-off between exchange-rate stability and macroeconomic policy autonomy; the second, the level of the exchange-rate itself, high/appreciated or low/depreciated.

Frieden argues that 'international traders and investors and the producers of export-oriented tradable goods tend to suffer from exchange market volatility, since it makes their business riskier', but they are less concerned about macroeconomic policy autonomy, since they are not tied to one national economy for their business (Frieden, 1991b, pp. 444–5). According to this specific-factors approach, the internationally-oriented firms will thus prefer a fixed exchange-rate, with industry preferring a weak currency and financial interests favouring a strong currency. In contrast, the producers of non-tradable goods and services, and those who produce goods for the national market that compete with imports, will both prefer national macroeconomic policy autonomy over stable rates, since their business is domestically-oriented.

Frieden predicts that the exchange-rate stability of the EMS, and the subsequent plans for monetary union contained in Maastricht, will thus find support from firms in the financial sector, major exporters and diversified multinationals; it will be opposed by domestically-oriented industries. He notes in support of his contentions that of the 12 corporate members of the British chapter of the Association for Monetary Union in Europe (AMUE), eight firms are in the financial sector, two are multinationals, and two are major exporter (Frieden, 1991b, p. 448).

The logic of Frieden's framework implies that the longevity of the EMS and the drive to full monetary union would be explained by support for monetary cooperation from the previously identified groups of economic actors because of the benefits they receive from exchange-rate stability. Governments are assumed to be highly motivated to participate in agreements designed to capture these benefits in response to domestic pressures from these interest groups.

How persuasive are these sectoral preferences in explaining the variation in cooperation from the failed Snake to the relatively successful EMS and the Maastricht Treaty? While Frieden's overall presumption is correct–internationally-oriented businesses prefer exchange-rate stability to instability–his highly differentiated framework of interests is disputable on both theoretical and empirical grounds. I first consider the high level of theoretical uncertainty over the distributional effects of different exchange-rate regimes, then turn to a preliminary assessment of the empirical record.

Uncertainty and institutional contingency

There is a significantly higher lack of certainty, both in theory and in practice, over both the size and the distribution of the gains from monetary cooperation among specific economic actors than that presented in Frieden's account. This is due to the highly contingent and complex nature of interactions between monetary policy actions, the level of the exchange-rate and the variability of the exchange rates which produces a highly unstable preference structure without a clear policy equilibrium.

For example, Frieden argues that producers of tradable goods should prefer monetary expansions, as reflationary policies generally lead to currency depreciations making exported goods cheaper on world markets. However, not captured in the analysis is the fact that undertaking a monetary expansion creates an inherent conflict with the tradeable sector's goal of exchange-rate stability. So what is an export-oriented firm to prefer?

The problem for the specific-factors approach is that the answer is difficult to formulate in the absence of highly specific information about the particularistic institutional and temporal context under which the decision is being made. This considerably complicates the task of generating an aggregated, single framework of European sectoral preferences. First, an export-oriented firm's preference will most likely depend on the overall macroeconomic situation of the national economy and its trading partners – is the exchange-rate highly overvalued or is it only moderately strong? Is the exchange-rate system relatively stable overall, and thus could perhaps withstand a one-time devaluation, or is the level of variability already excessive making exchange-rate-stability a first priority? While these questions are not unsolvable, it is apparent that the answers will be highly sensitive to contextual factors.

The firm's policy preference will also heavily depend on a second factor: the degree to which businesses believe inflation will be worsened by a monetary expansion and depreciation. For example, certain export producers who rely on imported inputs for production may find a depreciating national currency costs more than it benefits them, as it makes imports more costly. European public debates on exchange-rate and monetary policy have been dominated for the past decade by the view that a strong currency is necessary to protect against the 'vicious circle' effects of depreciation and inflation experienced during the 1970s (McNamara, 1998). Macroeconomic policy autonomy is not privileged as a worthwhile or realistic goal, as many business and government élites fear that expansionary macroeconomic policies in the highly open economies of Europe will only bring more inflation, not growth or employment. For example, Iverson and Thygesen (1998) note that in Denmark, the desire for monetary policy credibility explains more convincingly the sectoral coalitions and exchange-rate policies pursued than do the factors Frieden's framework predicts. These historically contingent, 'open economy' effects have had a major impact on the way social groups think about exchange-rate policy in Europe, but are not captured in the framework of the specific factors approach.

These obstacles in tracing out the distributional consequences of different exchange-rate regimes have been the focus of recent theoretical work by macroeconomists seeking to understand events in Europe. Alberto Giovannini has considered three major economic models that evaluate the effects of alternative exchange-rate regimes: the Mundell–Fleming model, the rules-versus-discretion model, and the transaction-costs model. He examines each model for its ability to identify the interest groups that should prefer one type of monetary regime over another, but concludes that the inability of the models to produce consistent hypotheses indicates that 'the economic interests in favour of a fixed versus flexible exchange rates are not easily identifiable' (Giovannini, 1992, p. 22). Giovannini points out that the economic effects of a monetary regime are often highly contingent on country-specific or time-specific institutional and contextual factors, and can change dependent on a range of variables such as the source of economic shocks or the business cycle (McNamara and Jones, 1996; Hall and Franzese, 1997) Thus, he concludes 'there are no stable constituencies for or against monetary union' (Giovannini, 1992, p. 18).

This view is echoed by Paul Krugman, who has written that the underdevelopment of the microfoundations of international monetary theory leaves us without 'anything we can properly call a model of the benefits of fixed rates and common currencies' (Krugman, 1993, p. 3). This uncertainty casts doubt on the view that economic benefits of monetary cooperation are compelling enough to stimulate strong and highly differentiated interest group pressures of the type proposed by Frieden, as the groups have trouble recognizing and acting on a fixed and compelling preference in this area.[5]

It should also be noted that this theoretical uncertainty has also led to consternation on the part of central bankers, for whom confusion over the effects of monetary policy action forms part of their daily routine (*The Economist*, 1992; 1994; Buerkle, 1993). Particularly over the past five years, as monetarist principles of targeting the growth of the money supply have been discredited as policy tools, central bankers have scrambled to find a convincing analytical framework within which to shape their national economies. As economist Benjamin M. Friedman stated at a recent conference of central bankers, 'It may be true that war is the human activity most vitally subject to chance and happenstance, but monetary policy runs a close second' (quoted in Greenhouse, 1993). Given the high level of uncertainty about the effects of monetary and exchange-rate policy, it is no wonder that an independent, European central bank has been sought by European leaders in lieu of macroeconomic policy autonomy. Simply put, it is far easier to give up the levers of policy if they appear to be out of order in the first place.

The empirical record

Second, an assessment of the empirical data does not support the contention that 'Europe's leading financial and multinational firms have been the stronghold of support for breaking down remaining barriers to EC financial and monetary integration' (Frieden, 1991b, p. 441). In fact, sectoral interest groups have *not* been a key causal influence in the development of European monetary cooperation. This conclusion is drawn from interviews with European Community observers and officials, as well as with the very representatives of the business interests

Frieden's theory would predict to be strongly in favour of monetary integration and exchange-rate stability.[6]

On the question of fixed exchange rates and European Monetary Union, for example, financial-services representatives demonstrate decidedly mixed reactions, not the positive endorsement Frieden predicts. In part, they dislike increased exchange-rate stability and a single currency because they are reluctant to lose lucrative foreign-exchange transaction business and the opportunity for large gains from currency trading, although they do favour the increasing investment opportunities that come with monetary integration.[7]

The remarks of the chief economist of a large, multinational bank are typical: he stated that his bank had undertaken several lengthy studies to determine the effects of monetary integration on its business, yet were unable to come up with a decisive position for or against.[8] This is echoed in a 1990 survey done by Ernst and Young for the Association for Monetary Union in Europe which concluded that while more than half the European non-financial businesses surveyed believed a European currency would have a positive impact on their overall business strategies, 'It is evident that a majority of the banks felt that the lack of a European currency has not been an obstacle to any aspect of their strategy.' On balance, the effect of monetary integration was judged in the study to be neutral for the banking sector (Ernst and Young, 1990, p. 47, figures 9 and 10).

While they may join organizations like the Association for Monetary Union in Europe (AMUE) so as to remain within the policy debate, some bankers will publicly state that their AMUE support does not extend to spending time and money to see monetary integration move forward.[9] An AMUE official himself states that

> the financial sector is involved in the AMUE because any change toward EMU obviously impacts them directly and they need to stay informed, but that is not the same as saying that they are pushing for EMU. They are most concerned with being well informed about the progress of the EMU project, so that they may plan accordingly.[10]

That being said, financial interests have not actively opposed steps towards exchange-rate stability or monetary union in the European Community. Interviews indicate that banking interests do not want to be seen as against the 'European project' because of their own 'selfish' interests, and because they also do not want to be excluded from the Community decision-making process in an area of importance to them.[11] Also, in line with the predictions of Frieden's framework, some specialized banks believe that they may gain markets with increased financial liberalization and a single currency, but these make up a minority of the European financial actors.

Have other, non-financial business interests been more active in pressuring their governments for increased exchange-rate cooperation? Here the evidence is equally unconvincing. Generally speaking, most export-oriented firms in Europe favour exchange-rate stability because of the possibility that wide swings in currency values could dampen trade within the European Community. Multinational industrial representatives have tended to be the most active members of the Association for Monetary Union in Europe, because they are the ones who would clearly benefit from a single currency (primarily through the reduction in transaction costs).[12] However, this preference, and its intensity, has remained constant over the postwar era, and thus cannot explain the differences in the degrees of cooperation in the Snake and the EMS.

The comments of a Brussels-based representative of an export-oriented, multinational beer and spirits company help explain why this is so:

> Multinational companies [like ours] would find a single currency a marginal improvement, but only marginal. [We] are already quite adept at dealing with currency risk through hedging and so on... Of course, if they ask us, we say we are for it, but it doesn't go beyond that.[13]

The speaker went on to point out that

> The people who would really be helped would be smaller businesses, who at present do not export because of the high barriers to learning about how to deal with different currencies and exchange-rate risks... however, they have not pushed for monetary integration because it is not in their immediate business interest.

These views, echoed in other interviews with multinational firms, directly contradict the predictions of Frieden's framework.

Generally speaking, the role of business groups in the European Community varies substantially over issue area and type of policy, and a preliminary assessment of the data seems to indicate that the level of collective action problems inherent in an issue works well in predicting the way business influences policy (Olson, 1965; Gowa, 1988; Greenwood and Aspinwall, 1998). For example, there is a great deal of interest-group activity, both in Brussels and at the national levels, on specific narrowly-drawn issues, such as food product regulations, that do not give rise to serious collective action problems. Some larger issues such as the reinvigoration of the single market programme, have been moved along with business input, but only through the actions of a select group of key industrialists on a very élite level (Sandholtz and Zysman, 1989). The role of Wisse Dekker, chief executive of Phillips, in providing a blueprint for the Single Act programme is an example of this (Cowles, 1995).

Yet while there has been a fairly constant base level of business support for exchange-rate stability, there has not been the type of highly differentiated sectoral demand for various macroeconomic and exchange-rate policies that Frieden's specific-factors approach predicts. The lack of strong preference articulation on the part of financial and industrial concerns indicates that the causal linkages between the firms' interests and government policies in this area may be too ambiguous, or indeed too contradictory, for interest groups to act decisively on these issues. Given the amount of uncertainty in the underlying economic theories about exchange rates, this is not surprising.

Reflecting this, even the Association for Monetary Union in Europe, which Frieden describes as the 'private-sector lobbying organization for rapid currency union', was in fact created as the Committee for Monetary Union in Europe in 1987 by former French President Valéry Giscard D'Estaing and former German Chancellor Helmut Schmidt as an 'elder statesmen's group'; the majority of the initial members were national and EC officials who were longtime supporters of political and monetary integration. Giscard and Schmidt in 1988 decided to try to encourage businesses to support the idea of monetary integration, and recruited Giovannini Agnelli of FIAT and C.J. Van der Klugt of Phillips, among others, to become active in the new, renamed group.

According to a senior AMUE official, the group has not been involved in the major policy initiatives, the Delors Committee and the Maastricht treaty negotiations, that have spurred EMU. In his experience, rather than lobby in the traditional sense, the AMUE has proved reactive in nature; the business representatives on the AMUE board hold the view that the most important benefits of monetary union lie in the political realm, as a way to further bind the EC countries together for peace and prosperity and thus do not act as a traditional interest group.[14]

Constructing actors' interests

Domestic political interests matter a great deal in the evolution of monetary cooperation in Europe, but not in the manner assumed by traditional analyses of sectoral interest theories. In other empirical settings, theorists have begun to focus on the role of institutions, broadly understood, in shaping preferences.

Focusing on the Japanese political economy, Steven Vogel has argued for the need for more attention to inductive research instead of assuming interests *a priori* based on economic theory (Vogel, 1999). He examines the case of Japanese consumer groups, who seem to act and advocate policies which do not conform to maxims of standard microeconomic theories. Vogel argues that the overzealous application of such theories has led political scientists to mischaracterize and misunderstand the contours of Japanese political economy more generally. He finds that Japanese consumers are neither 'abused nor confused', but view their policy interests in ways that are conditioned by institutions, broadly defined – their culture, history, and the networks of relationships and understandings which shape their identities. These identities, he claims, have evolved in ways not predicted by models of actors' interests based on their 'objective' positions in the economy.

Two historical studies further indicate the potential limitations of the sectoral-interest approach. Frank Trentmann (1998) has studied the case of free trade in late Victorian and Edwardian Britain, arguing that the sectoral-interests approach is inadequate without a broader focus on the cultural significance and interpretive framework underlying free trade. Instead, he proposes a focus on the 'formative role of ideology, historical memory and political language in constructing free trade as a collective good'. He contends that we should think about the political economy as a cultural institution. Efforts to understand the workings of the political economy based on exogenously constructed 'sectoral interests' can only be *post hoc prompter hoc* reasoning, or if *a priori*, can only sketch a very generalized, underdetermined framework which will falter when applied in specific institutional, temporal and cultural contexts such as the cases of turn-of-the-century Britain.

Similarly, Frank Dobbin (1992) studies the origins of American private social insurance in the period 1920–50 and finds that labour and capital's positions on social security policies in that period were unstable and varied significantly over time in response to changes in the broader institutional environment and efforts by salient political actors to shape societal groups' interpretations of their interests.

Elsewhere I have offered an alternative account of the progress of European monetary cooperation in which social institutions, or shared beliefs, are a pivotal source of political outcomes (McNamara, 1998). In this explanation, neither structure nor agency is given primacy, but rather actors must interpret their structural environment, be it made up of international economic structures such as capital mobility, or domestic institutional structures such as labour market institutions, or normative structures such as Keynesianism. By so doing, they have the potential to transform these structures through their interpretations and subsequent actions.

The importance of ideational factors in explaining the dynamics of monetary cooperation is not unique to the European cases, but follows a rich tradition in international monetary affairs. Policy-makers' perceptions of the costs and benefits of domestic policy autonomy versus international monetary cooperation, and the importance of common beliefs or, alternatively, conflicting interpretations about the role of monetary policy – both within and among states – are key themes in the literature. For example, Joanne Gowa points to 'shared images' among administration officials about the need for a reassertion of domestic policy priorities as a crucial determinant of the US decision to abandon Bretton Woods, an account congruent with John Odell's evidence about the importance of ideas in explaining US international monetary policies more broadly (Gowa, 1983; Odell, 1982). Barry Eichengreen has argued that an appropriate and effective international macroeconomic response to the severe worldwide depression of the 1930s did not occur primarily because national policy-makers had strongly divergent views, 'derived from the different historical experiences of the nations involved', on what type of action should be taken (Eichengreen, 1991, p. 150). Kenneth Oye's examination of the pattern of monetary conflict and cooperation during the interwar era likewise relies heavily on the role of 'changing economic beliefs' in altering 'perceptions of interest in international monetary arrangements' (Oye, 1985, p. 175).

The importance of ideas and perceptions across these cases is in large part a function of the continuing uncertainty over the fundamental workings of the macroeconomy and the lack of agreement over what constitutes 'correct' macroeconomic policy. Peter Hall has argued that 'policy paradigms', as he calls them, are critically important in macroeconomic policy-making because of the opacity of cause-and-effect relationships in this area of government policy (Hall, 1993). A policy paradigm serves as a crucial guide for government officials attempting to analyse the complex technical relationships that make up the macroeconomy, providing them with a means–end knowledge that allows for the development of economic policies.

The role of ideas in the formation of monetary policy is strengthened by the institutional setting in which EU and national monetary policy-making takes place. Control over monetary and exchange-rate policies has historically been highly concentrated in the national executives, national central banks, and insulated EU institutions such as the Committee of Central Bank Governors. These bodies constitute some of the 'strongest' state agencies of modern democracies, in the sense that they are highly insulated from societal pressures. This view is congruent with the majority of work in political science that has viewed monetary policy as an élite-driven issue area particularly insulated from direct societal or interest group pressures (Gowa, 1988; Krasner, 1978a; Moses, 1997).

Conclusion

Capital mobility and domestic politics do matter in European monetary integration, but not, as one might assume, through the inevitability of capital mobility prompting sectoral-interest-group pressures for government action. This theoretical approach to foreign economic policy-making and international cooperation, while offering important insights, loses its potency when applied to the realm of European monetary affairs. Instead, I have argued that continued uncertainty over what constitutes the correct prescriptions for monetary policy and the important role of institutional variation, both in terms of formal and social institutions, make more ambiguous the role of capital mobility in monetary cooperation.

Interests in monetary cooperation are underdetermined in the structural account offered by the sectoral-interest-group theories. I suggest that a more analytically and empirically sound account of European monetary cooperation would conceive of actors' interests as highly contingent *both* on the domestic and international political environment states face, *and* on the ideas that they have about the nature of the cost–benefit trade-offs in a given situation. We international political economists still have a way to go to fully explain the pattern of diverging and converging interests driving European monetary union. Attention to the role of changing ideas in defining national interests in monetary integration is one way to get us closer to such a goal, as is the consideration of institutions of a more formal nature. It may also bring us closer to understanding the relationship between structure and agency in international capital mobility.

Notes

1 The Snake's members included Belgium, France, Germany, Italy, Luxembourg, the Netherlands and Denmark, with Norway and Sweden participating for several years as non-EC members. Within the first two years, the United Kingdom, Denmark, Italy and France exited the agreement rather than abide by the Snake's rules, finding untenable the domestic policy adjustments and the level of coordinated interventions necessary for continued membership. France and Denmark both returned to the Snake, although France exited permanently in 1976. A limited version of the Snake, consisting of Germany and the smaller northern countries, persisted as a 'D-mark zone' throughout the 1970s. For a chronology of national participation in the Snake, see table 1.1 in Gros and Thygesen (1992, p. 17).

2 The EMS was founded by Belgium, Denmark, France, Germany, Ireland, Italy, Luxembourg and the Netherlands. The only then-EC member-state not participating in the ERM at the founding of the EMS was Britain, which entered the agreement in 1990 (Spain and Portugal also joined after entering the EC). Greece is the only EC country never to have joined the ERM.

3 See Clark (1998) for an opposing discussion of the structure–agency problem.

4 Frieden draws on the Mundell–Fleming model in his analysis of EMU, and more generally employs the Ricardo–Viner specific-factors approach (Frieden, 1991; Frieden and Rogowski, 1996). Rogowski's explanation for political conflict makes productive factors the unit of analysis, drawing on the Heckscher–Ohlin model and Stolper–Samuelson theorem (Rogowski, 1989).

5 Joanne Gowa (1988) asserts that different areas of monetary policy are subject to different levels of collective-action problems, with exchange-rate policy having the highest level.

6 Those interviewed included staff members from the Directorate General II of the European Community and expert observers of EC policy-making, as well as banking interests in London and Brussels, and officials from the Union of Industrial and Employers' Confederations of Europe (UNICE), the European Trade Union Confederation, the Roundtable of European Industrialists, and the Association for Monetary Union in Europe (London, September 1991; Brussels, October 1991, October 1993 and May 1994; and Paris, June 1994).

7 These conclusions are based on discussions with several chief economists and lobbyists working for large, multinational banks (London, September 1991; Brussels, October 1991; and Brussels, May 1994).

8 Interviews, Brussels, February and May 1994, and London, October 1991.

9 These views were expressed at a roundtable discussion, 'Is EMU Dead?' at The Philip Morris Institute for Public Policy Research, Brussels, Belgium, 6 May 1994. The banker in question advised examining the actual balance sheet of the AMUE to see who had given how much money for its activities, stating his view that the financial sector is not a major contributor.

10 Interview, Association for Monetary Union in Europe official, Paris, June 1994.

11 Interviews, Brussels, November 1991.

12 Interview, AMUE official, Paris, June 1994.
13 Interview, Brussels, May 1993.
14 Interview, AMUE official, Paris, June 1994. See also the initial statement of the AMUE, at that time called the Committee for Monetary Union in Europe, 'Un Programme pour L'Action' (Paris: AMUE, 1988); the founding membership list is on p. 56.

Part II

Developing the Scholarly Agenda

4

Bonded Polity: The Distributional Consequences of Relying More Heavily on Bond-Financed Social Policies*

Jonathon W. Moses

Over the past decade, European governments have become increasingly indebted. High levels of unemployment and low levels of growth have meant that politically timid governments have built up larger and larger debt-levels to placate their constituencies. Rather than scale back the welfare state, or increase the tax revenue base with which to pay for programmes that the electorate has come to expect, governments have chosen the path of least resistance: paying for today's policies with tomorrow's revenues. This chapter looks at the more significant distributional consequences of the shift to debt-financed social programmes.

The chapter is divided into three sections. The first section looks at the justifications for moving to more debt-financed policies. People and states do not usually plan as a first course of action their future indebtedness; debt-financed policies are the best choice, given the alternatives. The second section presents an empirical slide of a single country's move from one funding path to the other. Countries, for the reasons mentioned in the first section, have switched from a tax and money-financed path to one which relies more heavily on debt-financing. Sweden is chosen for a case study as it exemplifies the trend common

* An earlier draft of this chapter was presented at the 1995 Annual Meeting of the American Political Science Association in Chicago, and to the workshop on 'Structure and Agency in International Capital Mobility' (Princeton University, 29–30 March 1996). I would like to thank the ARENA (Advanced Research on the Europeanization of the Nation State) Project for research support in the early stages of this work. Thanks also to Karl-Orfeo Fioretos, Bent Sofus Tranøy, and the participants of the Princeton workshop for their thoughtful remarks on earlier drafts. Obviously, I alone am responsible for what follows.

to other industrialized countries: Sweden is an economy saddled with large public policy expenditures; one which relied heavily on tax and money financing throughout most of the postwar era; and one which has recently switched over to debt-financing its fiscal policy ambitions.

The third section attempts to sketch the new distributional fault-lines that are expected to result from a shift from tax and money-financed to debt-financed public policy. It sets up a relatively simple framework based on the arguments and data that were presented in the first two sections. This depiction, though informed by the Swedish example, is intended for application to a much larger sample. Whereas the institutional framework of the contemporary welfare state was built over class cleavages, the new environment might provoke new lines of conflict, potentially threatening the welfare state edifice. Besides the potential inter-generational trade-off assumed by loan-financed fiscal policies, borrowing (both foreign and domestic) encourages new factorial and/or internationalist fault-lines – for which welfare-state institutions are not suitably prepared. In particular, I conclude by suggesting that the most likely outcome benefits investors holding mobile assets, at the expense of those holding domestic – more immobile – assets.

Why borrow?

Why have the industrialized nations chosen to rely more heavily on debt-financing? This first section provides an explanation for the change, proposing a foundation from which to survey the remaining empirical landscape. In particular, I argue that increased capital mobility has seriously undermined the arsenal of economic steering mechanisms available to government leaders. As autonomous monetary policies have been sacrificed on the EMU altar, more and more of the national burden is being borne by fiscal policy measures alone. Tax bases cannot be expanded for fear of potential capital flight, and as a result lending has become the only viable revenue source for maintaining the popular welfare state. In short, states have not chosen their debt-financed path because of the economic gains such a strategy might offer; debt-financing is the result of three interactive developments – the collapse of autonomous monetary policy options; the threat of capital flight; and the politics of entrenchment. These are the three rubrics under which the remainder of this section is organized.

Throughout most of the postwar era, the developed economies have leaned heavily on money and credit policy instruments to steer their domestic economies (in and) out of recessions. In an international environment characterized by embedded liberalism, nations wielded relatively independent monetary policy instruments to maintain the growth levels which facilitated (and paid for) the development of modern public policies (Ruggie, 1982). The political pressures which formed the consensus at Bretton Woods were the same which drove national governments to adopt public policy measures for softening the blows of *laissez-faire* capitalism.

With the advent of freer (international) markets for capital, this regime has collapsed. While there is some disagreement about the impetus and reasons for the change, a near consensus has developed around the idea that monetary policies (and the monetary financing of fiscal policy), especially those of the smaller economies, have become much more costly in an environment characterized by increasingly free (financial) capital mobility.[1] If changes in the market itself cannot be held completely responsible for the absence of monetary policy autonomy, the European Union is providing its own pressures – though, arguably, the Union itself is conforming to the same market pressures. Over the most recent years, member-states of the European Union (and those on its periphery) have begun the pursuit of a single currency: a convergence path which, by definition, rules out monetary policy autonomy. In short, whether the changes are provoked by faceless market forces, or by those of the more impressionable Commissioners, European economies – in particular the smaller ones – have been under great pressure to jettison their autonomous monetary policies.

Obviously, autonomous monetary policies were not the only instruments available for maintaining economic stability in the postwar period; fiscal policies, generally, were widely and effectively wielded by industrial states. Why shouldn't these effectively fill the vacuum left by the jettisoned monetary policies?[2] Indeed, those who preach the benefits of freer capital markets often offer reconciliation (both implicitly and explicitly) in the form of increased fiscal policy effectiveness.[3] Thus, in theory, there was hope that this new economic environment – characterized by increasing levels of financial capital mobility – would not threaten democratic controls on the economy. Not only were fiscal policies unhampered by increased capital flows, but they were considered to be all the more efficient under the new international regime.

In theory, maybe. In practice, the record of the industrial states has not been all that promising. Along with increasing capital mobility, the 1980s brought with it a radical reorganizing of national tax policies,[4] which – despite the promise of greater ease, equity and efficiency – has led to greater downward harmonization.[5] Increasingly mobile factors of production have increased tax competition pressures. We might expect this downward pressure on revenues to lead to a corresponding pressures for reducing social expenditures, but the link is neither strong nor tight. In practice, what appears to be happening is the following. While there are decreasing real revenues available for social policy funding (because of the factors listed above), there has not been a concomitant drop in social spending levels. Instead, the ballooning gap between revenues and expenditures is being filled by government borrowing.

This international pressure for streamlining (in both monetary and taxation realms) has severely constrained the potential for government revenue generation. But the government budget constraint contains two elements: government revenues *and* expenditures. The third reason that states are increasing their debts is because of the electorate's unwillingness to jettison the public policy programmes for which their decreasing tax revenues are intended to pay.[6]

Recently, several authors have begun to study various political constellations used for the construction and defense of the welfare state edifice.[7] These authors' basic argument is that the politics of welfare-state retrenchment is different from the politics of welfare-state expansion. In the words of Stephens *et al.* (1994, p. 3):

> The broad social coalitions supporting the welfare state status quo prevent centrist and even right wing parties from implementing, or even advocating, significant cuts in entitlements. Thus, to the extent that economic difficulties mean the agenda in most countries is not expansion but rather retrenchment, one should expect narrower partisan differences than in the past.

We should expect the same sort of broad coalition to defend against cuts in the public policy edifice; there is, in short, little political gain to be made from carving up the welfare state. Public opinion is strongly in favour of maintaining the basic features of the contemporary welfare state, but its ability to control capital, to tax it, and to reap its benefits has decreased over time. In the short to medium term this vacuum is filled by borrowing. As a result, the burden of paying for these social benefits is now being borne more heavily by the average resident. As we will see in the third section below, the more mobile factors can escape taxation.

The Swedish record

Over the past decade, European governments have become increasingly indebted. Globally, government debt levels increased to more than 55 per cent of world GDP during 1981–93, from 45 per cent in 1960–72 (IMF, 1995, p. 208). High levels of unemployment and low levels of economic growth have meant that politically timid governments have built up larger and larger debt levels to placate their constituencies. Rather than scale-back public policy outlays, or increase the tax revenue base with which to pay for programmes that the electorate has come to expect, governments have chosen the path of least resistance: paying for today's policies with tomorrow's revenues.

To get a closer look at the nature of this regime-change, we now turn to the experience of a country that has been particularly hard hit by these events: Sweden. This section aims to quantify the discussions above by looking at developments in Sweden over the last decade. In particular, this section asks: Is it true that revenue sources have declined, while expenditures have largely remained constant? Has the gap been filled by increased borrowing? And who, exactly, is lending the money? Answers to these questions will provide a foundation from which to study the distributional dilemmas that result from them.

To begin with, we look at Swedish government revenues, expenditures and budget deficits over the last decade, which are shown graphically in Figure 4.1. As the first section hinted, revenues began to drop off from

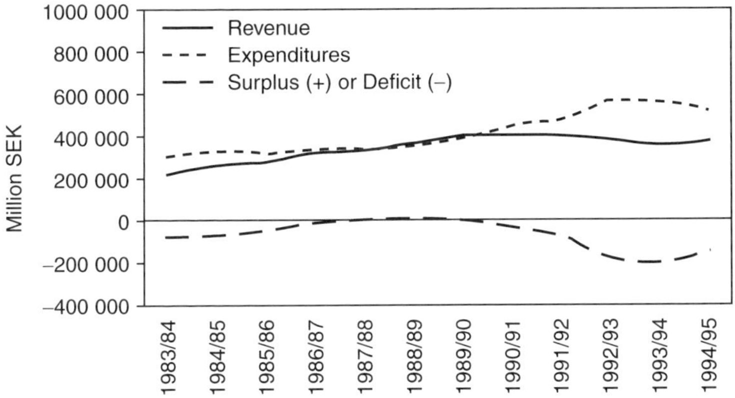

Figure 4.1 Swedish state revenues and expenditures, 1983–95
Source: Based on SCB (1995, table 269).

about 1989, while expenditures continued to grow. The result was a growing budget deficit, from about the same time. In per cent of GDP terms, government expenditures have stayed within a relatively small margin (between 25 and 30 per cent of GDP) over the past decade. Thus, there would appear to be strong political support for maintaining public spending levels, despite the drop in tax and money revenues.

Accumulated budget deficits become government debt. Thus, the difference between Sweden's falling money and tax revenues and its unchanging revenue level is reflected in the Swedish government's debt figures. Figure 4.2 details the extent of that debt over the entire postwar period. There are two significant elements depicted in Figure 4.2. First is the extent to which debt levels have grown since the mid-1970s; the level of Swedish public debt has grown to such an extent that it has surpassed the immediate postwar levels, and is setting new record heights.

The second significant element of Figure 4.2 is the growing degree to which foreign-denominated bonds make up the total debt burden. Foreign-denominated bonds now constitute approximately 30 per cent (and rising) of the total Swedish debt burden, and this reliance on foreign-denominated debt has unique distributional consequences which will be explored in the third section below.

With debt levels that are growing at unsustainable rates, it becomes important to ask about the cost of servicing this debt, and Table 4.1

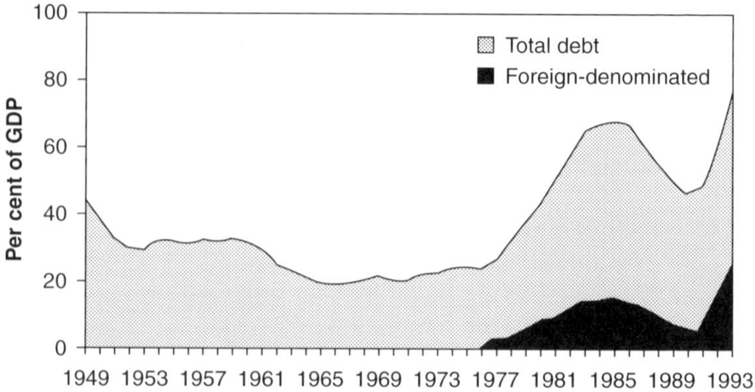

Figure 4.2 Swedish central government debt, 1949–93
Source: Based on Riksgäldskontoret (1977, 1994).

Table 4.1 Expenditures and incomes associated with Swedish state debt, 1983–93 (millions of SEK)

	Expenditures				*Income*				*Net expenditures*
	Interest on loans in SEK	*Interest on loans in foreign currency*	*Realized exchange-rate loss*	*Other expends., net*	*Interest on loans in SEK*	*Interest on loans in foreign currency*	*Realized exchange-rate gains*	*Other income, net*	
1982/83	33 990	9744	4 414	453	262	28	115		48 196
1983/84	39 875	12 245	7 700	998	229	75	127		60 387
1984/85	45 651	13 975	15 053	1 312	129	58	570		75 234
1985/86	49 002	12 537	6 816	1 149	315	32	2 648		66 509
1986/87	51 432	10 027	3 628	1 226	374	96	2 031		63 812
1987/88	48 826	9 783	2 924	505	422	295	7 911		53 410
1988/89	45 059	8 314	2 821	840	585	130	3 140		53 179
1989/90	53 505	8 551	4 035	929	1 273	300	1 751		63 696
1990/91	57 835	7 333	1 870		3 131	346	2 217	311	61 033
1991/92	59 840	6 720	4 048		3 576	411	3 432	3 146	60 043
1992/93	66 838	19 474	46 036		6 173	429	43 459	9 197	73 090

Source: Based on Riksgäldskontoret (1994, p. 12).

measures the nominal weight of the debt burden. Swedish net expenditures from both foreign and domestically-denominated debt have been increasing over the last decade. Although there is some income generated as well, the net figures are surprisingly large. However, to really capture the magnitude of these expenditures, we need to compare them to other expenditure items for the Swedish government.

Table 4.2 lists the departmental expenditures of the Swedish government in the fiscal year 1992/93. In that year, the expenditures associated with the national debt totalled SEK 73 090.2 million. There are only two other departmental expenditure items on the whole 1992/93 budget that exceed this amount: those for the Ministry of Health and Social Affairs and those for the Ministry of Finance. In other words, more money went to servicing the national debt in Sweden for the 1992/93 fiscal year than went to the Ministry of Defense, the Ministry of Education, the Ministry of Labour and all of the other remaining government departments.

In concluding this section, there are three main elements of the debt-financed Swedish regime worth mentioning. First, and most obviously: the overall size of the debt-servicing burden is enormous. Government

Table 4.2 Swedish government expenditures, 1992/93

State expenditures, by department		*SEK millions*
I	Royal Household and Establishment	65.0
II	Ministry of Justice	18 646.1
III	Ministry of Foreign Affairs	16 811.2
IV	Ministry of Defense	38 641.6
V	Ministry of Health and Social Affairs	133 043.6
VI	Ministry of Transport and Communications	25 483.0
VII	Ministry of Finance	124 039.5
VIII	Ministry of Education	53 093.5
IX	Ministry of Agriculture	8 457.4
X	Ministry of Labour	45 989.5
XI	Ministry of Cultural Affairs	14 639.4
XII	Ministry of Industry	8 617.7
XIII	Ministry for Civil Service Affairs	2 259.1
XIV	Ministry of Environment and Nature Resources	2 008.0
XV	The Riksdag and its agencies	649.8
XVI	Interest on the national debt	73 090.2
XVII	Unforeseen expenditures	13.6
Total		565 548.2

Source: Based on SCB (1995, table 274).

revenues used to service the debt are taken away from other public-policy areas. This, obviously, affects those who rely most heavily on current public policy expenditures. Second, the debt burden in recent years has been increasing at an alarming (and unsustainable) rate; it has become the current method of maintaining government expenditure levels. Third, and finally, it is noteworthy that a significant share of the Swedish debt is now being carried in foreign-denominated bonds. The remaining section looks at the distributional consequences of these changes.

Consequences of the regime change

As the first two sections of this chapter have discussed the reasons for (and the nature of) a fundamental regime change in the way in which countries fund their fiscal policy ambitions, this last section asks the more difficult question: What are the distributional consequences of this new regime? There is no easy answer to this question; indeed, there are several answers, each dependent on a multitude of variables. So where do we begin?

The previous two sections emphasized the degree to which debt was replacing other means of financing government expenditures, and the extent to which this debt was increasingly carried in foreign currency bonds. This seems like an appropriate starting point for our analysis: (1) what are the distributional consequences of a more debt-burdened public policy generally; and (2) what is the distributional significance of a growing *foreign* debt burden? From these two questions, I propose that three potential cleavages offer themselves: the first is an intergenerational divide; the other results from the price-trend effects that are a product of these changes; and the third cleavage goes across a spatial (internationalist) divide. These three potential cleavages are the organizing framework for the remainder of the chapter.

Intergenerational trade-offs

At first glance, the intergenerational consequences of a shift to debt-financed fiscal policy would appear obvious: tomorrow's generations end up paying for today's policies (of which, presumably) they obtain no benefit. But, as is often the case with intergenerational exchanges, first appearances can be deceiving. On closer inspection, the intergenerational consequences are far from clear-cut: those consequences can only be understood situationally and turn on (among other things) the generosity of the current generation in its bequeaths.[8]

Economists tend to discuss these issues in terms of the Barro–Ricardian Equivalence Theorem (BRET), despite the fact that Ricardo's musings on the matter were distinctly non-equivalent.[9] As there is no agreement as to whether or not the BRET holds in theory and/or practice,[10] it is difficult to trace the distributional consequences, among generations, of the policy shift. The potential intergenerational consequences of this change are dependent upon whether or not economic actors are benevolent and bequeath future generations with the means to payoff the debt. In economic theory, then, there may or may not be distributional trade-offs; in practice, however, we can say very little about its nature.

Nor can we say much about the apparent injustice associated with this intergenerational trade-off. Like economists, political philosophers cannot agree about the existence, let alone the nature, of intergenerational justice. Ball (1985, p. 322), for example, argues that '"inter-generational justice" is an oxymoron'. What little work that has been done by social scientists on the issue of intergenerational distributional trade-offs does not provide much guidance in our query.[11] In short, the social philosophers leave us with the same uncertainty and emptiness as did the economists.

Though we can say nothing with certainty about the specific distributional or just consequences (among generations) of choosing one regime over the other, we can say something about the likelihood of consequences from moving along the debt-financing path. What *is* certain is the fact that changes in the international economy have made debt-financing a more likely means of funding public policy ambitions. This was the argument of the first section. As a result, in this new environment, there are – *at best* – no intergenerational trade-offs: current generations bequeath future generations the money necessary to finance future tax demands on current borrowing. *At worst*, however, there will be hell to pay in the future. In short, we have moved to a path in which the likelihood of intergenerational trade-offs have increased, and yet we have neither the institutional nor the analytical approaches needed to accommodate them.

Price-levels: the regime consequence

The second distributional issue to arise in this new, debt-financed, regime is the tendency to move from an inflationary path to one emphasizing price stability and/or deflation. This change in price regimes has, in itself, distributional consequences. This section contains two parts. The first shows why the regime change encourages disinflationary price levels; the second looks at the potential distributional consequences of this change.

Why disinflation?

If we contrast the postwar inflation trend with today's, one is struck by the enormity of the recent change. Inflation, today, lies at record low levels; but this in itself is not evidence that the new regime is anti-inflationary. The fact that growth rates are now at (historically) very low levels, is also a symptom of the same problem. Deflationary pressures might simply be the result of a decline in aggregate demand. Also, international capital mobility may be pressing down the price regime, as they migrate from continent to continent in search of better returns (Stewart 1983). Another, not necessarily exclusionary, argument is the ideological one in support of independent central banks – one which has been growing in currency over recent years. In short, there may be several explanations for why the price regime has become less inflationary over time; but I would like to offer another. In addition to the potential explanations above, we can expect that debt-based regimes – by their very nature – encourage deflationary measures.[12]

When a country floats a bond to secure finances for its public policies, the price that it will pay, the interest rate, is generally assumed to cover two elements of risk:[13] the risk of default and the risk of devaluation. The market is said to evaluate the likelihood of these two risks, and set its price accordingly. The problem is, however, that there are no hard and fast indicators which telegraph the likelihood of these two risks. Generally, we assume that these risk elements are reflected in a series of economic variables which include (among other things) a country's inflation rate; the size of its budget deficit; its current debt level; its past record of exchange-rate adjustments; and so forth.

In particular, the market reads the following (rough) indicators as signals for creditworthiness: a low inflation rate; a small budget deficit; a small cumulative debt level; and infrequent exchange-rate adjustments. As states rely more heavily on debt-financing, creditworthiness indicators become increasingly important objects in the eyes of economic policy-makers. When debt levels are large, and interest-rate payments take up a larger and larger share of the government expenditure pot, creditworthiness indicators themselves become high-priority objectives.

What, then is the result of a country pursing these objectives? Obviously, they are disinflationary. Disinflation is the only acceptable response to creditors which are weary of past inflation. In addition, however, the size of the current and past budget deficits (that is, the debt level) will need to be restrained to satisfy creditors. There are (as any first-year economics student is aware) two means to better these imbalances: constrain expenditures and increase revenues. To the extent that revenues are increased by taxation (without being reemployed in an asset-improving manner), there will be less capital remaining to invest in productive activities. With less capital available, investment and growth are choked: the preconditions for a disinflationary regime. Alternatively, should other public-policy programmes be pruned back, and these revenues are instead funnelled to service the debt, the result on the economy will be just as depressing (assuming, of course, that these public-policy measures had at least some demand-stimulus, or investment consequences).

Distributional consequences of disinflation

Thus, the sort of policies that are demanded by creditors are those which encourage fiscal discipline and price stability. Debt (whether domestically or internationally denominated), then, will pressure governments to pursue restrictive, disinflationary policies in their attempt to try and limit the size of their future interest payments. What, then, are the distributional consequences of a disinflationary regime?

In answering this question it would be a mistake to think that the current situation is novel. In many ways, the movement from an inflationary to a disinflationary path parallels the experience of the interwar period. In the 1920s several European countries were heavily indebted, and the question of public finances and the value of money was the topic of frequent discussions among policy-makers and economists. Indeed, J. M. Keynes' writings on the subject provide us with a useful vantage point from which to view the current situation.

In *A Tract on Monetary Reform*, Keynes (1971 [1923]) concerned himself with the distributional consequences of price regimes which were either deflationary or inflationary. To study this, Keynes introduced a three-part classification of society, which he believed corresponded to society's main interest cleavages. Keynes focused on what he referred to as the investing, business and earning classes – recognizing that the three classes overlapped, and that a single individual could engage in the activities of all three classes.

In summary, Keynes describes his argument as follows (1971, pp. 29–30):

> We conclude that inflation redistributes wealth in a manner very injurious to the investor, very beneficial to the business man, and

> probably in modern industrial conditions, beneficial on the whole to the earner. . . . On the other hand deflation . . . is liable, in these days of huge national debts expressed in legal-tender money, to overturn the balance so far the other way in the interests of the rentier, that the burden of taxation becomes intolerable on the productive classes of the community.

Keynes' particular interest was in finding the effects of changes in the value of money on these three classes. The move to a deflationary regime in the interwar period parallels the current situation. During most of the postwar regime, inflation became one of the most usual ways of paying for current social policy ambitions; with money-financing, social policy programmes could be paid for with relative ease. The distributional consequences of this, as Keynes pointed out, were to the benefit of the business and earning classes. The shift to a less-inflationary path, Keynes argued, would bring with it relative distributional benefits for the investing classes, at the expense of the more productive classes (that is, the business and earning classes). It is not an exaggeration to expect the same distributional consequences from a similar regime shift today.[14]

In short, Keynes pointed to the degree that shifting from an inflationary regime to a disinflationary regime brought with it a distributional trade-off that benefited the rentier at the cost of the more productive classes. This we can call the *regime consequence*. But to what extent are the distributional consequences limited to intergenerational and intragenerational (but intra-national) cleavages? The empirical section, above (p. 77 ff) showed that a growing share of the national debt is being floated in foreign-denominated bonds. Does the nationality of creditors alter the relevant distributional consequences?

To pay for the policy ambitions of public officials, Keynes argued that there were three means of payment: an inflation tax, depreciation and/or a capital levy. The third and final section of this chapter will look at the distributional consequences that result from choosing one repayment option over the other. It is the argument of that section that the divisions which appear can be best understood in terms of a domestic–international cleavage. Choice of one repayment scheme over the other will benefit internationally-oriented or domestically-oriented interests.

The spatial divide

A third potential line of conflict involves a domestic/international divide; a cleavage which may seem quaint in a world with relatively free factor mobility. Nevertheless, elected governments are not (yet) mobile, so the domestic/international divide remains politically salient. Indeed, I have argued elsewhere that governments are spending more time and energy concerning themselves with the development of economic environments more suitable to international investors, at the expense of their domestic constituents (Moses and Tranøy, 1995). International interests have become powerful actors in national political arenas.

In order to consider the spatial cleavages that result from the new debt-based regime, we need to consider the problems associated with asset mobility and the growing tendency on the part of industrialized countries to rely more heavily on floating bonds in foreign-denominated bonds (as was seen in the Swedish case above). The internationalization of both creditors and debtors provides us with a matrix of potential spatial (that is, international/national) cleavages. One way to trace out these cleavages is to reconsider the three means of debt-repayment (following Keynes), and the two main types of debts incurred by nations today. In other words, there are six potentially different aspects of the new lending regime which bring to the surface the internationalist cleavage. These are shown in Figure 4.3. The text which follows takes up each repayment option in turn.

Future taxes

Under current international economic conditions, future taxes are the most likely option for paying off the national debt. With greater factor mobility, and falling support for utilizing autonomous monetary policies and adjustable exchange rates (at least in Europe), this line of cleavage will potentially become the most significant. Here the main distributional trade-offs will be between mobile and immobile (both long-term and short-term) assets. Taxing authorities will feel international pressure to harmonize national tax levels on the most mobile assets. Revenue

Payment options	Bond-type: *Domestic-denominated*	Bond-type: *Foreign-denominated*
Future taxes	Mobile/Immobile assets	
Devalution	Domestic/Foreign investors	Investors/Government
Money	Domestic/Foreign investors	Investors/Government

Figure 4.3 Spatial cleavages

short-falls will be supplemented with an increased tax burden on those assets unable to escape. In other words, land-owners and labour (although over the long run, taxes on these may converge as well) will be burdened with a heavier share of the tax burden, as the more mobile capital assets are able to reap the benefits of public policy while avoiding most of its costs. This mobility cleavage remains the same regardless of whether the original debts were incurred in domestic or foreign currencies.

Devaluation

Despite all the problems associated with devaluations, Keynes' advice to a heavily indebted interwar France was to devalue away large parts of its debt-burden (1971). His argument was not only based in terms of general economic effects, but also because it was the most politically expedient (though the distributional consequences are far from egalitarian). Elected governments may find it cheaper (politically) to pursue the devaluation option. This is true in part because a devaluation benefits domestic (that is, voting) bond-holders more than it does foreign bond-holders.

If the debt is domestically-denominated and there are some foreign holders, a devaluation benefits the domestic holders at the expense of international holders of the government's debt.[15] The reasons for this are as follows. For foreign holders of domestically-denominated bonds, a devaluation means an immediate depreciation of their return. Although this is a relatively easy way for governments to decrease their tax burden, it does contain credibility costs which makes its frequent use more costly. For domestic holders of domestic-denominated bonds, however, the devaluation does not affect their return, as it consists of nothing more than a nominal (scalar) change – the relative value of the debt has not altered. Indeed, the devaluation might actually aid the domestic holder of bonds if the devaluation contributes to bettering the general economic environment in which the domestic holder resides.

With the increased use of employing devaluations as a means to pay down debt, the market cover on the devaluation part of the risk increases. This is the primary reason that governments begin issuing debt in foreign currencies: to convince the market of their commitment to maintain fixed exchange rates.[16] With foreign-denominated bonds, the government itself bears the full brunt of the costs of a devaluation.[17] International creditors are unaffected by the change; and domestic holders of internationally-denominated bonds actually benefit from the devaluation.[18] In other words, the cleavage lines in this scenario (with foreign-denominated bonds) are between the government and domestic investors.

Money

Previously, this chapter (p. 84 ff) described the distributional consequences that result from a move from an inflationary to a disinflationary path, and touched on the distributional benefits of money-financing. There are, as pointed out, *internal* cleavages along factorial lines which are affected by the move from inflationary to disinflationary financing paths; the question now asked is, are there any spatial cleavages that might also result from the two different debt types?

In a scenario with domestically-denominated bonds, inflation can be used by the government to inflate away the real debt.[19] In other words, the debt can be repaid in inflated currency units (that is a currency unit of relatively less worth). Although this is not the best alternative for domestic bond-holders, as already discussed, it is not the worst alternative either. Inflation, *ceteris paribus*, is a scalar adjustment.[20] For international holders, also, the host (domestic) inflation level is of little consequence until inflationary pressures eventually pressure an exchange-rate change. At this point, the consequences of a devaluation kick-in (see above). In other words, the spatial cleavage lies dormant until inflationary pressures bring about an exchange-rate change. At this point, the lines of cleavage parallel those found in the previous, devaluation, scenario.

Alternatively, if the bonds are denominated in a foreign currency, the potential winners and losers of inflation are otherwise. In this scenario, the government does not benefit by domestic inflation, and it can actually be hurt should the inflation lead to a devaluation. At this point, as with the devaluation scenario above, the government bears the full cost of the devaluation. Alternatively, foreign holders of this debt are not affected by the host inflation, regardless of whether or not it ends in a devaluation. Finally, domestic holders are positively affected if the inflation eventually leads to a devaluation (see above), but are otherwise agnostic. In short, the distributional consequences along the spatial axis parallel those in the devaluation scenario.

To conclude this third section we should mention that these three options, under the spatial divide, are not equally likely in the current international economic environment. There is a greater likelihood that the first option, future taxes, will be the most likely one for paying off the growing debt burden. In this scenario it matters little if the debts are denominated in domestic or foreign currencies, the result will be a burden borne most heavily by the least mobile assets. To the extent that other two repayment scenarios are possible, the currency denomination of the bonds becomes more significant. In these scenarios (money and devaluation), the main distributional cleavages will be between different nationalities of investors and/or between investors and the government.

Conclusion

The argument of this chapter has proceeded in three steps. In order to examine the distributional consequences of a move to more debt-financed public policy ambitions, we needed to first look at the reasons for, and nature of, this new regime. The first section explained the current development in terms of a change in the international economy which limits government revenue options. In addition, on the expenditure side, we looked at the political difficulties associated with pruning public policy expenditures. The result, the first section argued, was a ballooning public debt.

The second section looked at the specific nature of the debt problem in one country: Sweden. In Sweden, revenues were constrained and expenditures maintained as we would expect given the argument in the first section. The second section detailed a new Swedish revenue regime, with two main characteristics. First, the debt-level which has developed in Sweden was shown to be quite large and costly. Second, Swedish debt is increasingly being held in foreign-denominated bonds.

The third section of the chapter has looked at the distributional consequences of this new regime. From the two unique elements of this regime (the very size of the debt burden and its international nature), I have proposed three potential lines of distributional cleavage: intergenerational; investor–producer; and spatial.

There is little we can say about the potential intergenerational cleavage. Simply said, a move to a debt-financed regime has increased the likelihood that there are some intergenerational cleavages. The exact nature (and existence) of that cleavage depends on the specifics of the situation. The rentier–producer divide was first illuminated by Keynes in the inter–war period. The change to a disinflationary price regime, which is partly a consequence of debt-dependency, benefits the investing classes at the expense of the productive classes. We can expect the same general consequences from the current regime change in so far as it mimics the interwar period.

The final, spatial, cleavage is the most difficult to map. International cleavages are found at the nexus of the various repayment means and debt types. To the extent that autonomous monetary policies (and thus, devaluations) have become less-utilized, we can expect that future taxes will be the primary means of paying off the current debt burden. If this is the case, we can expect that the future tax burden will be borne most heavily by those assets that do not have recourse to exit, regardless of the nationality of the creditor.

In the other two scenarios, however, the denomination of the bond has significant distributional consequences, depending on the government's plan of action. To the extent that the bonds are denominated in the domestic currency, governments can pursue the money-financing and devaluation paths as means to paying off their debt. In doing so, they themselves and their domestic investors benefit from the policy, at the expense of international investors. On the other hand, to the degree that debts are being increasingly held in foreign-denominated bonds, governments are increasingly subject to the potential costs of devaluation (even if they are not politically instigated), and forced to rely even more heavily on future taxes as the main means of repayment.

To the extent that postwar policies are understood as a compromise among competing, relatively equal class interests, these policies may become threatened by the new cleavages which result from a greater reliance on debt-financing. In the most likely scenario, mobile assets – particularly among the investing classes – will end up reaping the distributional benefits of a regime which is disinflationary and increasingly reliant on an overburdened tax base. Immobile, domestic producers have the most to lose.

Notes

1 See, for example, Goodman and Pauly (1993), Notermans (1993), Moses (1994, 1995b), Andrews (1994) and Helleiner (1994).

2 Herein lies another distributional quandary. Although, in theory, one can expect macroeconomic substitutability, different people, classes and sectors benefit more from monetary policy (say, interest-rate steering) than with fiscal policy measures. In short, there are also distributional concerns here which might be considered in the future.

3 This argument is furthered by evidence of policy variations among states within a monetary Union (e.g., the USA), as well as by economic theory based on the so-called Mundell–Fleming conditions. With international capital mobility, fiscal policies should be even more effective as the probability of 'crowding-out' diminishes significantly.

4 Indeed, the 1980s has been heralded by several as 'The decade of tax reform'. See, for example, Pechman (1987), Boskin and McLure (1990) and Steinmo (1993).

5 Although marginal individual and corporate tax rates first come to mind, the logic is equally consistent when applied to other types of taxes. Cross-border

shopping will almost certainly reduce international VAT differentials; tax rates on mobile labour are bound to equalize, given greater labour mobility; etc.

6 Though I focus on demand-side measures for explaining public-sector growth and entrenchment, I recognize other supply- or finance-side arguments as equally legitimate. They only bolster my argument about the difficulties associated with decreasing expenditures.

7 See, for example, Pierson (1994, 1995), Huber and Stephens (1993), Stephens (1994) and Stephens *et al.* (1994).

8 I would like to thank Tim Sinclair for challenging me on this point and referring me to Eisner's (1994) work on the subject.

9 See O'Driscoll (1977). Ricardo's discussion on these matters can be found in Ricardo (1951, 1, pp. 244–9); and his *The Funding System* (*ibid.*, 4, pp. 149–200).

10 See, for example, Leiderman and Blejer (1988), Poterba and Summers (1987), Stern (1987) and Dornbusch and Fisher (1994, pp. 587–93). The article which renewed interest in Ricardo and the subject is Barro (1974).

11 As far as I know, the intergenerational literature is more or less confined to the social scientists working in overlapping-generations economic models (e.g., Blanchard and Fischer, 1989; Sargent, 1987; and Stokey and Lucas, 1989); those working on public investment and state-owned enterprises (e.g., Arrow and Kurz, 1970; Freeman, 1989); those in the field of sustainable development (e.g., World Commission on Environment and Development, 1987; and Malnes, 1990); and a few curious social philosophers (e.g., Barry, 1978; Ball, 1985; and Coleman, 1990). A surprising exception is Lindbeck *et al.* (1994, pp. 164–7).

12 This is, of course, the inverse of Fisher's (1933) famous argument.

13 I believe that there are other, more ideological, factors involved when ranking a bond's creditworthiness. See Moses (1995a) for details of this argument.

14 One might object to the description of the earning classes benefiting from inflation, but – if anything – to the extent that wages and salaries are now largely indexed, it is not unreasonable to argue that earning classes benefit all the more (than during Keynes' time) from periods of inflation. Obviously, the specific benefactors of an inflationary regime are difficult to pinpoint with precision.

15 This distinction between domestic and international bond-holders is subtle in a world with free financial capital mobility. Still, investors have residence, even if their capital doesn't.

16 Indeed, this is one of two solutions offered by the influential Lindbeck commission (Lindbeck *et al.*, 1994, p. 47): issue foreign debt and employ debt-indexing.

17 Consider a government which has incurred X amount of debt in foreign currency f. At a 1:1 exchange rate, the domestic currency, d, is equal to the foreign currency; i.e., $d = f$. After a 10 per cent devaluation, the government will still own Xf, but it will need to pay them off in d units, where f is now equal to $1.1d$. In this way the government carries the brunt of the devaluation.

18 Consider a domestic investor which invests the amount X of domestic currency, d, in a foreign-denominated bond, under the same conditions as in the

previous note (i.e., $d = f$). After the government devalues its currency by 10 per cent, the investor's original investment $1f$ is now worth $1.1d$. If we assume that the domestic investor will exchange her foreign-denominated bonds back into the domestic currency, she has made, *ceteris paribus*, a 10 per cent profit.

19 With progressive tax schedules there is also the possibility of using inflation to encourage 'bracket-creep' revenues. See Steinmo (1993, p. 19).

20 Again, at the risk of labouring the point, I am not ignoring the issue of whether an investment in some other, more real, form would have been more profitable. The investing classes benefit relatively less than other classes under an inflationary price regime.

5
International Capital Mobility: An Endogenous Approach*

Timothy J. Sinclair

> Whether we are ready or not, mankind now has a completely integrated, international financial and information marketplace capable of moving money and ideas to any place on this planet in minutes. Capital will go where it is wanted and stay where it is well treated. It will flee from manipulation or onerous regulation of its value or use, and no government power can restrain it for long. (Wriston, 1992, pp. 61–2)

Rhetoric like this is the talk of our age. Capital mobility is the new Leviathan, and there is not a lot we can do about it, or so we are told on TV and by tabloid newspapers. Many serious commentators also seem to think international capital mobility (ICM) has reduced democratic governments to shadows of their former selves (Strange, 1996). Other scholarly critics, however, dissent, suggesting this view is significantly exaggerated. For these writers, ICM remains partial, constrained by public authority (Andrews and Willet, 1997; Watson, 1999). So, who is right here? Is international capital mobility as powerful and important as often portrayed, or is its importance overstated?

The impact of ICM has become an important contemporary political issue because it is widely perceived to threaten national economic sovereignty as this political framework developed during the Keynesian Welfare State (KWS) era subsequent to the Second World War (Martin,

* Subsequent to the Princeton workshop, parts of this chapter were given in revised form as a paper at the annual meeting of the American Political Science Association in San Francisco, September 1996. Thanks for useful comments to participants in the workshop and APSA panels, Michael Barnett, and especially Dave Andrews and Kenny Thomas.

1994). The specific form of sovereignty relevant here is not the legal notion of nominally equal states coexisting in conditions of anarchy (Pauly, 1997, p. 34); the type of sovereignty congruent with the KWS was sociological, not legal, in nature. At its centre was national policy autonomy, especially in economic and social matters. Threats to this policy autonomy from the exercise of external control compromised the domestic social distribution function, a core policy activity of the KWS. The social interests that benefited from KWS distributional patterns are, seemingly, threatened by ICM.

Given its *prima facie* importance, understanding how ICM works, its limits, and the institutions that support and promote it, are crucial to developing key explanations of contemporary politics. International Political Economy (IPE) scholars have tended, however, much like the authors of the popular literature, to conceive of ICM as if it were a law of nature, an automatic, non-social, mechanistic process let loose by states, limiting the full appreciation of ICM as a contingent phenomenon. I argue in this chapter that international capital mobility is made in concrete circumstances, that ICM is constructed by social actors. In my view, ICM is not an *external* force which impacts on states, constraining them in the way Waltz and other neorealists see inter-state anarchy pressuring states (Waltz, 1979). I am in broad agreement with constructivists, including Wendt, who question the notion of spontaneous social structures (Wendt, 1992).

The existence of ICM is, I argue, actually dependent upon states and other authoritative agents, which are implicated in the organization or constitution of capital. An accurate understanding of international capital mobility therefore necessitates an appreciation not just of the external constraint it places on states, but also of its internal, endogenous institutional qualities. Social scientists need, I argue, to develop an understanding of *capital* itself, in order to develop a viable understanding of capital mobility. Thinking about ICM as a structure, akin to the neorealist notion of anarchy, identifies an important feature of the relationship between states and capital – which has captured popular attention – but it also passes over the practical, essential characteristics of state and non-state authority which allow capital to exist, and that make markets work, enabling capital mobility to expand. Implicit in the 'ICM as structural constraint view,' is a spontaneous – and therefore unsustainable – conception of markets as non-social machines.

The double-sided perspective on ICM advocated is developed in three stages in this chapter. The first part of the chapter considers the evidence on ICM. Here, I argue that most accounts of capital mobility (such as

Watson, 1999) are really about capital flows, and do not consider the most important aspect of ICM: the impact the *potential* for capital mobility (and not necessarily actual flows) has on social practices – or ways of doing things – in order to attract these flows. I then provide evidence that there is considerable uneveness in these practices, which supports the view that ICM is not the uniform structure it is assumed to be. This observation supports the view that close attention needs to be given to the institutions and processes which underpin the creation and development of capital mobility in different contexts.

The second element of the chapter discusses what I consider the key IPE scholarship on international capital mobility. It examines the purposes and assumptions of these writings, and argues that these views are, in important respects, problematic in that they take an external, functionalist view of ICM purely as exogeneous constraint. Instead, I advocate refocusing on the endogeneity of ICM, on how it is created and subsequently develops This is what I term an institutional account of capital mobility.

In the last component of the chapter, I investigate the other side of ICM, the question of how ICM 'works', or its internal constitution, through the symptomatic case of credit-rating agencies. My objective here is to provide an example of how we can step beyond spontaneous, external conceptions of ICM, which assume ICM will automatically grow to constrain the rest of the world (if merely unshackled). Instead, I argue that ICM can only exist when supported by specific practices and principles generated by institutions, including state and non-state authorities. These institutions make ICM possible and give it different forms in diverse locations. Studying bond-rating agencies is supportive of this view. The way in which the processes and procedures of bond rating help to constitute ICM addresses the otherwise neglected internal dimension I am concerned to highlight here.

Evidence of international capital mobility

Much of the literature ostensibly about capital mobility is really about actual capital flows and not the potential for capital mobility, even though it is this potential for capital to move that gives rise to the greatest political consequences (Thomas, 1997, p. 53; Thomas, this volume). It is easy to come by data on the quantity of money that changes hands in contemporary capital markets, and this is frequently cited as evidence that ICM is a major force to be reckoned with in global politics, setting strict limits on government monetary and fiscal policy

(O'Brien, 1992; IMF, 1995; Keohane and Milner, 1996). Market turmoil in Asia, Russia and in the financial markets of the West during the 1990s reinforced this popular image. But this information on flows hides important discontinuities. The most obvious difficulty, identified by Epstein and Gintis, drawing on the research of Feldstein and Horioka (1980), is that there remains a strong connection between the quantity of resources saved in any particular jurisdiction and the amount invested there (1995, p. 694). There is, it seems, still a 'home bias' in investment. Citing data from French and Poterba (1990), Epstein and Gintis find that 94 per cent of US funds are actually invested in US securities and 98 per cent of Japanese savings are placed in Japanese securities. In addition, they cite Mussa and Goldstein (1993), who demonstrate that less than 10 per cent of the funds of the 500 largest institutional investors are placed in foreign securities (Epstein and Gintis, 1995, p. 694). In a subsequent paper, Epstein argues there is little evidence of profit-rate equalization between markets, as would be expected in a world of perfect international capital mobility (Epstein, 1996, p. 215). Evidence provided by Watson (1999) corroborates these findings. This is evidence oddly ignored by Held *et al.* (1999) in their discussion of financial globalization.

These conclusions suggest the model of perfect capital markets developed by financial economics does not correspond to the actual empirical parameters of ICM. Other considerations in addition to clearing prices seem to be influences on the incidence of ICM. What is going on here? Importantly, it would seem that information about, and confidence in, contracting parties is fundamental for capital mobility to occur. Financial markets – and we might say, investment over time generally, in contrast to simple exchange – is dependent on information about the intentions of other parties, trust, and the power to secure fulfilment of contractual commitments (Epstein, 1996, p. 216). In the real world, imperfect information abounds and parties may be opportunistic. Rather than ICM constraining everything in its wake, it seems that very real limits on ICM remain in our contemporary world order.

Processes of social intermediation – what Epstein calls enforcement structures – between those with capital and those seeking it, are therefore of vital importance to understanding real ICM. Although contracting uncertainties may have been solved (or at least lessened) within certain countries with major capital markets such as the USA, the uncertainties between countries remain sizable. What *has* fallen, Epstein argues, are the transaction costs within financial markets themselves,linked to information technology (1996, p. 217). This is important, as any lowering of costs has ramifications for the likelihood of ICM, by generating pressure to reduce the remaining barriers to mobility (Thomas, 2000). Over time this may promote the growth of ICM.

What follows from these observations? Despite the tentative agreement in the IPE literature that ICM is some form of structure in world politics, its existence remains fundamentally dependent on state and non-state institutions for key actions. This suggests that an understanding of international capital mobility requires investigation of the supports for capital mobility, in addition to study of the manifestations and downstream consequences of ICM. Attention only to flows of capital has been myopic as far as understanding the causal mechanisms in ICM are concerned, because this has been underpinned by a functional understanding of markets as spontaneous, self-regulating systems. How markets are made, or what constitutes them and makes them possible at all, are crucial issues scholars of ICM need to consider.

Where does this conclusion lead us? It pushes IPE to develop an institutional account of international capital mobility. By an institutional understanding, I mean one that discards the neo-classical notion popularized by Hayek that markets are spontaneous systems rather than evolving, social institutions which reflect concrete circumstances and the consequences of path dependency (Hayek, 1949). The spontaneous account of capital mobility is premised on the idea of a simple cause–effect power relationship between those with resources and those that want these resources. The evidence cited above suggests meaningful barriers persist in the global economy which prevent such a direct or behavioural form of power being exercised by the holders of capital in the way popularly imagined.

An institutional account pushes us to think about the power of capital more broadly. The power of capital is the generation of action (and, of course, inaction) based on the anticipated preferences of people we can term capital controllers, amongst those seeking access to their resources (Winters, 1996; Gill and Law, 1989; Lukes, 1974, pp. 16–17). This view of where to start investigating ICM leads us to examine evidence of change in ways of doing things by those seeking resources, most obviously in finance and the creation of the rules of the game surrounding investment and speculation in different jurisdictions. But the investigation might potentially look outside the traditional business realm to matters, such as central bank control, which were shielded from international pressures during the KWS era (Gill, 1992). In the next part of this chapter I examine the basis for an institutional account of ICM in more depth.

An institutional account

The largest literature on ICM has, of course, purely an agent focus. This is the literature of financial economics, that activity within business schools which offers a guide to maximizing behaviour in the financial markets.[1] It is perhaps the quitessential problem-solving theory (Cox with Sinclair, 1996, p. 88). Based on Utilitarian assumptions, this way of thinking about ICM has typically viewed institutional and other issues associated with capital-market transactions as problems or rigidities introduced by rent-seekers, often located in governments. In this view, capital markets are transparent in that they provide venues for agents to meet and conduct forms of exchange. For financial economics, it is important that no obstruction be allowed which might frustrate maximization objectives; such an outcome is assumed to be socially optimal.

The extreme agent-centredness of financial economics is less evident in the economics literature outside the pragmatic environment of business schools. Here, the new institutional thinking has focused on the transaction costs of contracting between agents (Williamson, 1985). This literature assumes the context in which exchange occurs is problematic, and that great attention must be given to designing appropriate interventions which solve information problems, allowing parties to reduce uncertainty amongst themselves. In this more dynamic tradition, capital markets are problems of organizational design, although organizational execution may – and generally should – be achieved via private parties, as this is assumed to be usually the most efficient means. International capital markets, in this view, are social phenomena only in a narrow sense, in that they must be organized by states to work efficiently. The nature of the exchange taking place within them, however, and the implications of those decisions are private to the agents concerned, and not thought appropriately subject to societal intervention. Capital therefore remains pre-social in this account.

The fundamental problem with these ways of thinking about ICM is that they reduce what must be explained to what Wendt has called 'ontologically primitive units,' not subject to explanation, in this view of things (Wendt, 1987, p. 339). As with states in international-relations theory, the agent-centred approach to ICM, 'precludes an explanation of the essential properties' of capital as an institution (Wendt, 1987, p. 340). The nature of capital, the preferences that constitute it, the mix of material and normative dimensions capital encapsulates, capital's development over time and its spatial differentiation are eliminated from consideration in this formulation, in which 'capital' is assumed to be of a universal, timeless and aspatial character. By imputing a defining set of overly parsimonious assumptions to capital *a priori*, analysis can only be developed on the basis of the implications or effects of some change that is exogenous to capital. Capital, therefore, is reduced again to a 'black box' about which we need know nothing.

While agent-centred, undersocialized views of ICM are dominant within business schools and economics departments, political science has generally considered structure paramount. During the cold war, the high politics of defense and foreign policy dominated realist accounts of the world, precluding serious consideration of ICM outside the (then more marginal) liberal institutionalist and critical schools. The capital mobility hypothesis (CMH) – a recent hybrid neorealist model – is discussed by Webb (1991), Andrews (1994), Cerny (1994) and others (see contributions to this volume).[2] The CMH retains the state-centric ontology of neorealism, but introduces the idea of ICM as a creator of 'structural incentives' for states to pursue certain, amenable policy objectives (Andrews, 1994, p. 203). Both states and capital have fixed, universal preferences (or characteristics) here, as in the agent-centred approaches discussed above. Capital remains something we do not need to explore because it is assumed we know what it is already. But is this so?

The neoliberal institutionalist approach to IPE has developed this hybrid neorealist contribution to international-relations theorizing (Milner and Keohane, 1996, p. 257). These authors also see ICM as undermining governmental autonomy in macroeconomic policy, and as imposing potentially 'enormous costs' on states (*ibid.*). A major contribution of this approach has been to focus attention on the potential *mediation* of ICM by institutions (Garrett and Lange, 1996), and an important feature of this institutional perspective is the question of asset specificity (Frieden, 1991b; Garrett, 1996).[3] Frieden argues that asset owners 'prefer' it when input prices fall and output prices rise, changing relative prices in their favour (Frieden, 1991b, p. 19). But the extent to which an asset holder attempts to influence policy depends 'on how policy will affect returns on the asset, and on the availability of other uses to which the asset might be put' (*ibid.*). The range of these other uses can be a function of many things: 'mechanical or technical factors... less tangible personal ties with suppliers or even less tangible reputations with consumers' (Frieden, 1991b, p. 21). Incentives for the owners and controllers of capital to influence local policy rise with increasing specificity and fall to zero for liquid assets which are non-specific (*ibid.*). Here, the lowest-cost choice is always assumed to be mobility rather than lobbying. Accordingly, asset specificity is generally associated with industries with high barriers to entry, unique technology, associated skills and significant interpersonal networks (*ibid.* p. 22). Despite Winters' identification of a 'locational revolution,' Frieden suggests that at least in some forms, capital may actually be more specific and less mobile as it becomes more knowledge-intensive (Winters, 1994, p. 446).

It is, of course, financial capital with the greatest capacity for exit that is the primary constraint on government policy in a world of mobile capital (Garrett, 1996, p. 88).[4] The great advantage of thinking about the relative mobility of different instances or types of capital is, of course, that this begins to peel back the outer surface of capital, and forces us to ask what mechanisms influence capital's modalities. Rather than assume capital to be essentially undifferentiated, the asset-specificity approach looks at the institutional manifestation or concrete form of capital, and attempts to examine the consequences. There are two difficulties here though. First, this remains a very simple characterization of form: the '*economic* characteristics of assets determine the policy preferences of their owners' (Frieden, 1991b, p. 22, emphasis added). Second, it is not clear why non-specific asset holders would always choose mobility rather than lobbying (that is, exit rather than voice). The specific costs of lobbying – which are contingent – must be set against the costs of mobility in an environment of diverse investment opportunities about which there is uncertainty (Thomas, 2000). Accordingly, even if we know the specificity of the asset we do not necessarily know the strategy likely to be chosen by capital controllers. That depends on circumstances, Thomas rightly argues. Although Frieden does qualify asset specificity somewhat by incorporating what he calls 'social networks' into his account, his view remains very parsimonious. He does not help us explain the non-intuitive data cited by Epstein and Gintis about the location of financial assets, which would seem to be caused by what, on Frieden's definition, are non-economic factors. Capital then, remains in Frieden's account largely an *a priori* construct. It is just that for him, it can take broadly two forms rather than merely one. The only institutional characteristic of capital which is allowed, if we follow Frieden, is an economic one, and considerations of time, place or other factors remain irrelevant to understanding capital in his view.

The basic problem with this sort of thinking about ICM is that, as noted, it continues to assume what has to be explained. The nature of capital, its propensity to be mobile, and the implications of its mobility need to be thought out in ways that acknowledge an awareness of the agent–structure problem at the heart of ICM. This problem is central because although, on the one hand, we can identify entities (states, firms, capital controllers) which are purposeful actors, and on the other, understand that society is made up of social relationships, which structure interactions between these purposeful actors, a 'self-evident way to conceptualize' these entities and their relations (and thus understand ICM dynamics) does not exist (Wendt, 1987, p. 338). Neorealist explanation instead sees system structure as constraining pre-given agents, a form of determinism in which all action is conditioned by the structure of the situation facing the actors. Because agents are given in most writings about ICM, there can be no *theory of capital* in these accounts analogous to Wendt's notion of a theorization of the state. As Wendt claims in relation to the international system, we need such a theory (or theories) to understand the internal mechanisms of capital, so as to derive views of interactions between international capital mobility and other actors and processes that are not simply arbitary (Wendt, 1987, pp. 342–3). In other words, without a theorization of capital itself we cannot hope to understand the complex interactions between states, private institutions and ICM.

Approaches that are more successful in agent/structure terms are those that step beyond cause/effect understandings of action and incorporate the dualism or interdependence of the capital/state relationship (such as Harvey, 1999). On the one hand, we have the power of international capital mobility. Here '*anticipation* by policymakers plays a central role in the power dynamics' (Winters, 1996, p.10). But this does not mean that ICM simply constrains the action, as in the capital mobility hypothesis, because over time anticipation gives rise to change in the constitution or identity of the actors themselves. On the other hand, international capital mobility itself remains dependent on legal authority for the supports and rules that allow for its existence (Gill and Law, 1989, p. 479). Capital needs authority, just as authority (in a capitalist world) clearly needs capital. Linear structural models of cause and effect between ICM and the state are, therefore, likely to be inadequate understandings of what is really a reciprocal or dialectical process. Institutional understandings based on the internal dynamics of the relevant elements are necessary beginnings to persuasive explanations of ICM. The final section, which makes three arguments about the way credit-rating agencies constitute capital, supports this institutional perspective on ICM.

Constructing international capital mobility

Perhaps more than any other institutions, bond-rating agencies sit at the confluence of structure and agency in international capital mobility. I argue that the rating agencies comprise a central mechanism within ICM; they discipline corporations, municipalities and states directly as they seek resources, as well as being part of the more systemic data-gathering and surveillance logic of international capital mobility. Rating agencies both constrain the seekers of capital and shape what capital is itself. They are structure and agency.

Rating agencies have become important institutions only in recent years as bank lending has come to be viewed as a relatively more expensive way of obtaining finance by comparison with the securities markets in globalized conditions (Sinclair, 1994a, b, 2000a). The prime rationale for the existence of the agencies has been to solve the information problem between buyers and sellers of debt securities. They claim to provide intelligence in the form of a credit rating which captures how financially sound the borrower is, allowing the lender to estimate whether the risk of default is rewarded by the return offered. Although developed in the USA, disintermediation is now, like many other ostensibly more efficient processes, increasingly being adopted around the world in the context of globalization and concerns about the lack of transparency in many markets. The two major agencies, Moody's Investors Service (Moody's) and Standard and Poor's (S&P), currently rate around $14 trillion at any given time (*Far Eastern Economic Review*, 1998). Both headquartered in New York, they have branches around the world and are experiencing rapid growth in staff numbers and revenues.

I make three arguments about rating agencies and the construction of international capital mobility. The purpose of these arguments is to illustrate the interdependence of ICM and authority and therefore to demonstrate how capital is institutionalized. In doing so, I draw upon literature (Sinclair, 1995, 1999) which sketched out some of the core operating dynamics rating reproduces inside the social relations which comprise capital. In each case, what I identify is a challenge to pre-existing norms and attributes which have constituted the hegemonic structure through which investment takes place. So, far from being a technical or merely static data-gathering system, what I hope to demonstrate is that rating agencies are an agent of reengineering inside the system of capitalist social relations. Capital emerges from these stories as a social phenomenon with its own history, rather than the ontologically primitive entity most IPE thinking assumes it to be. In making this claim I wish to assure readers that it is not my contention that rating agencies are the only means through which the social construction of capital takes place (although I *do* argue they are increasingly important in this process). Site-location consultants, for example, are vital in direct investment (Thomas, 2000). There are many other stories to be told about capital mobility (see other contributions to this volume); my purpose is merely to demonstrate that capital is made, and that it is best investigated as an institutional phenomenon, a social relation and not a 'thing'.

The initial argument I make concerns the role of ideas in hegemony. Too often, ICM is interpreted as a technical matter; but when we look at ideas we see just how political ICM really is, how ideas are constantly deployed in the pursuit of capital's position and how this deployment can subsequently change capital itself. Ideas can be thought of in two relevant ways here: as intersubjective meanings which tend to cut across social divisions, and as rival collective images of social order which are specific to particular alliances of social interests (Cox, 1986, p. 218). The former act as breaks on social conflict by reinforcing the hegemony of a particular social alliance of interests. They may have been established by a dominant fraction within the alliance, but the set of ideas offer a way of understanding the world that the whole set of social interests can ascribe to. Rival collective images, on the other hand, may exist when hegemony is in crisis, when dominant fractions seek to reestablish their position, or when aspiring social forces try to establish an alternative to the dominant way of thinking about the political and economic order (Cox, 1987).

A key contemporary intersubjective idea – or understanding – is the diminishing salience of non-economic, non-financial thinking in public policy, empowering those social groups with mastery in the economic and financial ways of analysing what then come to be deemed the major societal problems. This intersubjective tendency reduces the scope for social conflict around ideas to those that fit within the particular assumptions of contemporary economic and financial analysis. Those who argue outside of these assumptions can be patronized, or if that fails, can be written off as 'irrational', not to be listened to. This process of knowledge definition is a vital political battle.

How do rating agencies contribute to this construction of knowledge? The agencies shape this process by making it appear their decisions are the product of a scientific process of determination that is impartial in terms of the interests of all involved. Rating agencies acknowledge in their publications that a rating reflects a mixture of qualitative and quantitative information and analysis, and that ratings are therefore inherently subjective. However, they do not make an issue of this subjectivity in their press releases. They talk a great deal more about deteriorating financial ratios than management skill in their press outputs, presumably because, from their point of view, it is a lot easier to defend a ratio-justified downgrade than one which centres on the capacity of management to avoid problems. By not making it clear that their decisions are judgments, the agencies contribute to the creation of a popular (and élite) myth that rating actions reflect simply the facts of the situation, as revealed by incontestable economic and financial analysis. In turn, this reinforces the validity of economic and financial thinking by making it seem that any clear- thinking person, possessed of all the facts and the right sort of knowledge, would come to the same view (as if replicating an experiment in the natural sciences).

Let us consider the rival collective dimension. What is this, how do raters contribute to it, and why is it important? Here, economic and financial analysis can be understood in more tactical terms as a tool that dominant social groups use to blunt challenges and that counter-hegemonic forces use to initiate those movements. A less-noticed dimension of the Michael Milken junk bond scandal story was his constant effort to propagate and justify an alternative set of ideas about credit, which suggested that access to credit was being artificially constrained, and that high-yield (junk bond) financing was a legitimate way of channelling funds to start-up companies (Bailey, 1991; Sinclair, 1995). Milken can in retrospect (but only up to a point) be understood as representing growth-seeking firms with few ties to the great oligopoly-like US corporations of the 'old economy'. He created and projected a set of ideas that justified more acceptance of access to disintermediated finance by firms previously shut-out of the markets by the rating agencies. Rather than categorize risks into acceptable and unacceptable (or investment and speculative grades in the rating terminology) there was a greater concern in Milken's approach with the specification of risk in graded terms, allowing the purchasers of debt issues to make their own judgments about the costs and benefits, thus putting pressure on a rating framework that implicitly focused on creditworthiness as a state of kind (with inside and outside dimensions) not degree (*The Economist*, 10 April 1993). Despite the fact that Milken and the LBO (Leveraged Buyout) movement came to an end, this greater concern with finely specifying risk as an aid to investor analysis seems to have made a lasting impression on global finance. It has, in fact, changed capital.

The junk-bond market has subsequently become a core feature of modern finance despite Milken's demise as a financier. Capital can be transformed; what 'it' is, is not predetermined.

The second argument I make is about the role of bond-rating agencies in 'privatising' capital. The emphasis on certain types of data by the agencies reflects prevailing assumptions about the relationship between governments, fiscal affairs and civil societies. My argument is that the intellectual tools developed for application to private financial dealings seem increasingly to be those also considered appropriate to public finance. Indeed, the very idea of public finance as a separate intellectual and pragmatic field, with its own assumptions and prescriptions no longer seems sustainable, just as the idea of intervention in markets no longer has the status of policy orthodoxy.[5]

The pressure on what we can term a socially-centred view of capital's role in the KWS political economy is reflected in the concern of politicians and populations alike with the problem of government deficits (Cameron, 1993; McCarthy, 1993; Crane, 1993). Although there is no universally agreed analytical criteria for determining that any particular deficit level is more troublesome than any other – except that bigger deficits are generally understood to be worse than smaller ones – the idea that deficits are out of control and likely to compromise both public and private initiatives assumed a hegemonic position within public discourse in the OECD during the 1990s (*The Economist*, 28 August 1993; Sinclair, 2000b). With a few exceptions, it is again commonsense to believe, as was the case prior to the Depression, that governments must manage their affairs in the same way that individual households do – on a cash basis (Walkom, 1993). Bond-raters have helped to establish this view, despite their occasional comments to the contrary (Grogan-Green, 1993).

What is at stake here? In broad terms, the mix of public and private interests in western societies. Public goods are a key issue in this struggle. Public goods are those for which no market can exist; any provision of them must be made by government if they are to be produced at all (Bannock *et al.*, 1987, p. 335). However, debates persist over whether any particular good or service is really a public good, or can in some form (or at some level) be provided by the market, or some combination of market and government. These policy debates often revolve not so much around the question of provision as such, but over the price and quantity of supply. Different resolutions of these conflicts emerge, as anyone who has driven on freeways in southern Ontario and western New York state can affirm. Traditionally, in Ontario these roads have been free, in the sense that the driver pays no fee for travelling any particular distance.[6] It is a very different story when the driver crosses the border into the Niagara frontier region of western New York state (despite the dramatic deterioration in the road surface); almost immediately, the driver is required to pay to use the I-190.

Bond-rating agencies reproduce this more privatized American pattern of supply of social goods. Their focus on the financing arrangements for new infrastructure, and the judgments they make in light of this focus, reinforces a pattern of provision with heavy emphasis on identifying 'revenue producing' projects that are not dependent on general taxation.[7] From a raters point of view, this makes sense when taxation sources are perceived to be less reliable than other types of income because of their vulnerability to political gridlock and recessionary contraction, amongst other things (Moody's, 12 August 1992). However, dedicating revenue has implications beyond public finance. Influencing the public/private goods distinction impacts on the access different social forces have to government-provided goods. For example, financing the Verrazano Narrows bridge in New York City from tolls rather than taxes rations access to the bridge to lower-income drivers living on Staten Island.

In contrast to the orthodox account of ICM, my third argument is that capital, like the state, is actually a *place* in which social and cultural conflicts are worked out in a context of the pressure globalization generates for homogenization of policy. Capital is contested within itself, and whether it is dominated by transnational or local logics in any particular context is a matter for research not assumption. As capital markets tend to displace traditional bank lending, as the US rating agencies establish a wider list of rated entities in Europe, Asia and Latin America, and as domestic rating agencies are established in these countries which receive 'technical assistance' from the major agencies, a process of displacement has developed in which knowledge based on history, location and tradition exemplified by what used to be called 'names' in London, is giving way to more abstract, verifiable and 'transparent' knowledge forms. Increasingly and paradoxically, this form of knowledge is the starting point for the generation of new sources of authority.

Outside the USA, borrowers have a strong incentive to adopt Anglo-American forms of codified knowledge such as GAAP (generally accepted accounting principles), despite US agency assurances that they interpret preexisting local accounting practices. Because rating agencies want comparability across the world, we can anticipate the development of an 'operating system' around which rating judgments will be derived, centred on hegemonic norms and values, despite explicit assertions of the value of local knowledge (Lipschutz, 1992, p. 418). As the US agencies reflect this global framework most convincingly, they represent the norm around which the non-US domestic rating agencies organize their analysis.

The tendency toward convergence around powerful norms is illustrated by rating expansion in Europe and Japan. The hegemonization of investors seems to be more complete in Japan yet to have fewer consequences than in Europe, where there is a more critical view of rating but greater utilization of ratings in the Euromarkets where ratings are now required. Several domestic rating agencies exist in Japan which compete with the global US agencies. Apart from Fitch-IBCA and three minor German firms, there is little significant competition for Moody's and Standard and Poor's in Europe. These different patterns of institutional arrangements reflect distinct histories of capital market growth.

In Japan, rating agencies were introduced as a result of the yen–dollar negotiations between the US and Japanese governments during the early 1980s (Rosenbluth, 1989, p. 68). While the crash of the so-called 'bubble economy' of inflated asset values weakened bank–corporate relations and has increased volume in the domestic Japanese bond market, there are major differences between the forms of knowledge connected to rating in the USA and those that influence the judgments of the Japanese rating agencies. These agencies have readily assumed the outward form of their US counterparts and have sought SEC recognition,[8] but they utilize more local knowledge in their determinations, such as the incorporation of what American raters consider 'vague' so-called 'hidden' financial reserves not listed on financial statements.[9] These reserves have not been used by the US agencies in making their Japanese ratings. The Japanese agencies 'tend to judge a company by size and how much profit there is if the company sold its land and securities holdings,' according to Toshiaki Nakano, manager at Asahi Mutual Life Insurance Company's bond-investment division (Bloomberg, 8 April 1994). The different pattern of knowledge production reflects the greater local character of the Japanese domestic agencies in comparison to the domestic agencies now developing in emerging markets, whose organization and knowledge acquisition have been tightly linked to the norms that predominate in Moody's and S&P (often through ownership ties or alliances).

Japan remains a battleground between US-originated transnational knowledge structures and the local forms of knowledge nurtured by the circumstances of postwar reconstruction. This battle is being fought within capital markets as the state-sponsored process of disintermediation generates disembedding pressures and the need for more 'independent' forms of knowledge which do not reflect implicit guarantees of risk socialization (a feature of the Japanese postwar system of social relations). It remains the case, however, as Pauly argues, that major differences in economic and financial practices persist between nations (Pauly, 1994, p. 344). The US model is catching on gradually as the Japanese state, in cooperation with major financial interests including banks, is intimately involved in building the knowledge infrastructure of a different form of capital allocation as a consequence of the decade-long Japanese economic malaise. The final product of these developments is likely to be a hybrid of local and transnational practices.

In Europe, Underhill also observes a process of liberalization in the EU that places increasing pressure on domestic European regulators to accept market-based capital allocation (Underhill, 1995, p. 22). Because of monetary union, there is the expectation that a deep corporate bond market based on credit differentials spanning the continent will develop as it has in the US (Ball, 1994, pp. 18–21).[10] The logic of rating analysis has seeped into EU directives on capital backing for investment banks, which 'explicitly recognises the ratings of bonds', following similar incorporation of rating agencies into regulation in the UK and France (Waters, 14 May 1992, p. 21). As noted, there are few substantial local rating agencies in Europe but some hostility to the American rating institutions and their ways of thinking.[11] This hostility is most strongly expressed in Germany where the demand for cross-border finance is growing and where practices such as Moody's unsolicited ratings are strongly disapproved.[12] A Frankfurt banker suggested Moody's and S&P 'display a colonial attitude and often fail to take into account the special characteristics in European accounting, disclosure and management practices' (Engelen, 1994, p. 46). We might yet see a German-backed ratings agency emerge in response to these tensions (Shirreff, 1999). Although rating is increasingly the norm in Europe, especially within the Euromarkets, this does not constitute a wholesale importation of American norms. In important respects, capital, and how it is made, is likely to remain conditioned by local circumstances in Europe.

In Japan and Europe, capital is changing form; but how it changes, the pace of change and the results are not predetermined. Capital, like other social relations, takes particular forms in particular places (Thrift, 1996); understanding international capital mobility requires a rejection of a functional, overly parsimonious or universal model of capital.

Conclusions

International capital mobility is a key feature of our age. To come to a full understanding of ICM, however, requires an appreciation of it as a social process or institution with its own history and social and political constraints like any other phenomenon. ICM is not a law of nature or a machine. Evidence of the qualification of international capital mobility presented here demonstrates that it is limited in extent and dependent on key social supports.

Examining the effects of bond-rating agencies provides an illustration of these processes. Not only do rating agencies act as disciplinary agents on corporations, municipalities and states that seek capital, they also institutionalize capital itself, as the Milken story and the Japanese and European rating cases support. Capital is not always the same; it develops and has spatial features which mean there are 'capitals' just as there are a variety of capitalist states which vary in key ways. The preferences and expectations implicit in capital are subject to change, and capitals are places of contestation where competing tendencies work out their differences.

No doubt most research into capital mobility will continue to focus on its perceived effects as a conquering force within globalization. A fuller, more accurate and necessarily less parsimonious understanding of ICM will only emerge, however, once IPE scholars acknowledge that capital is not the inert thing they mistakenly thought it to be, but a social relationship (just like states), with a history and a variety of endogenous motivations and modalities which depend on local circumstances and the challenges of the context. Within this broader understanding, middle-range theories of specific modalities of ICM constitute a crucial research agenda.

Notes

1 Consensus is not evident on the purposes of business-school departments of financial economics (or indeed, on the purposes of business schools themselves). It is certainly the case that some academicians within these institutions see themselves as social scientists with the maximization of societal welfare as their objective. Despite this self-perception on the part of some business school faculty, it seems to be the case that at least in terms of grants and private contracts, business-schools are more widely perceived to be creators of pragmatic, partial, franchisable knowledge.

2 According to Andrews, 'The central claim associated with the capital mobility hypothesis is that financial integration has increased the costs of pursuing divergent monetary objectives, resulting in structural incentives for monetary adjustment' (1994, p. 203). Also see the articles in Helleiner (1994).

3 I view the issues raised by asset form as being similar to those raised by institutional form. Both are forms of organization of social relations and, in the liberal insitutionalist view, constrain action in crucial ways. It is therefore reasonable to see assets, broadly speaking, as part of the liberal institutionalist ontology.
4 For a less financially-focused view of ICM, see Thomas (this volume).
5 Reflecting this development, university courses in public finance are being retitled as public-policy courses.
6 Toll roads have recently been introduced to Ontario.
7 Interview with Hyman C. Grossman, Standard & Poor's, New York, NY, 18 August 1992.
8 Interview with official, Securities and Exchange Commission, Washington, DC, 20 March 1994.
9 Interview with Koyo Ozeki and Reiko Toritani, IBCA Ltd (now Fitch-IBCA) Tokyo, 17 May 1994.
10 Rating is in its infancy on the continent where banks still dominate: 7 of the top 20 French companies have a Moody's bond rating, while only 8 of Germany's top 30 have such a rating (Ball, 1994, 18–21).
11 A corporate finance officer for a major British-based multinational observed that Moody's is more centralized, bureaucratic and New York-based compared to S&P, which is perceived to be more European, less aggressive and more academic, which 'makes a difference'. Confidential source, London, December 1992.
12 Interview with Richard Waters, *Financial Times*, London, 8 December 1992.

6
Expanding the Debate on Capital Mobility

Kenneth P. Thomas

Most discussions of capital mobility have been dominated by conceptions derived from analysis of international finance that are inappropriate for the analysis of direct investment. Such notions are inappropriate because financial analyses of capital mobility rely on assumptions of perfect competition,[1] whereas deviations from perfect competition are central to the existence of multinational corporations. This predominant focus on finance is problematic: while most literature on capital mobility correctly identifies the constraints thereby placed on governments' monetary policy, too many analysts overlook the other constraints on government policy that result from foreign direct investment (FDI). These constraints are substantial, and have profound political consequences. In particular, while the rapid growth of financial markets and foreign-exchange markets has created a deflationary bias in the world economy (Stewart, 1983) and reduced barriers to the movement of financial capital, the competition for direct investment (whether from foreign or domestic sources) has led to falling taxes on capital and the rich (Steinmo, 1993; Webb, this volume) and is the linchpin for a host of deregulatory exercises and potential 'races to the bottom' in environmental, social welfare, health care and other policies.[2] In other words, while the mobility of finance affects monetary policy, the mobility of production constrains fiscal and regulatory policy. If we construe capital mobility as solely about international finance, this second set of constraints on government policy, and its connection to the first set, fall from view. This chapter tries to redress this imbalance and argues for a definition of capital mobility that emphasizes the *ability* to move capital (as distinct from actual movements), in a manner that is neutral as between financial and productive capital. Part of this process involves recapturing previous insights into the multinational corporation and inserting them into the present debate.

Besides expanding our definition, we need to enquire about the *status* of capital mobility. The oft-made distinction between relational (or direct) and structural power suggests that there are at least two senses in which capital mobility could be important: as a power resource and as a structural feature of the international political economy. Are these two possibilities contradictory or complementary?

Finally, we need to ask about the implications of capital mobility. Why is capital mobility *analytically* so important to an understanding of international political economy? What are the practical consequences of rising capital mobility, such as we are currently witnessing?

This chapter suggests that capital mobility is both a source of power for individual owners of capital and a structural feature of the international political economy. In particular, capital mobility is the primary determinant of the relative power of states and firms in structuring the world's political economy. Seeing capital mobility this way lets us problematize the centrality of the state, rather than simply assume it, as Realism does, or claim that it is withering away, as theorists as diverse as Kindleberger (1969) and McKenzie and Lee (1991) have done.

Moreover, as we shall see, rising capital mobility has clear distributional consequences in its economic effects. Bringing capital mobility to centre-stage in our analysis of international political economy requires that we be attentive to these impacts.

Defining capital mobility

When analysing the issue of capital mobility, economists tend to limit their discussion to portfolio investment, and base their understanding of it on assumptions of perfect competition. For instance, in his influential textbook, Rudiger Dornbusch (1980, p. 176) defines 'perfect capital mobility' as a situation with perfect substitution of domestic and foreign bonds and instantaneous adjustment of actual to desired portfolios. Economists are not alone in limiting their discussions of capital mobility to portfolio or financial investment. Many of the leading recent works on capital mobility focus exclusively on finance and ignore the mobility of productive investment. For example, Geoffrey Garrett (1995) discusses and measures capital mobility purely in financial terms, while Jeffry Frieden (1991b) notes the greater mobility of financial capital and thereafter ignores other types of mobile capital.

Viewing capital mobility as coterminous with the mobility of financial capital is, however, quite distorting. Economists view capital mobility as the extent to which capital flows across international borders in search of higher marginal returns to capital in a competitive capital market; if capital were 'perfectly' mobile, the market would also be perfectly competitive. But in the case of multinational corporations, the motivation for such investment revolves precisely around market imperfections. As Stephen Hymer argued, 'The control of the foreign enterprise is desired in order to remove competition between that foreign enterprise and enterprises in other countries. Or the control is desired in order to appropriate fully the returns on certain skills and abilities' (1960, p. 24). In other words, the motivation for foreign direct investment, as opposed to portfolio investment, is to create and extract monopoly rents. It is necessary, therefore, to define capital mobility in a way that does not assume perfect competition.

A wider view of capital mobility

Since capital mobility is a concept which applies both to financial and productive investment, we need a definition that does not discriminate between the two. Most important of all, it is necessary to view capital mobility as a potential,[3] akin to potential energy: the potential to transfer financial capital and to coordinate production on a wide-ranging geographical scale.[4] Why is the distinction between potential mobility and actual capital movements so important? Three reasons stand out. First, the two do not always move in tandem, which is why measuring mobility is relatively difficult: movements give only a partial picture. Second, it is mobility, rather than movements, which causes changes in markets and constrains governmental choice. Focusing on capital movements, then, obscures the real causal processes at work. Third, and related to the previous point, it is the increased *options* represented by mobility that strengthen firms in their bargaining with states, particularly in terms of increasing the credibility of threats to move.

The first of these points is empirical in nature, and fairly easy to demonstrate. Within finance, it is easy to see how currency convertibility, the rise of the Euromarkets, improving technology and the dismantling of capital controls have increased capital mobility in an ever-increasing fashion since at least the late 1950s. Yet financial flows have not risen by the same amount or by the same percentage every year: for example, international lending fell from a peak of 728 billion SDRs in 1989 to 208 billion SDRs in 1991 (Webb, 1995a, p. 40, table 3). Did this mean capital had become less mobile? Of course not. As Webb (1995a, p. 40) points out, this decline was mainly attributable to the recession causing reduced demand for funds. More generally, even in a situation of high capital mobility, there may be relatively low international flows of capital 'due to the (relative) absence of profit incentives deriving from differential rates of expected return in different states' (Andrews, 1994, p. 195). In terms of productive capital, there can be similar divergences between the trend of mobility and actual capital movements. Falling transport and communications costs (real international telephone costs have fallen over 95 per cent and real international air travel costs are down more than 80 per cent since the Second World War) and GATT-driven declining trade barriers have made more production locations substitutable for one another. Yet the actual internationalization of individual firms' operations can be significantly reduced under certain circumstances, as a variety of examples in the auto industry make clear. For example, when Chrysler came close to bankruptcy in the late 1970s, it had to sell or close production facilities on four continents in order to avoid collapse. A less-dramatic example can be seen for any of the Big Three US automakers: when they experience a sales boom in the United States, it reduces measures of internationalization such as the proportion of workers or sales abroad, or the Herfindahl index of geographical dispersion (Thomas, 1997, pp. 85–92).

A deeper issue is that focusing on actual capital movements is an obstacle to understanding. As Cerny (1994, p. 332) persuasively argues for the financial markets, 'price sensitivity is at the heart of globalization of markets'. For Cerny, price sensitivity means the responsiveness of market actors to changes at the margin of the price of various financial instruments. He specifically contrasts price sensitivity with the volume of capital movements. From the point of view of government decision-makers, constraints come from the potential reaction to their decisions, and these reactions will rise with the responsiveness to prices signals or, in my terms, with capital mobility.

Finally, it is mobility which creates options and strengthens threats, but threats need not always be carried out to achieve their goal. As capital mobility increases, the number of potential uses for capital increases. This decreases the cost of switching from one use to another, thereby strengthening credibility of the threat to disinvest in response to some government decision or in negotiations with workers. Because such a threat is increasingly credible due to rising capital mobility, it may well bring success to an actor using it without actually having to carry out the threat. In such cases, there is an obvious divergence between mobility and movement.

A note on asset specificity

Asset specificity is a concept similar to capital mobility, in that it relates to the ability to transfer assets from one use to another. There are important correlations between the two concepts, but they are not the same thing. Most obviously, non-specific assets will be highly mobile if transportation and communications costs are reasonably low and if there is no prohibitive government policy. While specific assets are less mobile than non-specific assets, they will vary in mobility not due to their particular level of specificity, but due to the extent to which they benefit from lower transportation and communications costs. Most importantly, this is a function of their value/weight ratio. There is a world market for computer chips, and a world market for production sites for them, because they are so valuable relative to their weight. By contrast, production of mass-market automobiles is only regionally mobile, due to their lesser value/weight ratio. Indeed, it may well be that financial assets are mobile not because they are non-specific, but because their value/weight ratio is so high and because financial innovation makes it possible to accept computerized transfers without moving physical assets at all. Thus, it is the factors I identify below that determine their mobility, as well as the mobility of productive physical capital. Finally, the foregoing discussion of threats illuminates another important distinction between the two concepts. Asset holders have bargaining power with governments not because they might threaten to transfer assets from one form to another, but because they threaten to move them outside a government's jurisdiction altogether. Thus, it is mobility and not specificity that gives these threats force.

Sources of capital mobility

For both portfolio and direct investment, capital mobility makes it easier to overcome the problems distance poses for both asset allocation and production. I argue that there are four main determinants of mobility: economic feasibility, strategic (non-technological) innovation by firms, political arrangements, and the effect of 'sinking' or committing an investment.[5]

Economic feasibility relates to the costs of operating at a distance, and is heavily a function of technological innovations which reduce these costs. The most important of these developments are communications (including computer) and transportation advances. The former are especially important for financial investments, but they are also relevant to the operation of multinational firms since they make it easier for corporate managers to monitor operations at a distance, provide feedback and directions to their subsidiaries, and so forth. Transport cost declines are especially important in the mobility of production facilities as they facilitate the movement of components and finished products from one location to another as well as reducing the cost of on-site supervisory visits to subsidiaries. In general, communications and transportation cost reductions increase the number of options available to holders of capital.

Strategic innovation by firms can increase capital mobility independent of technological change and its effect on economic feasibility (Andrews, 1994, p. 198). In financial markets, innovation has been constant (see the Holt-Dwyer chapter in this volume), helping firms evade regulation and increase mobility. In the realm of production, adopting a strategy of plant-level specialization, as has taken place in the North American automobile industry since the 1960s, could be seen as increasing capital mobility. Note that this shift was also driven by technologically-induced changes in transport costs (Rubenstein, 1992, pp. 153–68, 197). Just-in-time production is another strategic innovation in production, which should have the effect, however, of reducing capital mobility since it constrains firms to locate closer to final markets (Thomas, 1997, p. 144).

Political arrangements further affect capital mobility. Tax rates, tariff levels, and the presence or absence of exchange controls all affect the ease with which capital can move from one location to another. Reducing tariffs, for example, makes countries more substitutable for each other as location sites. A Tobin tax on foreign-exchange transactions would reduce the desirability of such transactions. While governments can, therefore, put up roadblocks to technologically-based capital mobility, increasing mobility also drives up the efficiency costs of such policies (Thomas, 1995, p. 9; Frieden and Rogowski, 1996, p. 35).

Finally, the effect of 'sinking' an investment is an important element of capital mobility. All other things equal, the more difficult and costly it is for the investor to move invested capital after it has been invested, the more 'sunken' it is, and the less mobile it is. The extent of this effect obviously varies with the type of investment in the case of FDI; however, a loan that has been expended is also quite sunken in this sense (Gilpin, 1987, p. 307). In addition to varying with the type of investment, the cost of disinvesting and relocating will naturally be affected by general transportation costs, as well as by differences in government policies (contrast, for example, the relatively higher cost of laying off employees in Europe compared to the United States).

This aspect of capital mobility is the core of the obsolescing bargain, although earlier theorists such as Vernon (1971) or Moran (1978) focused instead on related political phenomena or changes in uncertainty. Sinking an investment at a particular site not only affects the agreement for the initial investment, it affects bargaining for future investments as well by possibly making the location more desirable because of economies of scale, the creation of a trained workforce, or similar factors.

Capital mobility, thus understood, is central to understanding the bargaining relationship between states and firms. Rising capital mobility should increase firms' bargaining power in their negotiations with host states (and also with their workers) in five main ways:

1 It increases the number of feasible investment options open to firms. This has the consequences both of strengthening corporate threats and of reducing states' ability to cooperate with each other in their policies toward firms by increasing the number of potential production locations. As the number of potential sites increases, cooperation among states becomes more difficult to achieve.
2 It improves firms' ability to disinvest or withhold investment (by lowering the costs of these options) and thereby increases the credibility of threats to do so.
3 The potential and actuality of spatial diversification reduce the impact of threatened sanctions by any one host government.
4 By increasing the number of potential production sites, capital mobility also introduces bidding dynamics into the competition among states for investment.
5 The internal financing options for firms are also increased by growing capital mobility.[6]

Agency, structure, or both?

The relative importance of agency and structure in international interactions and explanations is a central problem that was brought to prominence by Alexander Wendt's 'The Agent–Structure Problem in International Relations Theory' (1987). As he argues there (p. 365), 'Agents are inseparable from social structures in the sense that their action is possible only in virtue of those structures, and social structures cannot have causal significance except insofar as they are instantiated by agents.' This claim that agents and structures are 'co-determined' would seem to be borne out by an analysis of capital mobility.

At the level of an individual firm, mobility is clearly a power resource for owners of capital. A mobile firm is in a stronger position to resist or evade government regulation than an immobile firm, because its greater ability to threaten evasion or relocation (or to not invest in the first place) increases its bargaining power with the government. Yet, as we have seen above, the development of capital mobility to a large extent is a function of technological developments in the wider economy over which governments have no power. Moreover, the power of firms to invest or not invest is a consequence of a deeply structural factor, the capitalist organization of production.[7]

At the level of the entire economy, however, capital mobility represents a structural constraint. The case of Mitterand's France (Stewart, 1983; Goodman and Pauly, 1993; Andrews, this volume) is an oft-cited example of the effect of financial capital on government policy. As capital flight increased the costs of following an expansionary macroeconomic policy, the policy was ultimately reversed. The example has no doubt made other governments more hesitant to aim for higher growth than their trading partners. Such effects are not, however, limited to cases where an impact on financial capital might be expected. In a world of many states, the result of one state following policies unfavourable to capital is that investment is lower than it would have been in the absence of such policies.[8] Increased regulation of foreign direct investment will, *ceteris paribus*, lead to a fall in inward FDI; as a result, governments will be deterred from certain types of regulation. Although comparison with a counterfactual case is difficult, the closest proxy is comparing investment levels with their historical level prior to a policy change. Several examples showing how a policy change affected direct investment are:

1 When India 'improved' its bargaining position *vis-à-vis* multinational computer companies, it also witnessed a slowdown in inward FDI relative to its prevailing world proportion, which I argue undermines Grieco's (1984) conclusion that the Indian government was successful in its bargaining (Thomas, 1997, pp. 57–8).
2 After the Gray Report was leaked to the press in December 1971 and Canadian Prime Minister Pierre Trudeau confirmed that foreign investment screening was imminent, inward FDI fell both absolutely

and as a percentage of all inflows to developed countries. After having already declined from its mid-1960s peak of 17.6 per cent of all advanced country FDI inflows to 11.7 per cent in 1970 and 1971, it dropped precipitously to 6.1 per cent in 1972, and never reached even as high as 7 per cent again (Thomas, 1997, p. 58).

3 Ironically, while the OPEC nationalizations of the 1970s helped stimulate theories showing increasing host power in their bargaining relationships with multinational corporations, they also helped redirect oil exploration to the North Sea and Alaska. Similarly, the result of intense host-state pressure in a variety of mining industries during the same period was that mineral investment went to the USA, Canada, Australia and South Africa (Thomas, 1997, p. 59). Moreover, this avoidance of investment in developing countries had the desired effect, as nationalization fell dramatically (to virtually nothing by the mid-1980s) and as host governments increasingly accepted international arbitration of investment disputes (UNCTC, 1988, chapter XIX).

What is important to note in these examples is that the structural effects came about through the uncoordinated decisions of individual firms.[9] Thus, as suggested above, there does appear to be mutual determination of structures and agents.[10]

Implications for realist theory

The examples above suggest that considerations of the potential impact of today's actions on future investment may inhibit governments from pursuing policies they might otherwise prefer, in order to maintain the flow of investment. This implies that capital mobility is a structural constraint on government policies, as Webb (1991, 1995a) and Andrews (1994) have most prominently argued. As the former originally put it, 'According to Kenneth Waltz, if different states act similarly in response to similar phenomena, we are justified in thinking that there may be some kind of structural effect at work' (Webb, 1991, p. 312). But unlike anarchy, which for Waltz has major structural effects, the structural constraints which capital mobility imposes on states are not based in the actions of other states. The constraint is a result of the behavior of private actors, who are given an independent basis of power by the structure of the capitalist economic system. If, however, a major structural feature of the global system is determined by the actions of private, rather than state, entities, it calls into question the central role that

Realism accords the state. This is hardly to say, as Charles Kindleberger once did, that 'The state is just about through as an economic unit' (Kindleberger, 1969, p. 207). But it does mean that we cannot follow the Realist approach that makes states the central (indeed, the only truly important) actors in the international system. Instead, seeing capital mobility as a structural aspect of world politics lets us ask the question, 'How important is the state in shaping international outcomes?' In other words, it allows us to *problematize* the role of the state in international political economy, rather than assuming either its centrality or its imminent demise.

I propose seeing the global political economy as structured by both states and firms, rather than, as Realists would have it, by states alone (see Gilpin, 1975, p. 4; and Krasner, 1978b, p. 348, for the classic statements of this argument). Governments, for their part, want to channel economic activity, support particular producers, achieve geopolitical objectives, etc., through their attempts to regulate markets. But since capitalism gives producers a power resource that is not reducible to states or state activity, governments must concede to firms some ability to structure economic activity. As Lindblom (1977) suggests, it is for that reason always the case that firms must be induced to perform their 'public' functions. My argument implies further, however, that the relative importance of states and firms in ordering the world political economy will vary with capital mobility: as it increases, firms have increasing ability to achieve their goals even when they run counter to the preferences of state managers.

The reason capital mobility tells us the relative contribution of the two parties to structuring the world economy is that it is a crucial, perhaps the most important, factor determining the relative bargaining power of firms and states. That is, even in situations where all other variables affecting bargaining power between MNCs and host states have changed so as to favour the host, increases in capital mobility outweighed them and led to improved bargaining outcomes for the firms involved (Thomas, 1997, chapter 5). This has quite broad implications because the same factors which theorists have previously identified as determining the outcome of MNC/host bargaining are also crucially relevant for government ability to regulate firms in general. Thus, this analysis points to the centrality of capital mobility as a method by which firms can avoid or blunt regulation. The fact that capital mobility represents a power resource for the owners of capital that is independent of states is why we can see it as the central index of the relative contribution of states and firms to the structuring of the global system.

To show that states were not alone in structuring the world economy, I have elsewhere (Thomas, 1997, pp. 34–40) analysed the growth of foreign direct investment since 1897 and show that its rapid increase since the Second World War has not been the result of US hegemony, as argued by many Realists. World foreign direct investment stocks have grown more rapidly in the period since 1970 than during the height of American hegemony from 1950–70, while American FDI growth has slowed since then. This implies that economic conditions, especially the growth of capital mobility, are at the root of the rapid growth of FDI, rather than a favourable climate created by American hegemony, power or security interests. Moreover, it highlights quite clearly how firms are jointly responsible for the structure of the global political economy, far more so than Realists would admit.

The centrality of capital mobility

Why is capital mobility so important? As noted above, four major factors stand out: it increases options available to the firm, it reduces the cost of withholding investment or disinvesting, it directly reduces the power of state sanctions against firms, and it introduces bidding dynamics into the process of obtaining investment. All of these strengthen firms in their bargaining with states. Moreover, all of these considerations are relevant to the relations of the companies to their workers. We now consider each of them in more detail:

1 At the most basic level, capital mobility increases the options available to firms. It makes more and more locations technically feasible for a given economic activity serving a particular market or markets, which in turn has two major consequences.

First, the increased options increase the credibility of a firm's threats to use some other option when it negotiates with a state over the conditions for an investment.[11] Second, by increasing the number of feasible locations for economic activity, capital mobility creates more actors on the state side of the firm/state equation. This makes the collective action problem faced by those countries in regulating firms more severe. As the number of relevant actors increases, cooperation among them becomes more difficult. This is important because states need to cooperate if they wish to undertake actions limiting the power of large corporations; otherwise firms will use their mobility to play one nation off against the others in search of lower taxes, fewer regulations, and so on. This exemplifies how differential ability to achieve collective action can be a source of power in state/firm interaction, just as Offe and Wiesenthal argue it is in capital/labour relations (Offe and Wiesenthal, 1980, pp. 74–5).

2 International capital mobility reduces a firm's prospective cost from not investing in any one country. That is, a company that withholds investment is likely to see a cost as a result of doing so, because presumably it would have to put the money it would have reinvested in its business into something (such as financial instruments) with a lower expected rate of profit. If its investment options were widened by international mobility, especially to its same line of business in other countries, it would lose less than if it could only choose from alternative investments within its home country. Similarly, it reduces the cost of actually relocating. By reducing the cost of not investing or of disinvesting, it makes the *threat* to do so more credible. In this way, too, capital mobility improves companies' bargaining power.

3 Capital mobility similarly reduces the force of threats that states can make against firms. As Gill and Law (1988, p. 92) argue, 'The threat of nationalisation is less crushing to a transnational company, since it is likely that only a small proportion of its assets would be expropriated by a single country.' Moreover, if a plant only represented one piece in an integrated process, the threat to take it over would be less credible. As Kobrin predicted in 1987 (pp. 635–36), industries with integrated production processes may well witness increased firm bargaining power over time, a claim that was borne out in my study of the automobile industry (Thomas, 1997).

4 Capital mobility is also important because it introduces bidding dynamics into state/firm relations. If a firm succeeds in receiving bids from several states for an investment, it will generally do better than if it had simply negotiated with a single state. States may try to limit competition among themselves (for the reasonably successful EU attempts to do so, see Thomas, 1996, and Thomas, 2000), but as we saw above, capital mobility increases the number of states which must cooperate to do so.

As noted above, these factors are also relevant for a corporation's relationships with its workers. A firm can threaten to shut down a plant if workers' wage or other demands are more than it wants to pay. If capital mobility increases, the credibility of these threats becomes greater. A company can locate new plants in areas where its workers' union is not strong, as in GM's 'Southern strategy' in the mid- to late 1970s (Rubenstein, 1992, pp. 238–41). It can build duplicate plants in other locations, making closure threats more credible since it has another source of production, and making it less vulnerable to strikes for the same reason. Finally, bidding dynamics apply between union locals as well as between governments, especially when companies state they will close one or more of their operations; the auto industry in North America has provided numerous examples in the past decade (Rubenstein, 1992, pp. 263–6).

Practical consequences of rising capital mobility

As can be documented for both financial and productive capital, capital mobility has risen throughout the postwar period (Thomas, 1997, chapter 3). Since states and labour are both relatively immobile, this implies that the power of capital has risen relative to that of both the state and labour. At the very broadest levels, this suggests distributional consequences that favour capital over labour (Frieden, 1991b, pp. 434, 442). In addition, increasing capital mobility has reduced states' ability to regulate firms and to carry out expansionary macroeconomic policies (Helleiner, 1995b). This reduces their ability to redistribute income towards labour, although some supply-side policy options may remain available to labour-oriented governments (Garrett and Lange, 1991). This systematic shutting-off of policy options that democratic governments have chosen in the past and might want to again follow raises questions about the implications of rising capital mobility for democracy (Helleiner, 1995b; Held, 1991).

That capital mobility has had the predicted distributional effects is hard to dispute. In the United States, real weekly wages for nonsupervisory workers (80 per cent of the workforce) fell 17.3 per cent from 1972 to 1997.[12] In Europe, where institutional factors make it more difficult to reduce wages, the effects of capital mobility have instead been manifested in an increase in unemployment, with joblessness increasing from 2.9 per cent of the European Union labour force in 1973 to 10.3 per cent in the first quarter of 1998.[13] Capital mobility has also allowed firms and wealthy individuals to reduce their share of national tax burdens.[14] Overall, then, the increase in the mobility of capital has indeed strengthened capital relative to labour as well as the state.

Because this is so, moving capital mobility closer to centre-stage of our work in international political economy means that we must also pay attention to such distributional consequences. They are not marginal phenomena, and are intimately bound up with a structural feature of the global system.

Conclusion

This chapter has argued that past discussions of capital mobility have been heavily weighted towards analysis of the mobility of financial assets only, thereby tacitly accepting the economist's baseline of perfect competition as a background condition. However, this is highly distorting when we consider the motivation for foreign direct investment, the instantiation of the mobility of productive capital. FDI exists precisely because of imperfect competition, so a definition that assumes perfect competition cannot be adequate for understanding all types of capital mobility. Instead, I have proposed a definition based on the *ability* to transfer capital across geographical locations as a more inclusive way of treating financial and productive capital.

This work also suggests that we need to enquire about the status of capital mobility, that is whether this concept functions most fundamentally on the individual level, the structural level, or both. The analysis here, though preliminary, tends to support Wendt's claim that agency and structure are co-determining.

Finally, the practical result of increasing capital mobility is a redistribution of resources away from labour and towards capital, and a reduction in the regulatory capacity of the state. As capital mobility occupies an increasingly important role in IPE analysis, these distributional consequences will necessarily be highlighted. Future work needs to determine how states and labour movements can effectively respond to the problems raised by increasing capital mobility, perhaps most importantly through international cooperation in regulation (see the Porter and Webb contributions to this volume; Thomas, 1996; and Thomas, 2000).

Notes

1 An important exception to this, however, is Sinclair (1994), which analyses the extent to which credit-rating agencies coordinate the efforts of capital holders.
2 For example, there is a rapidly growing comparative politics literature on policy convergence, especially in the industrialized world. Some sample contributions include Leibfried and Pierson (1995) and Berger and Dore (1996).
3 As David Andrews (1994, p. 195 fn. 7) points out, this distinction is often overlooked but is not, in fact, new.
4 The latter half of this definition is drawn from Cowling and Sugden's (1987, p. 12) treatment of multinational corporations as organizations which coordinate production across national borders.
5 Andrews (1994) makes a similar argument, but does not include degree of commitment of capital as a factor in mobility, nor does he differentiate

between financial and productive capital. Frieden and Rogowski (1996, p. 26) is also similar, but they implausibly link the incentives to engage in international transactions with the *ability* to do so in their concept of the 'exogenous easing of international exchange'.

The difference between technological change and strategic innovation is a very fine line, but it seems that there are at least some innovations which are not based in technological changes. Douglass North (1990, pp. 125–6) discusses several non-technological innovations affecting capital mobility. For more contemporary examples, see further below. Finally, war and war preparations tend to reduce capital mobility, often sharply.

6 I owe this suggestion to Michael Webb.

7 See Thomas (1997, pp. 43–5) for an elaboration of this. Fred Halliday (1995, p. 39) points out that international-relations theory has an extraordinarily striking silence about capitalism.

8 This has been disputed, however. For example, Barbara Jenkins (1992, chapter 2), suggests that states have much greater ability to regulate firms than is suggested by my analysis. While accepting that investment flows lead to changes in regulatory policy, she claims that regulation of investment by Canada and Mexico has not affected foreign investment inflows into those two countries. While I accept her point that economic conditions (in which I include capital mobility) are the most important determinant of FDI, they are not the only one. If rising investment regulation is followed by increased FDI inflows, it only means that the economic effects were greater than the regulation effects, not that regulation effects were zero. For example, her claim that FDI increased after Canada adopted the Foreign Investment Review Act (FIRA) is dubious because she looks for regulation effects only after FIRA went into effect in April 1974, rather than after the government confirmed in early 1972 that it would increase regulation of foreign investment. As I show below, FDI inflows fell sharply in 1972 and never regained their 1971 level as a proportion of advanced-country inflows; her finding of an increase in 1974–75 is only possible because of that previous decline.

9 This is not to say that all the 'disciplining' effects of capital mobility come about through uncoordinated action. As Sinclair (1994) has pointed out, the decisions of capital owners can be coordinated through knowledge-brokers such as credit-rating agencies. One could also add site location consultants and business-climate raters to this list.

10 It might appear that this discussion of structural constraints falls prey to the criticism Wendt makes of Waltz, namely that his structure is ultimately reducible to the properties of agents (see also Ashley, 1984). As Wendt suggests, though, if neorealism were to incorporate all three of Waltz's elements of structure into its definition, rather than focusing exclusively on the distribution of capabilities among agents, it might be possible to construct a generative interpretation of neorealism (1987, p. 341 fn. 9). The following analysis suggests one such reconstruction: instead of seeing anarchy as a constraint, perhaps it can be considered a way of socializing states to act in a certain way, i.e. to follow the prescriptions of 'self-help'.

11 For a more detailed analysis of the importance of threats, see Thomas (1997, pp. 25–7).

12 U.S. Council of Economic Advisers, *Economic Report of the President*, 1998, table B-47, p. 336.

13 Organization for Economic Cooperation and Development, *Quarterly Labour Force Statistics* (Paris: OECD) 1995, no. 1, p. 82; and 1998, no. 2, p. 104. Unemployment had been as high as 11.3% in the first quarter 1994.

14 Steinmo (1993, chapter 6). Although this pattern is not monolithic, as his discussion indicates, it is the main trend.

Part III

Responses to International Capital Mobility

7
Reconciling Practice and Structure: US Regulation of Transfer Pricing by Transnational Firms

Michael C. Webb

Introduction: structure, practice and the potential for change

How seriously does international capital mobility constrain national economic policy-making? Since capital would not be internationally mobile if states did not support mobility through their practices, could states not change their practices to deal with the undesirable effects of capital mobility? These are key questions for the political-economic analysis of globalization. This chapter explores these questions in the context of a study of US regulation of transfer pricing by transnational corporations (TNCs). The growth of TNCs depended on state practice in a variety of areas, one of which was favourable tax treatment of transnational earnings. States supported foreign direct investment (FDI) at home and abroad in part by relieving double taxation of profits earned outside their home countries. Yet the practices followed by states had the undesirable consequence of facilitating tax avoidance by TNCs, which could reduce their profits in high-tax jurisdictions by setting internal transfer prices to shift profits to low-tax jurisdictions. As more and more industry became transnational, the consequent loss of tax revenues became less tolerable to deficit-strapped governments. The US government, which had taken the lead in encouraging the spread of FDI, also took the lead in the 1980s and 1990s in searching for new practices that would curb abuse of existing tax regulations. Yet after a few years of debate, and in the face of transnational and foreign opposition, the United States made only minor changes to its international tax policy, changes that will likely have only a modest impact on the effectiveness of that policy in collecting tax revenues from TNCs.

This case provides an excellent opportunity to examine the questions posed above. Was US tax policy seriously constrained by international capital mobility and the structural power of transnational corporations? Could the United States, as the state whose practices matter most to the global economy (Strange, 1988), not alter its practices to cope with an undesirable consequence of capital mobility? Indeed, this can be considered a crucial case study of the impact of international economic structure on national policy autonomy, and a most-likely case (Eckstein, 1975; Collier, 1993) for the hypothesis that states retain the capacity for effective autonomous policy-making in the face of open capital markets. If even the most powerful state (also the state that did the most to shape existing international practices) is constrained by the international economic structure, then one can safely conclude that smaller states also are similarly (or more strictly) constrained.

A useful point of departure for investigating these issues is the literature on the structural power of capital. This literature argues that the ability to move capital across national borders increases capital's power *vis-à-vis* states (Gill and Law, 1988, chapter 7; Gill and Law, 1989). Capitalist economies depend on the private decisions of the owners of capital for the investment necessary for future economic prosperity. The state is structurally dependent on capital because it can realize its own objectives only if private capitalists invest enough to maintain economic prosperity. But capitalists will do so only if the state provides favourable conditions (on the structural dependence thesis, also see Przeworski and Wallerstein, 1988). In an insular economy, investors facing unfavourable policies would reduce the rate of investment. Such an 'investment strike' would punish the state, but it also involves costs for investors. Reducing investment may be detrimental to the enterprise's own future success, and funds diverted from investment to consumption may be subject to higher tax rates. International capital mobility provides investors with additional options for responding to unfavourable policies, thus making the level of investment more sensitive to government policies and increasing the structural power of capital. Adverse policies would be met with an immediate outflow of capital in search of more favourable policies and higher returns.

The degree of international capital mobility can be considered a structural feature of the international system to the extent that the degree of mobility systematically influences the behaviour of state and non-state actors and would be difficult or costly for actors to change (Webb, 1995a; Andrews, 1994). It is the *conjuncture* of an international political system of separate sovereign states with an economic structure dominated by transnational capital that gives rise to the international structural power of capital. The division of political authority among competing states means that TNCs are 'not accountable to any public authority that matches [them] in geographic reach and that represents the aggregate interests of all the countries the enterprise[s] affect' (Vernon, 1971, p. 249). Instead, states compete with each other to attract internationally-mobile investment, though they may also cooperate to limit that competition (on the 'competition state' see Cerny, 1990). Structural constraints, it should be noted, arise out of the independent, non-coordinated actions of private actors responding to the opportunities and constraints that they face. Thus, structural power is distinct from lobbying and other overt political action, which is sometimes labelled behavioural power (Gill and Law, 1988, chapter 7).

At the same time, it is important to recognize that claims about structural constraints and the structural power of capital are not claims that these constitute exogenous constraints on the practices of states. Constructivist arguments such as structuration theory (Wendt, 1987; Giddens, 1984) emphasize that structures such as the global economy are not separate from the practices of states – that is, they should not be viewed as 'primitive ontological units' (Wendt, 1987). Instead, we need to recognize how structural features of the global economy arise out of the practices of state and non-state actors. As I argued in an earlier study of how structural changes in international financial markets influence macroeconomic policy, 'those structural changes were themselves the product of policy choices to liberalize trade and trade-related capital flows and not to regulate international capital markets when regulation might have been feasible' (Webb, 1995a, p. 16; see also Andrews, 1994). Nevertheless, I argued, those earlier choices and the practices they encouraged had created an international economic structure that had persisted over time, that systematically influenced (though it did not determine) policy choices in all of the industrialized countries, and that would be difficult for governments to reverse (Webb, 1995a, pp. 15–18).

There is considerable debate about the severity of the constraints that capital mobility imposes on national policies and about the ability of governments to alter their practices to ameliorate any problems that might arise (for different views on these issues from that presented in this chapter, see the contributions by Tony Porter and Eric Helleiner in this volume). In the area of corporate taxation, most analysts argue that international mobility is an important constraint. When capital is not internationally mobile, high tax rates might dampen investment, but the effect will be limited because investors have few other options. But if firms are able to invest in more than one country, high-tax countries are likely to see an exodous of investment to lower-tax countries. Alternatively, firms may continue to invest in the high-tax country but use transfer pricing and other income-shifting strategies to reduce the profits they declare in the high-tax country. The opportunities for capital to escape a government's jurisdiction – by investing abroad or shifting profits to lower-tax jurisdictions – limit the ability of governments to use corporate taxation to finance their spending. Most tax economists argue that international capital mobility undermines all forms of capital taxation and encourages governments to focus taxation on relatively immobile tax bases such as labour income, consumption and land (Frenkel, Razin and Sadka, 1991; Tanzi, 1995; Gordon and MacKie-Mason, 1995).[1] Sven Steinmo highlights the political implications of this dynamic; reduced taxation of internationally-mobile sources of wealth and income undermines redistributive taxation, a central element of the Keynesian welfare state (Steinmo, 1994; see also Tanzi, 1995; and Frenkel, Razin and Sadka, 1991, pp. 213–14).

From this perspective, governments face international structural pressures to reduce effective tax rates by statutory means (lowering tax rates, providing incentives) and by weakening enforcement of tax laws (Tanzi, 1995, p. 110). Most of the debates in the literature about the impact of international pressures on corporate taxation have focused on statutory elements of tax policy, including tax rates and the definition of the tax base. Analysts have come to different conclusions about the impact of internationalization, with some finding that capital taxation has been eroded (Steinmo, 1994; Tanzi, 1995; Lee and McKenzie, 1989) but others arguing on theoretical and empirical grounds that governments retain considerable autonomy to tax corporate income in response to domestic political considerations (Garrett, 1995; Rose, 1986; Wallerstein and Przeworski, 1995).[2]

In this chapter, I will focus on a different element of tax policy, namely enforcement. Transfer-pricing regulations are a particularly important element of enforcement as far as international competitive pressures are concerned. Strict enforcement by high-tax countries to prevent companies from using artificial transfer prices to shift profits abroad could seriously undermine these countries' attractiveness as a location for investment. Thus, theoretical arguments that emphasize the constraining impact of international capital mobility might expect relatively weak administrative efforts to enforce national tax laws on TNCs.[3]

But international pressures for relaxed enforcement of regulations restricting income-shifting run up against domestic political considerations emphasized in the comparative political economy literature on taxation. Domestic politics generally encourage governments to tax corporate profits, since this form of taxation is more popular among voters than alternative sources of revenue such as personal income taxes or sales taxes (Peters, 1991, p. 31). Strict enforcement of existing tax laws may be particularly attractive to contemporary governments, most of which face vociferous opposition to overt tax increases yet desperately need to raise revenues to reduce budget deficits. Stricter enforcement can raise revenues without raising tax rates, and cracking down on tax avoidance by multinational corporations (especially foreign-owned corporations) is always popular among wage and salary earners who face few opportunities to avoid taxation of their income. Thus, while international competitive pressures generally should encourage lighter regulation of transfer pricing and other income-shifting strategies, domestic political pressures generally encourage stricter regulation of tax avoidance by corporations.

These questions about international structural constraints and international versus domestic determinants of policy are examined in this chapter through a case study of US government efforts to reform its policy on transfer pricing in the late 1980s and 1990s. Deficit pressures, continued growth in the overseas manufacturing operations of US firms, and the flood of FDI into the United States in the 1980s all generated concern that US corporate tax revenues were being undermined by TNCs manipulating transfer prices to shift taxable profits out of the United States. Congress, the Treasury Department and the Internal Revenue Service (IRS) proposed some dramatic alterations to US international tax policy to address these perceived problems. In addition to administrative reforms, a central theme of many of the proposed changes was to focus more attention on the distribution of profits between parent firms and their subsidiaries, rather than on trying to ensure that TNCs set transfer prices at levels equivalent to prices for similar transactions between unrelated firms – the so-called arm's-length standard. But the changes implemented in 1993–4 essentially abandoned this approach in favour of a modest revision of existing practices. These changes actually increased taxpayers' flexibility in setting and justifying transfer prices, though taxpayers also had to document their methods more carefully and financial penalties for non-compliance were introduced.

What does this case suggest about the ability of the US government to alter international practices that enable capital mobility, yet which have negative consequences for other US policy goals? The dependence of capital mobility on state practice did not, in this case, give even the most powerful state sufficient lattitude to alter those practices to ameliorate negative effects of capital mobility. But was the outcome due to structural constraints and the international structural power of transnational capital? Tracing the process (George and McKeown, 1985) by which US proposals were developed, revised and implemented suggests that the kinds of structural pressures often emphasized in the literature were not decisive. There is no evidence that transnational investors threatened to shift investment out of the United States in response to adverse changes in US international tax policy. Most TNCs have strong incentives, regardless of US tax policy, to be active in the United States, which makes the US much less vulnerable to international structural pressures than smaller states. But the US was constrained by the international practices it had previously developed to support the growth of an open international economy, and specifically to support FDI by American TNCs. Existing international arrangements for relieving corporations of double taxation would have come under severe strain had the US profit-based proposals been implemented, exposing US TNCs to foreign retaliation and double taxation. Despite its clear leadership role in international taxation, the US government lacked the power to change deeply-embedded international practices, and was not willing to accept the costs of pushing ahead unilaterally.

Before describing the US proposals and their reception by TNCs and foreign governments, some description of prior international practice is in order. Therefore, the second section briefly outlines how TNCs could shift income to reduce their global tax burdens, the US regulations prior to 1986 that sought to prevent tax-motivated transfer pricing, and international norms in this area. The third section describes the regulatory changes proposed by the IRS, the Treasury Department and Congress beginning in 1986. The fourth section describes the international debate about these proposals and the US compromise which left corporate taxpayers with greater freedom for choosing and justifying transfer prices, albeit at the cost of a modestly-increased compliance burden. The final section concludes the chapter.

Transfer pricing and its regulation before 1986

The disjuncture between the territorial segmentation of the international political system and the territorial spread of modern corporations creates serious problems for corporate taxation. The income and profits of a TNC are generated by operations that span the borders of more than one state. Each government has an interest in taxing some portion of TNCs' income and profits, but there is no apolitical criteria that could be used to determine which portion. In order to avoid double taxation (that is, when two or more governments tax the same income of a TNC), the industrialized-country governments long ago decided to rely on the method of separate national accounts based on arm's-length prices (Webb, 1995b). TNCs are required to keep separate accounts for their operations in each country and to pay taxes to each national revenue authority based on the profits reported in each country.[4] Taxpayers are supposed to use arm's-length prices for inter-affiliate transfers of goods and services – that is, prices that would prevail for equivalent transfers between unaffiliated firms operating at arm's-length.

This shared understanding was codified in Article 7 of the 1963 OECD 'Draft Convention on Double Taxation of Income and Capital', which has served as the basis for many bilateral tax treaties. The OECD countries recognized that this method created opportunities for TNCs to set internal transfer prices to shift profits from high-tax to low-tax countries, but argued that this problem 'should not be given undue weight. Much more importance is attached to the desirability of interfering as little as possible with existing business organization' (OECD, 1963, Article 7 commentary, paragraph 9). This balance between facilitating FDI and preventing tax evasion reflected the political priorities of the 1950s and 1960s, as well as the extensive involvement of TNC representatives in the consultations since the 1920s. Western governments were not unduly concerned about losing tax revenue at a time when most industry was organized nationally and thus did not have the opportunity to evade taxes by international income-shifting.

Widespread concern in the United States about the potential for manipulating transfer prices to avoid taxes emerged in the 1960s. As American multinationals expanded abroad, some Democrats and trade union leaders became concerned that these firms were taking advantage of favourable tax treatment for FDI to evade US taxes, export jobs, and worsen the US balance-of-payments deficit. Regulations specifying arm's-length pricing had been in place since the 1930s, but these were vague and rarely enforced by the IRS. In 1968 the Treasury Department released new regulations under Section 482 of the Internal Revenue Code that defined rules for establishing arm's-length prices for intra-firm transactions (GAO, 1981, pp. 2–3; Langbein, 1986, p. 645). Prices for all transactions should be determined by reference to 'comparable uncontrolled prices' (CUP) – that is, arm's-length prices – whenever possible. Alternative methods were specified for cases in which CUPs were not available, including resale price minus an appropriate profit mark up (which subsequently came to be known as resale-price minus) and cost of production plus a profit mark up (cost plus) (Picciotto, 1992, p. 187). This approach to regulating transfer pricing was endorsed by other OECD governments in 1979 (OECD, 1979; Langbein, 1986).

American proposals for new transfer pricing rules, 1986–92

The arm's-length approach was bound to come under pressure as the number of TNCs grew. The range of firms that had to be watched to ensure against international tax avoidance increased, and TNCs were developing much more highly integrated cross-border operations as part of the trend towards more global corporations (Dunning, 1993). Production, finance, management services, research and development, and other functions within corporations were becoming more transnational. Transfer prices no longer mattered just for a few raw materials or intermediate products transferred among relatively autonomous enterprises, as was generally the case in the 1950s and 1960s. Now, a much wider range of corporate functions is 'traded' internationally within TNCs and the issue of transfer pricing has become much more important (Pagan and Wilkie, 1992, p. 301). Especially important is the growing role of intangibles in intra-corporate relations. With the shift towards post-Fordist industrial structures, knowledge and other intangibles have become more important sources of competitive advantage. TNCs' choices of transfer prices for high-profit intangibles – such as process and product technologies, brand names, organizational and managerial innovations, and shared business services – can have a huge impact on the distribution of profits among its operations in different countries. These intangibles also tend to be unique and are rarely sold in open international markets, which makes it difficult to attach an appropriate arm's-length price to them (US Treasury and IRS, 1988, chapters 3 and 4).

Political concern about transfer pricing after the mid-1980s focused on two distinct problems, the first concerning US-owned firms and the second concerning foreign-owned – especially Japanese – firms. First, it appeared that some US-owned firms were shifting profits abroad by setting low prices for intangible assets transfered to foreign subsidiaries in low-tax countries. Firms were alleged to underprice exports of trademarks, patents and other intellectual property to their foreign manufacturing subsidiaries, which would then earn high profits from exporting products incorporating these intangibles back to the USA and to third-country markets (interviews with Treasury officials, Washington, D.C.,

March 1997; Birnkrant and Crocker, 1994b, p. 336). In response, the 1986 Tax Reform Act (TRA) added to Section 482 a sentence specifying that the income generated by the transfer (or license) of intangible property should be 'commensurate with the income attributable to the intangible' – the so-called CWI standard (Bischel, 1990, pp. 83–4; Quigley, 1992, p. 282).

The CWI standard was aimed at tax avoidance by US-owned TNCs. The second concern, which became more prominent in the early 1990s, focused on alleged tax avoidance by foreign-owned firms. The nationalist backlash against the flood of FDI, particularly from Japan, included allegations that foreign-owned firms underreported profits in the United States to evade US taxes. Japanese automobile and electronics firms with distribution and manufacturing operations in the USA were said to overprice imports into the USA from their Japanese parents. This was identified as a possible reason for the failure of the 1986 TRA to raise corporate tax revenues enough to offset the planned cut in personal income tax revenues (*New York Times*, 4 March 1990, p. D19; on the 1986TRA, see Conlan *et al.*, 1990).[5] In widely-publicized Congressional hearings, politicians and analysts estimated that foreign-owned firms were avoiding as much as $30 billion per year in taxes that should have been paid to the US Treasury; and presidential candidate Bill Clinton claimed in 1992 that he could increase US tax revenues by $45 billion over four years by cracking down on tax abuse by foreign corporations. Taking into account other factors that might legitimately reduce the taxable profits of foreign-owned companies, the IRS and outside experts eventually settled on a figure of about $3 billion per year in lost tax revenues due to international income shifting by foreign TNCs (Matthews, 1992, pp. 577–9; Grubert *et al.*, 1993). These figures compare with total US federal government corporate income tax revenues of approximately $100 billion annually during this period.

These political concerns highlighted serious administrative problems with the arm's-length price method. Arm's-length prices can be determined only through an inquiry into the facts and circumstances specific to each transaction; the tax examiner must choose which of a myriad of transactions to audit in detail and search for comparable uncontrolled prices. Studies by the General Accounting Office (GAO) have found that CUPs can be identified only for a small number of the transactions being audited, and that in roughly half of the cases it examined, none of the methods specified in the 1968 regulations could be used. Thus, the tax examiner often must construct an arm's-length price based on detailed information about the firm and its industry. International examiners often faced major obstacles getting the information they needed to assess transfer prices. Many firms did not prepare any documentation to support their choice of transfer prices until a request came from the IRS, and some used delaying tactics in the hope that the IRS would simply give up (GAO, 1981, 1992).

Auditing transfer prices is therefore a very labour-intensive process, and the growth of TNCs threatens to overwhelm IRS efforts. The IRS's 540 international examiners and economists audited more than 3000 corporate returns with international issues in 1991, but this was a small proportion of the total (GAO, 1994, 1995). The IRS tries to deal with the imbalance between returns needing examination and the resources available in part by concentrating on larger firms where the amount of tax revenue at stake is greater, but this may have contributed to a decline that has occurred in the level of voluntary compliance by smaller corporate taxpayers; in 1991, for example, more than 60 per cent of corporations with assets less than $100 million paid no tax (GAO, 1995, p. 39; GAO, 1997).

Two types of responses to the problems of regulating transfer pricing were considered in US debates in the late 1980s and the 1990s. Potential responses were basically of two types; improved enforcement of the arm's-length price standard, and new methods that would allocate the profits of a TNC to its US and foreign operations on some basis other than prices for intra-firm transfers, with that basis presumably being less-vulnerable to manipulation by taxpayers. Policy debates proceeded simultaneously on both fronts, and a number of steps were taken to make enforcement of the arm's-length standard more rigorous. The IRS responded to Congressional concern about international tax avoidance by foreign-controlled corporations (FCCs) mainly by reallocating existing audit resources, reducing those devoted to auditing the returns of US-controlled corporations (USCCs).[6] The number of international examiners and economists rose to 700 by 1994 (Lyons, 1996, p. 100). New reporting requirements for FCCs and penalties for firms subject to transfer price adjustments were introduced by Congress in 1989 and 1990 (the penalties became significant only with new regulations in 1993, and they are discussed more fully below).

Increased attention to auditing the accounts of foreign-owned firms did have an impact. The IRS imposed substantial tax adjustments on such firms as Nissan (whose US profits over an 11-year period were adjusted up by $1.85 billion) and Toyota (profits adjusted by $850 million for a 5-year period) (*International Tax Review*, September/October 1995, p. 2; *Globe and Mail*, 30 August 1990, p. B6). While the overall value of the proposed adjustments fluctuates sharply from year to year,

GAO data suggest a trend in 1989–94 of larger adjustments proposed for FCCs and smaller adjustments proposed for USCCs (GAO, 1995, p. 19).

A less-contentious approach to improving administration of the arm's-length standard adopted by the IRS in 1991 was the advance pricing agreement (APA) programme. An APA is an agreement with a taxpayer and, potentially, one or more foreign tax authorities, which specifies in advance the method to be used for determining prices for specific cross-border transfers within firms. The APA initiative was favourably received by most tax advisors and foreign governments (Cole, 1991; Boidman, 1992, pp. 256–7, 260). In practice, however, it appears quite limited as a solution to problems of transfer pricing and international tax cooperation, mainly because of the enormous administrative effort required of both tax authorities and taxpayers. APAs appear to be restricted to a small number of large taxpayers, and perhaps to taxpayers that were relatively compliant to begin with (GAO, 1992, pp. 64–6). As of mid-1995 – four years after the programme was introduced – only 33 APAs had been concluded, and only 12 of these formally involved a foreign tax authority (approximately 100 other APAs were then under negotiation) (Cole, 1995, pp. 220, 222). Furthermore, the IRS was granting taxpayers seeking APAs even more flexibility in setting transfer prices than they already had under the new regulations (Birnkrant and Crocker, 1994a, p. 335; Boidman, 1992, p. 256; Franko *et al.*, 1994, pp. 33–4). While the long-run potential to reduce the administrative burden of annual audits exists, in the short run the APA programme has consumed an enormous amount of IRS resources for a relatively small number of agreements (GAO, 1994, pp. 13–14).

All of the initiatives described so far – intensified audits of foreign-owned firms, new documentation requirements, and APAs – were attempts to improve compliance with the 1968 transfer-pricing regulations. During the same period, Treasury and the IRS were also working to develop new regulations intended to ensure an appropriate division of *profits* between US firms and their foreign parents or subsidiaries rather than calculating accurate arm's-length *prices* for intra-firm cross-border transactions. The problem of tax avoidance by American TNCs setting low transfer prices for exports of intangibles to their foreign subsidiaries generated one such proposal. In a 1988 white paper, they proposed that in cases in which arm's-length comparables could not be found, the profit attributable to the intangible (after assigning a market rate of return to those functions performed by the foreign affiliate) should be assigned to the parent firm and taxed in the USA (US Treasury and IRS, 1988; Picciotto, 1992, pp. 218–19; Rothschild and Rae, 1989, pp. 178–9).

This was portrayed as an arm's-length method because it attempted to estimate the distribution of profits that would have occurred with respect to a similar transaction between unrelated firms, but critics decried the shift of attention away from the pricing of transactions. They also criticized the white paper's call for periodic adjustments to the compensation paid for transfers of intangibles as information on the profits earned from those intangibles became available.

A more fundamental reform was proposed in January 1992, when the IRS released proposed transfer-pricing regulations that moved sharply toward a profit-based approach. This approach was driven mainly by the concern that foreign-owned firms were not paying a fair share of taxes, though the regulations would also apply to US-owned firms and would subsume the method for pricing intangibles just discussed. The central element of the January 1992 proposals was their definition of a new concept, the comparable profit interval (CPI). The basic idea was to define a range of profits comparable to what a similarly situated but uncontrolled third-party taxpayer (that is, a firm operating at arm's length to the overseas firm in question) would earn from a comparable business transaction (Pagan and Wilkie, 1992, p. 302; Cole and Rubloff, 1992, p. 292). The CPI would then serve as the basis for determining whether specific transfer prices for tangibles and intangibles proposed by TNCs were acceptable.[7] Essentially, if the transfer price assigned by the firm resulted in a profit that fell within the CPI calculated for that firm, the IRS would accept the price; if the profit fell below that interval, the IRS would require an adjustment. This would be a radical departure from the arm's-length methods specified in earlier regulations, since the price for a specific transfer would be determined by attributing to a firm the profit level that other comparable firms reported and then setting prices so as to achieve that profit level, rather than by trying to estimate the price that such a transfer would command in an open market (Cole and Rubloff, 1992, p. 294). The focus on comparing the taxable profits of FCCs with those of their US competitors closely reflected Congressional concerns that FCCs were declaring much lower taxable profits relative to their assets than were USCCs (interviews with Treasury Department officials, Washington, D.C., March 1997).

Transnational and international opposition and American retreat

The release of the proposed new Section 482 regulations in January 1992 triggered a storm of opposition. TNCs and their tax advisors feared that the proposed regulations would severely restrict the freedom that the arm's-length standard had given TNCs to shift taxable profits to low-tax jurisdictions (though this concern was not stated so bluntly), saddle them with a heavy compliance burden, and threaten them with heavy penalties. But the most influential complaint was that TNCs would face a serious risk of double taxation if the United States forced them to use a profit-based method to determine transfer prices while other states used the traditional arm's-length price method. Since this problem is at the heart of the reason why the USA abandoned the proposed CPI method, it is necessary at this point to explain the arcane procedures by which international double tax issues are resolved. These procedures are the most extensive and fully-developed element of international tax cooperation, though they attract little political attention. Even when all tax authorities use the arm's-length method, disputes can arise when different tax authorities use different transfer prices to increase the profits and taxes of the TNC's operations in each of their countries. These disputes are resolved through the mutual agreement procedure defined in bilateral tax treaties. So-called 'competent authorities' of each country negotiate a settlement whereby one or both governments would adjust their determination of transfer prices to eliminate this form of double taxation (the relevant procedures are in OECD, 1996, Articles 9 and 25). For example, an American auto firm that exported parts to its Canadian subsidiary for final assembly could face double taxation if the IRS adjusted its transfer prices, insisting that it charge a higher price for those parts. The higher price would increase the profit the firm declared in the United States, but the firm would face double taxation because it had already declared and paid taxes on that profit in Canada. At the firm's request, the US and Canadian competent authorities would meet to discuss how to relieve the firm of double taxation. Revenue Canada might accept the transfer price determined by the IRS and make a so-called 'corresponding adjustment' to the profits and taxes of the Canadian subsidiary, the IRS might abandon its proposed adjustment, or the two authorities might reach a compromise agreement.[8]

The mutual-agreement procedures have generally worked well to relieve firms of double taxation (Cole, 1991, p. 385; Pagan and Wilkie, 1992, p. 300; Boidman, 1995, p. 292). But the number of double-tax disputes escalated after the mid-1980s as US audits of foreign-owned TNCs intensified, and some foreign tax authorities (most notably Japan's) became less willing to accept the reduction in their tax revenues that would occur if they made the corresponding adjustments needed to relieve TNCs of double taxation resulting from IRS transfer-price adjustments (*International Tax Review*, March/April 1994, pp. 10–11). US adoption of a profit-based method would both increase the number of disputes and make them more difficult to solve, since different authorities would be using different methods to determine an appropriate division of profit (Birnkrant and Crocker, 1994b, p. 269). Shared norms were key to the kind of pragmatic cooperation that had existed between the US and foreign competent authorities.

American proposals also met with intense, concerted opposition from foreign governments. Foreign governments were responding to the concerns of nationally-owned TNCs and believed that the American proposals posed a threat to their own revenues. If the IRS adjusted transfer prices to increase the share of a TNC's global profits and taxes that appeared in the United States, a necessary correlate would be to reduce profits declared outside the United States and therefore the tax revenues of foreign governments. Furthermore, the transfer-pricing penalties created an incentive for TNCs to overreport income in the United States and underreport income elsewhere, since the financial risk of US penalties outweighed the risk of double taxation that would occur if the non-US authority required the TNC to correct its underreporting of income and pay higher taxes (Boidman, 1995). Some governments appeared to be willing to reject transfer-price adjustments demanded by the IRS in mutual agreement proceedings, thereby subjecting TNCs to lengthly disputes and double taxation (Birnkrant and Crocker, 1994a, p. 333). Key governments – including those of Japan, Britain and Germany – threatened to retaliate by auditing US-owned firms more intensively (*International Tax Review*, January/February 1994, p. 4; *Globe and Mail*, 25 November 1996, p. B4).

The OECD's Fiscal Committee established a special task force to review the proposed US regulations and formulate a joint response, an indication of the seriousness with which other governments and TNCs viewed the US threat. The task force also consulted with the International Chamber of Commerce and the Business and Industry Committee of the OECD, which voiced the stong opposition of non-US TNCs to the proposed regulations (Pagan, 1993, p. 181; interview with US Treasury official, Washington, DC, March 1997). The views expressed in the OECD consultations coincided with direct lobbying in Washington by TNCs and tax professionals, and these together helped move the Treasury Department away from the proposed regulations (Pagan, 1993, p. 181; Hay *et al.*,, 1994, p. 510; Birnkrant and Crocker, 1994b, p. 268). Treasury Department officials confirm that foreign opposition was central to the Department's decision (interviews, March 1997, Washington, DC).

The OECD task force argued that the US proposals were inconsistent with the existing international consensus in favour of arm's-length pricing and that this could lead to double taxation and disrupt international commerce (OECD, 1993, pp. vii–viii). International consensus, in the task force's view, permitted the use of profit comparisons for determining whether a transfer price proposed by a taxpayer was consistent with the arm's-length standard, whereas that the CPI method relied too rigidly on profit comparisons for determining transfer prices, neglecting other variables that could account for differences in profitability (OECD, 1993). Tax professionals made similar arguments (Granwell *et al.*, 1992).

Thus, opponents were able to portray the proposed regulations as inconsistent with international norms, and that portrayal was important in persuading US authorities that they, rather than foreign authorities, had to back down to prevent double taxation. American critics of the arm's-length price method have argued that the USA could take the lead in forging a new international consensus around better methods of income allocation such as formula apportionment, just as it had earlier played a key role in developing the international consensus around the arm's-length standard (GAO, 1981, p. 53; interviews, Washington, DC, March 1997). But the arm's-length method for pricing intra-firm transactions drew support from many sources outside the United States long before the USA drafted its regulations in 1968, and subsequently took on a life of its own by being incorporated into numerous international agreements and the practices of most governments. Particularly important is the network of bilateral tax treaties based on the OECD model tax treaty, first published in draft form in 1963. The OECD model clearly favours arm's-length pricing, though it does not rule out other methods when arm's-length pricing is not viable (see especially Article 7 and the accompanying commentary; OECD, 1996). A major change in the method for allocating income would necessitate renegotiation of treaties with many different partners, or legislation to revoke or override provisions of bilateral tax treaties. Any of these moves would be extremely disruptive and costly for the state making the change (on the inertia of tax treaties, see Williams, 1991, chapter 4). Perhaps for these reasons, the United States apparently did not even consider trying to change international practices by negotiating revisions to its tax treaties or seeking changes in the OECD model treaty. Instead, the proposals were presented in a purely unilateral fashion, with a complicated rationalization of how they were consistent with the international arm's-length norm.

The severity of foreign opposition to the CPI proposals put the USA in a difficult position. If it went ahead, it could expect chaos in international tax relations as foreign competent authorities rejected transfer-price adjustments proposed by the IRS and retaliated by subjecting US-owned TNCs to greater scrutiny. US officials place a high value on the pragmatic cooperation on international taxation that had existed among OECD governments and were loathe to undermine that cooperation. Not only would the IRS and US TNCs find themselves embroiled in far more international disputes, but Treasury officials also feared that foreign tax authorities would become less willing to cooperate with the US on other important issues such as exchange of information and tax havens. Consequently, Treasury decided to seek a compromise that would retain some elements needed to improve enforcement of arm's-length pricing while dropping those features that were least consistent with international norms (interviews with Treasury officials, Washington, DC, March 1997).

The US retreat from the CPI proposals was announced in January 1993, in the form of new temporary section 482 regulations.[9] These had been drawn up with foreign concerns in mind, and subsequently were accepted in new OECD transfer pricing guidelines (OECD, 1995). The US and foreign governments had been anxious to reach agreement on new guidelines to ease the mutual agreement proceedings and to prevent double taxation, and the USA was not the only government that had to compromise. In essence, the proposed regulations abandoned the profit-based approach specified in the 1992 proposals in favour of a revision of the arm's-length price method that provides greater flexibility for taxpayers in setting and defending transfer prices – the opposite of the original intent of US tax authorities – but that demands more extensive justification for and documentation of their transfer-pricing methodologies than was previously the case (these temporary regulations, with some minor changes, were made permanent in 1994; Birnkrant and Crocker, 1994b, p. 268; Hay *et al.*, 1994, p. 510).

The new regulations dropped the hierarchical listing of methods and the mandatory test of prices against the CPI standard, instead specifying a 'best method rule' which provided that the method which produced the most 'reliable' arm's-length value for a transaction should be used. The comparable profits method was now listed as one of the possible methods that the taxpayer could use, whether for tangibles or intangibles, alongside the traditional comparable uncontrolled prices, cost-plus, and resale-price-minus methods and the profit-split method, which was new to the US regulations but common in US and international practice (Ruchelman, 1993; Birnkrant and Crocker, 1994b, p. 270).[10] Some governments had been reluctant to accept the comparable profits method in any form in the new OECD guidelines, but eventually did so to prevent the worse outcome of no agreement (the OECD renamed it the transactional net margin method) (*International Tax Review*, September–October 1995, pp. 6–8; interviews with Treasury officials, Washington, DC, March 1997).

Taxpayers therefore now had a much wider range of methods to choose from in setting and justifying their transfer prices. In exchange for this enhanced flexibility, they had to provide extensive documentation to show that they had chosen the most reliable method. Treasury and the IRS had decided to emphasize this as the key element of their strategy to administer the existing method more effectively. The documentation requirement, backed by penalties if transfer prices were subsequently adjusted, was designed to force taxpayers to justify and document their choices when those decisions were made, thereby preparing a paper trail that an international examiner could more easily follow. This would hopefully ease the resource crunch facing the IRS.

The penalties for non-compliance with the new Section 482 regulations were detailed in revised Section 6662 regulations issued in February 1994. If the IRS determined that a taxpayer had misrepresented transfer prices by a factor of two (or reported prices that understated profits by more than 10 per cent of its gross annual receipts), a penalty equivalent to 20 per cent of the tax underpayment would be imposed. The penalty would be doubled to 40 per cent if the transfer price was misrepresented by a factor of four (or if profits were understated by more than 20 per cent of gross annual receipts). These are heavy penalties, but they would be waived if the taxpayer had met the IRS's documentation requirements (Cole, 1995, p. 216; Bonfiglio, 1995, pp. 12–13). Additional revisions to the penalty regulations issued in February 1996 – partly as a concession to foreign critics of US policy – further reduced the likelihood of taxpayers being penalized (interviews with Treasury Department officials, Washington, DC, March 1997).

Since tax years covered by the new regulations are only now being audited, it will be some years before definitive judgements can be made about their effectiveness. Nevertheless, one can assess the likelihood that the new approach will overcome problems with the arm's-length standard, and can examine the views and behaviour; of taxpayers and their advisors. The new regulations give taxpayers greater flexibility in choosing transfer-pricing methods, and it is difficult to see how this could restrict taxpayers' freedom to use transfer prices to shift income abroad. Similarly, it is difficult to imagine how the greater flexibility that taxpayers now have to choose and justify transfer prices could improve the IRS's ability to sustain adjustments proposed by its examiners through the appeals process and the courts. In recent years the sustention rate for proposed adjustments – the adjustment amount determined after the issue has been resolved through the IRS's own appeals process or the courts, relative to the adjustment originally proposed by international examiners – has often been below 30 per cent (GAO, 1995, p. 24). The low sustention rate reflects the inherent indeterminacy of the arm's-length standard in the absence of exact comparables. Courts have often been unwilling to accept the IRS's judgement, a problem that is reportedly compounded by inadequate case preparation by the IRS and by an imbalance between the legal resources available to the IRS and the much more extensive resources marshalled by taxpayers (GAO, 1992, pp. 45–7, 62; GAO, 1995, pp. 25–8; interview with tax lobbyist, Washington, DC, March 1997). The requirement for contemporaneous documentation will reduce the problem of taxpayers not providing sufficient information quickly enough to permit IRS examiners to assess transfer prices. But the information taxpayers are now required to provide still has to be reviewed, and the complexity of the regulations combined with the inherent facts-and-circumstances nature of transfer pricing mean that a heavy administrative burden remains (GAO, 1992, pp. 63–4). Indeed, one Treasury official interviewed said that the real problem facing the IRS was its lack of resources, and that the new approach did not really address this issue (interview, Washington, DC, March 1997).

The new regulations encourage taxpayers to draw on outside experts, such as tax accountants, lawyers and economists, in preparing their transfer-pricing methods and documentation. Treasury and IRS officials intended to educate tax professionals about the new rules in the hope that this would lead to greater voluntary compliance by taxpayers (Lyons, 1996, p. 101). This downloading of some of the administrative burden of regulation to the private sector is consistent with trends in other areas of international financial regulation (see Tony Porter's contribution to this volume), but it is a risky strategy. Tax advisors' knowledge of complex tax laws may encourage compliance with regulatory requirements and discourage outright fraud, but their main objective is to minimize the taxes their clients pay. Published advice about how taxpayers should deal with the new US regulations is generally couched in terms of what a taxpayer can get away with, hardly an orientation likely to increase tax collections (see, for example, the advice offered by Price Waterhouse partners in their newsletter for clients, *International Tax Review*). Consistent with this, a survey of TNCs by international accounting firm Ernst and Young found that 44 per cent of the responding firms had discovered 'tax planning opportunities' (a euphemism for ways to avoid taxes) as a result of their efforts to meet the documentation requirements! (Ernst and Young, 1996, 'Documentation Issues', pp. 1, 3).

The impact of the penalties specified for taxpayers who fail to meet the documentation requirements and are subject to large transfer-price adjustments is also uncertain. IRS officials argue that threats of penalties 'have served . . . as deterrents that altered taxpayer behavior' and reduced abuse of transfer pricing, but a study conducted by the General Accounting Office in 1995 concluded that it 'remains to be seen' whether the new flexibility available to taxpayers is offset by the documentation requirements and threat of penalties (GAO, 1995, p. 4). Risk-averse taxpayers may respond as the IRS hopes, but some tax specialists suggest that

> many corporate taxpayers will now be able to take more aggressive international tax positions, realizing that so long as the position staked out can be explained with basic legal and economic reason and it is contemporaneously documented the new harsher penalties can be completely avoided.
>
> (Bonfiglio, 1995, p. 13 [quotation]; interview with tax lawyer, Washington, DC, March 1997)

In fact, by encouraging taxpayers to pay more attention to transfer pricing and to consult professional tax advisors, the new regulations could lead to more systematic efforts to use transfer prices to shift income to low-tax jurisdictions.

It is also important to consider the international context when evaluating the likely impact of the new US approach. The United States was the first major state to introduce substantial penalties for transfer-pricing violations. This gave risk-averse firms an incentive to overreport income in the USA to reduce the likelihood of being subject to an adjustment by the IRS. Thus, the penalties may have served the US government's interest in increasing corporate tax revenues, though by encouraging distortion of arm's-length pricing in a direction favourable to the United States rather than by improving the accuracy with which the standard was implemented. However, many foreign governments have responded to the threat of erosion of their own tax bases by introducing their own penalties and stepping up their own enforcement efforts. This could eliminate the incentive for cautious firms to shift income into the United States. Thus, the impact of the penalties also depends on the reaction of foreign governments, and on taxpayers' perceptions of the risk of transfer pricing in different countries.

Conclusions

This review of American tax authorities' efforts to reform their approach to transfer pricing by TNCs shows that corporate tax policy in even the most powerful state is highly constrained by international pressures. Growth in FDI and in the complexity and volume of transfers within TNCs generated concern that US tax authorities were losing the ability to prevent TNCs from artificially manipulating transfer prices to shift taxable profits abroad. The existing arm's-length price method had become very difficult to administer effectively. The US Treasury Department proposed a new method – the CPI method – based on comparing the profits TNCs earned from their internal cross-border transactions with profits earned by firms making similar transactions at arm's length. It retreated from this proposal in response to a storm of protest from TNCs and foreign governments, and instead adopted modestly-revised Section 482 regulations that provided taxpayers with much greater flexibility in setting and justifying transfer prices, but also required them to document their transfer pricing methods under threat of penalty.

International dynamics were central to the approach finally adopted by the United States, but the structural power of capital emphasized by some recent theories of globalization was not. There is no evidence in the extensive literature on debates surrounding the US proposals that internationally-mobile capital threatened to withdraw investments from the United States if the US government adopted the proposed profit-based method. Treasury Department officials confirmed in interviews that the potential impact of the proposed policy changes on the attractiveness of the United States as a location for FDI was not a major consideration. Indeed, some recognized that the USA had certain advantages as a big country, in that it could pursue a tougher line against transfer pricing than smaller countries that faced, as one official put it, a higher elasticity of supply of capital than the USA (interviews with Treasury Department officials, Washington, DC, March 1997).

Thus, the US government was not very vulnerable to the international structural power of capital in this narrow sense. The US market is the largest and wealthiest in the world, and despite very open trade policies, TNCs in leading sectors recognize that if they want secure access to the

US market they need to make substantial real investments in that market. This was demonstrated in the 1980s and 1990s by the influx of investment by Japanese TNCs, particularly in autos. Japanese firms maintained and expanded their US manufacturing and service operations in the late 1980s and early 1990s, even though they were subject to intensified IRS surveillance and substantially larger tax bills. Most smaller countries are more highly constrained by the structural power of TNCs; companies could much more easily withdraw their investments from countries such as Canada, Ireland and the Netherlands if they withdrew favourable tax regimes for TNCs. In this sense, the United States has a uniquely favourable structural location in the international economy, and this makes it much less vulnerable to the structural power of transnational capital.

But the US government was constrained by the very high costs that would have accompanied a unilateral adoption of a new method inconsistent with existing international practice. International practice in the tranfer-pricing area was based on establishing arm's-length prices for intra-firm transactions. Prior US policy, international guidelines at the OECD level, bilateral tax treaties, and tax administration in other OECD countries were all based on this approach. Inconsistency between the existing arm's-length standard and the proposed US profit-based CPI approach would have generated innumerable triangular conflicts among the IRS, foreign tax authorities and TNCs. Foreign governments threatened to retaliate against American-owned firms, and threatened to refuse to make the adjustments to their own corporate taxation needed to avoid saddling TNCs with double taxation. Conflict between the USA and foreign governments would have caught TNCs (especially American-owned) in the middle and created major obstacles to international capital mobility.

This meant that from Washington's perspective, the costs of a unilateral shift away from the arm's-length approach would have far outweighed the benefits. The US government – a key agent in the creation and maintenance of the international economic structure – could have chosen to alter the state practices that supported that structure, but did not do so because the costs were too high. The absence of threats by TNCs to withdraw investments therefore does not mean that US policy was unconstrained by international capital mobility and the global economic system that had emerged under US leadership. But it does mean that the constraints on US policy were more complicated than sometimes described. Interestingly, the constraints arose out of the need for international cooperation to eliminate obstacles (that is, double taxation) to international capital mobility. While it is often argued that international cooperation has the potential for restoring effective market regulation in the face of globalization (see for example Kapstein, 1994b), in this case international cooperation served mainly to *prevent* a government from adopting measures that make national policy more effective in the face of international capital mobility.

While international considerations did prevent the USA from adopting radically different transfer-pricing regulations, efforts to improve enforcement of the arm's-length pricing standard were implemented, most notably the new documentation requirements and transfer-pricing penalties. The flurry of US international tax initiatives in the late 1980s and 1990s did give the IRS new instruments for enforcing transfer pricing within the traditional arm's-length framework and new documentation requirements for US and foreign-owned firms should provide the IRS with better information to assess the validity of transfer prices proposed by taxpayers. New penalties for transfer-pricing violations may have a deterrent effect, though there is considerable evidence that tax planning by sophisticated TNCs will not be constrained and may even be facilitated by the new combination of regulations and penalties. Moves in these areas (documentation requirements and penalties) were not inconsistent with international norms – indeed, they were consistent with the long-standing emphasis on verifying transnational taxpayers's accounts through national means rather than international cooperation. This eased their adoption even in the face of strong opposition from TNCs and foreign governments. The IRS has used its new instruments and resources to enforce the arm's-length standard in a discrimatory fashion, auditing foreign-controlled corporations more intensively than American-owned firms. International competitive pressures clearly matter here, though in a different way than in most OECD countries. Smaller countries are primarily concerned with maintaining their competitiveness as a location for internationally-mobile investment. Because the United States has such strong non-tax locational advantages, its government has greater freedom to target foreign investors for stricter tax enforcement to enhance the competitive position of domestic firms.

The arm's-length standard for transfer pricing was originally adopted in part because it was a method that appeared to require very little international cooperation, as governments could agree that market prices were usually an appropriate benchmark for transfer prices and it was expected that governments could assess transfer prices independently. The growth in the volume of FDI and the complexity of cross-border transactions within TNCs makes this standard very difficult to apply. The new world of international capital mobility clearly poses major challenges to the effectiveness of existing government policies, even in the most powerful state. OECD governments negotiated more precise transfer-pricing guidelines after the 1993 IRS proposals were issued, and these moved in the direction of the revised regulations the United States adopted in 1993–94 (OECD, 1995). As noted earlier, this approach leaves TNCs with considerable scope to set transfer prices to shift income and minimize taxes. Thus, neither unilateral nor cooperative responses to the problem of transfer pricing have yet clearly enhanced governments' ability to tax transnational corporations.

Notes

1 Economists generally argue that when capital is mobile, corporate income taxes will be borne in large part by non-mobile labour and land, as the returns to those factors must fall by enough to maintain the after-tax rate of return to capital at the world level.

2 My own research in progress suggests that large volumes of FDI are significantly associated with lower corporate income tax revenues, but the association is substantively smaller than strong versions of the structural power argument would expect.

3 Some evidence to support this view can be found in the modest resources devoted to transfer-price regulation by most governments in the 1980s, despite widespread public concern about alleged transfer-price abuses in the 1970s; Picciotto, 1992, pp. 188–92, 200. In Canada, Revenue Canada devoted few resources to transfer pricing before the 1990s (interviews with Revenue Canada officials, Ottawa, March 1997), despite longstanding concerns about the potential for tax avoidance by the many TNCs active in the country (Canada, 1972, chapter 13).

4 This is called 'source' country taxation. Many governments, including the United States, also tax the profits that nationally-owned TNCs earn on their foreign operations. In order to ensure that this 'residence' country taxation does not cause double taxation, TNCs are allowed to credit foreign taxes paid against domestic taxes owing on their foreign income, and TNCs are also allowed to defer domestic taxes owing on foreign-source income until it is repatriated in the form of dividends paid by the foreign subsidiary to the domestic parent.

5 The claim about Japanese-owned firms shifting profits to Japan is paradoxical, since corporate tax rates were higher in Japan than America and the Japanese government largely exempted foreign profits of Japanese TNCs from Japanese taxation; this meant that income-shifting from the USA to Japan could *increase* Japanese firms total tax bills!

6 International audits of FCCs rose from 673 to 3048 over this period, while international audits of USCCs fell from 3010 to 2084 (GAO, 1994, p. 12). Since there were far more USCCs with foreign operations than there were FCCs, this meant that FCCs were now much more likely to be audited than USCCs.

7 If exact arm's-length comparables could be found, transfer prices could still be set by reference to them. However, as discussed earlier, this was possible only in a small minority of cases.

8 The mutual agreement procedure is in Article 25 of the OECD Model Tax Convention, and is described in the accompanying commentary. Article 9, paragraph 2 of the OECD Model Tax Convention provides for corresponding adjustments by a state (eg., a state in Canada's position in this example) if it believes that the adjustment to arm's-length prices by another state (eg., a state in the USA's position in this example) is justified; see Articles 9 and 25 and the accompanying commentaries in OECD (1996). This description also draws on interviews with Canadian and American tax officials, Ottawa and Washington, DC, March 1997.

9 The Bush administration rushed to announce these before the inauguration of President-elect Bill Clinton. Treasury officials publicly denied that they were trying to put new regulations in place to constrain President Bush's successor administration, but it is no secret that the Bush and Clinton campaigns had clashed sharply over taxing foreign businesses and that the Bush campaign had aligned itself with business-group critiques of some Clinton campaign positions (Matthews, 1992; Turro, 1992, 1993).

10 The profit-split method attempts to assign a transfer price by splitting the profit attributable to a particular transaction (in contrast to formula apportionment, which splits the total profit of a TNC among its various parts according to some formula). TNCs often favoured the additional flexibility the profit-split method gave them for justifying particular transfer prices, even though they rejected formula apportionment, and the method also found favour among many OECD governments (Langbein, 1986, p. 671; Picciotto, 1992, pp. 211–12; Ernst and Young, 1996, 'Documentation Methodology', p. 1; OECD, 1993, p. x).

8

Negotiating the Structure of Capital Mobility

Tony Porter

This chapter argues that the notion of *structure* can provide insight into the impact of capital mobility on states, but that it can also obscure certain important features of global finance and should therefore be used cautiously. Most seriously, it overstates the immutability of the structural constraints imposed by capital markets on states and encourages us to neglect the degree to which states and other actors construct and negotiate those structures. It also obscures variation in the degree and ways in which states have exercised control over different types of financial flows. This variation is important because it shows that the structure of capital mobility should not be thought of as an attribute of the international system as a whole and because it provides insight into types of state initiatives that are likely to be successful in altering the structure of capital mobility.

Three types of international financial flows are examined here: bank loans, intra-firm financial flows brought about by transfer pricing, and foreign-exchange trading. It will be argued that states have enjoyed considerable success in exercising control over the first two of these relative to the third. *Structure* and its components are of little use in explaining the variation in their success: these variations can best be explained by differences across the cases in the process of negotiation and institution-building.

The argument is developed in three steps. The chapter starts with a discussion of structure and its limitations in analysing global finance; it then proceeds through each of the three cases; and in the final section conclusions are drawn by comparing the cases.

The advantages and disadvantages of structure in analysing capital mobility

Three of the best-known attempts to apply the notion of structure to global finance provide a useful starting point in evaluating it: Strange (1988, 1990); Gill and Law (1989) and Andrews (1994).

The three differ in the perceived basis of structural constraint. Strange sees structure as originating in the actions of powerful states. States, especially the US government, played a key role in bringing about the globalization of finance (Strange, 1990, p. 263). The centrality of the state to her notion of structure is evident as well in her reference to the continued ability of the USA to use to its advantage such features of 'structural power' as the leading role of the dollar and the English language. Gill and Law, by contrast, see structural power as arising from and benefitting transnational capital as a social class. While 'capital as a social relation, depends on the power of the state to define, shape and be part of a regime of accumulation' (Gill and Law, 1989, p. 479), capital's increasing mobility 'can swiftly force governments which deviate from policies seen as suitable by the "market" to change course' (Gill and Law, 1989, p. 486). Finally, Andrews emphasizes the ability of finance, conceived primarily as flows rather than a form of power, to systematically constrain states.

Despite these differences, all three analyses indicate that the distinguishing feature of structure is that it is systematic rather than behavioural. For instance, Andrews (1994, p. 193) notes that capital mobility is structural in that it 'systematically constrains state behavior by rewarding some actions and punishing others'. For Strange (1988, p. 25), structural power 'confers the power to decide how things shall be done, the power to shape frameworks within which states relate to each other, relate to people, or relate to corporate enterprises'. Gill and Law (1989, p. 480) refer to a 'deeper, socio-structural dimension, inherent in the capitalist system'.

The great advantage of this type of structural analysis, as its proponents argue, is that it highlights certain vehicles for and constraints on power that are obscured by a narrow focus on power as involving the deployment of resources by states to directly alter the behaviour; of other states. Andrews, for instance, by evoking Waltz (1979), is suggesting to structural realists that expanding models to acknowledge the constraints imposed by capital mobility is consistent with the assumptions of those models. Moreover the three analyses suggest that these forms of structural power and constraint may be more fundamental and thus more important than traditional forms of power.

Unfortunately the notion of 'structure' – as compared to 'constraint' for instance – brings with it certain meanings that may act rhetorically to reinforce unintended, premature or unsubstantiated conclusions. Four such implications in particular stand out: that capital mobility is irreversible; that it is a singular feature of the system as a whole; that it is outside (or underneath) the field of action of most if not all state actors; and that once present it acts as a casual variable and not as something that needs to be continually reproduced and therefore to be explained. This concern is similar, then, to criticisms levied by social constructivists at Waltz's structuralism. Ruggie (1986, p. 152), for instance, has argued that in the Waltzian model 'continuity – at least in part – is a product of premise even before it is hypothesized as an outcome'. Similarly Wendt (1987, p. 342) has criticized the tendency of neorealists to see 'system structures in the manner in which they appear to states – as given, external constraints on their actions – rather than as conditions of possibility for state action'. Both critics are concerned that the notion of structure leads to overstating and reifying the sources of continuity and constraint.

The remainder of this essay seeks to substantiate these concerns by looking more concretely at the practices and institutions that have allowed states to increase their control over global finance; by revealing the countertendencies to those revealed by structuralist analysis of capital mobility – and indeed that would be obscured by structuralist analysis. This will be done with reference to three factors which Andrews (1994) has usefully identified as sources of structure of capital mobility: technological change, competitive pressures on states' regulatory processes, and socialization.

The three cases examined

The above section has argued that each of the three types of financial flows share the features that contribute to the structure of capital mobility as identified by Andrews (1994). One would therefore expect in each case that state efforts to regulate these flows would be equally futile. In this section it will become apparent, as we examine the cases in more detail, that this is not what occurred.

International bank regulation

The strengthening of international bank regulation has been primarily carried out at the Basle Committee on Banking Supervision, formed in 1974 by bank regulators from 12 industrialized countries. Broadly speaking the accomplishments of the Basle Committee are of two types. The first is the establishment of a division of labour and agreed general principles for the regulation of multinational banks. The adoption of consolidated supervision in a 1983 Concordat required a home regulator to obtain information on, and supervise, all the operations of the banks headquartered in its jurisdiction. This concordat clarified the division of responsibilities among regulators and reduced the ability of banks to escape regulation by shifting funds to more lightly-regulated jurisdictions.[1] This policy was reinforced in 1992 by the adoption of a set of standards for adequate supervision and by commitments by home and host regulators to refuse entry by banks into markets that did not meet these standards.

The second major accomplishment of the Basle Committee was to agree upon a fairly complex and specific set of common standards for bank capital in July 1988. These standards were based on risk-weighted capital–asset ratios which enhance stability of banks by (a) limiting the growth of loans and other assets by requiring banks to maintain a certain level of capital relative to those assets;[2] (b) shifting more of the responsibility and cost for monitoring riskiness to shareholders by increasing the amount of their capital that is available to offset problems with solvency; and (c) forcing banks to hold more capital to offset the greater riskiness of some types of assets. By September 1992, the Basle Committee (1992, pp. 20–1) had noted that

> the capital agreement has now been fully incorporated within the supervisory framework of all member countries . . . Virtually all countries outside the membership of the Basle Committee with international banks of significant size have introduced, or are in the process of introducing, arrangements based on the capital agreement.

The Committee has carried its agreed standards into other jurisdictions by fostering nominally independent but effectively subordinate regional groups, the most important of which is the Offshore Group (Porter, 1993, chapter 3).

Despite the vociferous opposition of some critics to the Basle Committee's capital standards (for example Litan, 1992) there seems to be a widespread support among market actors and regulators for the concept ('A Who's Who', 1992). It is now widely recognized and accepted by the Basle Committee itself, however, that the original capital standards were too crude.[3] The Committee is therefore increasingly moving towards reliance on data generated by banks' own internal risk-management systems in an ongoing estimation of the minimum levels of capital which they must maintain. Penalties in the form of higher required levels of capital will be imposed if these calculations subsequently prove to be inaccurate. In short, the Committee's regulations have been made more sophisticated and have not been weakened in response to market developments.

These accomplishments of the Basle Committee show that it has made it possible for states to overcome the difficulties associated with bank-intermediated financial flows to an important degree. The downward pressure on regulatory standards resulting from competition among jurisdictions was halted and reversed; and compliance with the standards is strong despite the considerable cost which they imposed on many national banking industries. The concern that, with the assistance of technological innovation, the regulations would be undermined by a shift from bank-intermediated lending to securities markets, has not proven to be a serious problem.

The regulation of transfer pricing

Both multilateral and unilateral measures to control transfer pricing have been strengthened in recent years. Mutlilateral acknowledgement of the problem of transfer pricing dates back to the work of the Fiscal Committee of the League of Nations which produced a major study of the taxation of MNCs (Picciotto, 1989, p. 25). Concerns over transfer pricing were also raised in the context of customs valuation: assessing the value of imported goods for the imposition of duties (Verlage, 1975, chapter 6). During the 1970s it was targetted by developing countries which saw the ability of MNCs to shift profits among various offices as depriving host governments of taxes owed. More recently, developed countries have become alarmed at transfer-pricing problems relating to the taxation of profits. The US General Accounting Office, for instance, estimated that in the USA in 1991 over 73 per cent of foreign-controlled domestic corporations and 60 per cent of domestic corporations that were controlled by US persons paid no tax (Ruchelman, 1996, p. 42). US President Clinton estimated in his initial economic plan that he could raise $45 billion in four years by strengthening transfer-pricing regulations (Harper, 1994, p. A2). Also, tensions over transfer-pricing have exacerbated US–Japan trade tensions with both sides taking tough measures against each others' corporations (Reed, Holyoke and Harb, 1994, p. 55; Humphreys and McCrodan, 1995, p. 32).

In July 1995, in the midst of this heightened concern about the issue, the OECD, the primary multilateral forum for developing such international standards, issued its new draft Transfer Pricing Guidelines for Multinational Enterprises and Tax Administration. Most significantly the standards represented a commitment on the part of OECD governments to enforce transfer pricing based on arms-length principles and a rejection of an alternative of allocating an MNC's taxes on the basis of a more arbitrary but more easily measured indicator such as the distribution of revenues or salaries across jurisdications.

While the OECD guidelines must be implemented through changes in domestic tax regulations and therefore do not themselves directly control transfer pricing, they do signify a heightened level of cooperation among the world's most powerful governments to address the problem. The OECD guidelines are also used in resolving differences between governments over transfer-pricing issues (Cole, 1995, p. 216). The guidelines also provide procedures for Advanced Pricing Arrangements (APA) in which the MNC and tax authorities agree on transfer-pricing methodology before the transactions occur. Regulations consistent with these APA procedures are being introduced in a number of countries. The Pacific Association of Tax Administrators (Australia, Canada, Japan and the United States) has APA procedures that are consistent with the OECD's (Cole, 1995). These international changes are further reinforced by changes at the national level.

The most significant of these changes given the weight of its MNCs in the world economy are those of the USA. Between 1992 and 1994 the Internal Revenue Service (IRS) issued dramatically strengthened regulations. One analyst (Bonfligio, 1995, pp. 1–2) commented with respect to these regulations:

> Given the amount of money at stake, the only reasonable course of action for a multinational corporation is to bring its international tax planning to the top of its priority list and to begin implementing a documentation system for playing by the new transfer pricing rules. Other options include waiting for the IRS to arrive, hiring international tax counsel, and hoping it is not too little too late – or having the company's controller issue an eight- (or nine) figure check made payable to the IRS to help reduce the US budget deficit.

The new IRS regulations make two key changes from previous ones. First, they offer more options for MNCs in calculating transfer prices. Second, there are sharply increased penalties for firms that do not comply with the regulations: from 20 to 40 per cent of the additional tax depending on the size of the adjustment. The costs to firms of compliance is not trivial; according to some tax professionals 'most taxpayers agree that the penalty regulations present a tremendous burden' (Kral *et al.*, 1995: 28). The onus is on firms to show that they have adequate documentation and have selected the 'best method' of those available. Criteria for selecting the best method include the availability, comparability and quality of the data and the consistency of results with those obtained by other methods. Adjustments under the new regulations totalled \$2.2 billion in 1993 and \$3.5 billion in 1994: 62 per cent of these involved US-controlled enterprises and the rest foreign (Kral *et al.*, 1995, p. 28). One of the higher profile transfer-pricing cases is an \$880 million bill demanded by the IRS from PepsiCo Inc. for 1985–89 (Reed, Holyoke and Harb, 1994, p. 55).

Since 1991, Advance Pricing Agreements in which MNCs receive approval in advance for transfer prices have been offered by the IRS as a reliable but cumbersome alternative to risking an unfavourable IRS audit. In 1995 the IRS began using proposed revisions of APA procedures to encourage agreement among the MNC, and all relevant tax authorities and not just the MNC and the IRS (Cole, 1995). As of 1995, 12 of 33 APAs concluded with the IRS also formally involved at least one other country and a number of the other APAs involved some international cooperation (Cole, 1995, p. 220–there were about 100 additional APAs in process). Particularly important in this regard was a joint statement issued by the IRS and the UK Treasury that emphasized the importance of APAs as a key tool for addressing transfer pricing and tax-base erosion. This joint statement also called for making international tax compliance a high priority in the coming years (Cole, 1995).

Japan, in part in response to the strengthened US rules, has also enforced its regulations more vigorously. Coca Cola was hit with a \$145 million tax deficiency for 1990–92 and a subsidiary of the insurance company American International Group Inc. was told to pay \$37 million more in taxes. German and Canadian authorities are also stepping up enforcement (Cole, 1995). Australia, Belgium, Denmark, France, Italy, the Netherlands, Spain and the UK also have rules in place to regulate transfer pricing (Humphreys, 1994; Business International and Ernst and Young, 1991).

In the European Union the key document is a convention on the elimination of double taxation which was approved in July 1990. Although the main thrust of the convention is to create a common tax base to facilitate integration it also strengthens measures against the use of transfer pricing to avoid taxes, stating that if 'legal and administrative proceedings have resulted in a final ruling that by actions giving rise to an adjustment of transfers of profits . . . one of the enterprises concerned is liable to a serious penalty' (Coopers and Lybrand, 1993, 1006). All EU members individually have further defined the term 'serious' which is left vague in the convention itself. The convention is also significant because it is seen by the EU as a model for worldwide resolution of transfer-pricing issues (Coopers and Lybrand, 1993, p. 1011).

The above developments indicate that states have taken a number of significant initiatives to strengthen their control over MNCs' tax evasion through transfer pricing. As in the banking regime the features of these private financial flows which might be thought to contribute to a structure of capital mobility have not prevented such initiatives.

Controlling foreign-exchange transactions

In currency markets the counterpart to the above efforts to regulate banking and transfer pricing is the increasing interest among policy-makers and academics in using an internationally coordinated tax on foreign-exchange transactions tax (FET) to reduce capital mobility, an idea first promoted by Nobel Laureate James Tobin in 1972 and 1978 addresses (Tobin, 1978, 1987, 1996; ul Huq, Kaul and Grunberg, 1996).[4] Such a tax, if set low enough, would reduce the attractiveness of short-term speculative investments without discouraging long-term flows of investment. For traders of real goods the benefits from reduced exchange-rate volatility could outweigh the cost of the tax.

There have been no international negotiations to develop a FET in contrast to the other two cases.[5] The most significant recent expression by policy-makers of interest in a FET was in the run up to the June 1995 Halifax G-7 summit which took place in the wake of the Mexican peso crisis that broke out in December 1994. Before the summit its host, Canadian Prime Minister Jean Chretien, publicly expressed interest in an FET. In consulting with Canada's Ministry of Finance, the Prime Minister's staff was told, however, that the tax was impractical. This may have contributed to a waning of enthusiasm for the tax and in the end it did not appear on the agenda. A lack of strong support from the rest of the G-7 was undoubtedly a factor as well – only France had publicly expressed interest in the FET.

Prior to the Halifax Summit the most significant instance of political interest in an FET was in the activities associated with the 1995 World Summit on Social Development in Copenhagen. The FET was seen by its supporters as beneficial not only because of its effects on the economy, but also because the revenues raised could potentially be used to promote development. The Australian government was a particularly vigorous supporter of an FET in the pre-summit preparations (Langmore, 1995, 193). Some other governments supported the Australian lead, including the Canadian government. In the period before the Summit several international institutions issued reports which either seriously considered the FET (International Labour Office, UN Development Program) or explicitly advocated it (the Commission on Global Governance).[6]

There are also signs of growing academic support for the FET. When Tobin initially suggested the tax 'the idea fell like a stone in a deep well' (Tobin, 1987, p. 155). By contrast there are now a number of influential economists who have, at one time or another, endorsed the idea including Lawrence Summers, US Under Secretary of the Treasury; Joseph Stigliz, head of the US President's Council of Economic Advisors; and New York investment banker Felix Rohatyn (Langmore, 1995). Others, including the IMF's chief economist, Stanley Fischer, E. Gerald Corrigan of Goldman Sachs and former chair of the Federal Reserve Bank of New York and the Basle Committee on Banking Supervision, and the participants in a session of the 1996 meetings of the American Economic Association on monetary policy have indicated that the Tobin tax might be useful if enforcement problems could be solved (Tobin, 1996; Berry and Chandler, 1995). Similarly, economist Rudiger Dornbusch noted that 'speed limits for world financial markets would be a very useful thing', but added that 'it would have to be worldwide' (Shirreff, 1993, p. 60). In July 1996 the first scholarly collection of articles focusing on the Tobin tax was published (ul Huq, Kaul and Grunberg, 1996). This change in attitude appears to be driven both by the increasingly evident negative effects of capital mobility in practice, especially with the East Asian currency crises of 1997 and 1998, as well as by the demonstrated theoretical weaknesses of older economic models that treated financial markets as perfect. Indeed a renewed interest in the FET in the 1990s intersected with growing concern in the USA about the problem of investors' and managers' short-term horizons in highly-competitive US capital markets. We do not know the degree of public support for an FET, although one survey in the USA found about two-thirds of respondents in favour of it (Langmore, 1995, p. 192).

Despite the growth in interest in a FET it presently is not likely to be implemented. While some oppose the tax because they are enthusiastic about high capital mobility, there are others who argue strongly that it is not feasible given the ability of market participants to evade the tax by switching to assets or jurisdictions for which the tax is not applied. Thus the FET would appear to fit more closely than the other two cases the notion that there is a structure of capital mobility.

The three cases compared: is there a structure of capital mobility?

The above three cases indicate that there is substantial variation among them in the degree to which states have contemplated and implemented measures to control cross-border financial flows. Both the banking regime and the measures taken to control transfer pricing have been growing in strength in recent years and there is no indication that states are likely to weaken or dismantle these measures. By contrast, while scholarly and political support for a foreign-exchange tax to slow down currency markets has been growing, it is unlikely that the tax will be implemented in the near future. The first conclusion to be drawn from the cases, then, is that there *is* considerable variation in the ability of states to control capital flows that would be missed by a notion of a single structure of capital mobility.

Because it is notable that neither the banking nor the transfer-tax measures erect barriers at borders it is important to ask whether they really represent instances of increased state control over global financial flows. Indeed it could be argued that by increasing systemic stability and levelling the playing field these measures are merely smoothing the way to greater capital mobility. There are two ways in which such arguments underestimate the importance of these measures however.

First, the notion of a structure of capital mobility is only interesting because of the possibility that it can lead states to adopt policies to which they would otherwise be averse. The aversion is because the policies are perceived as costly, as in the loss of tax revenue, the potential for financial collapse due to competitive deregulation, or declining support among citizens for the state as a result of austerity measures. If states and citizens were indifferent to the effects of capital mobility – as might be the case with the cross-border mobility of birds for instance – then it would be of little analytical interest. To the extent that states, by banding together, are able to reimpose these costs on private actors, then it can be said that the structure of capital mobility is of declining significance.

Second, it is possible that states could build on their experience with these measures to further expand their control over capital flows. The variation in the degree to which states have developed such measures across the three cases suggests that the process by which a structure of capital can be reversed should be treated as a continuum and not a wholesale transformation from structure to no structure. The successes enjoyed by states in regulating banking and transfer pricing indicate that states can, at a minimum, initiate the process of dismantling a structure of capital mobility.[7]

Given that the three cases all shared the features associated with the structure of capital mobility – technological change, regulatory change and socialization – it would seem that we need to search elsewhere for explanations for the differences in the success of state regulatory initiatives. The differences among the cases suggest three relevant factors.

The first factor is that, unlike foreign-exchange trading, both the banking and transfer-pricing initiatives were facilitated by a US desire to alter the regulatory framework in response to a perceived advantage enjoyed by Japan. While, as I have argued elsewhere (Porter, 1993), the US followed European initiatives through the most important parts of the Basle Committee negotiations, it is clear that they also wished to alter the playing field to offset the dramatic rise to dominance of Japanese banks and that their threat to conclude a bilateral deal with the UK helped restart negotiations when they were bogged down. Japanese compliance with the standards did contribute to the subsequent retreat of their international banks. Similarly, Japan has been an important target of the strengthened US transfer-pricing regulations (Reed, Holyoke and Harb, 1994). Foreign-exchange trading does not involve a perceived competitive threat as is the case with banking or the US offices of Japanese MNCs.

The second factor is differences in the institutional arrangements that facilitate cross-border financial flows. The banking and transfer-pricing initiatives were built on traditions of regulatory cooperation; the Basle Committee, for example, is a Committee of the Group of Ten, a vehicle for central bank cooperation since 1961. Similarly, the transfer-pricing initiatives built on a legacy of tax coordination that had developed at the OECD. Additionally there is a long tradition at the domestic level of monitoring and enforcing prudential and tax regulations on banks and firms. By contrast, a tax on foreign-exchange trading would require coordination among both tax authorities and foreign-exchange market regulators which do not have a tradition of cooperation at the international level.

Institutional arrangements at the private level differ across the three cases as well. Both banks and MNCs engaging in transfer pricing are facilitating financial flows that are internal to a firm structure while foreign-exchange trading is an arms-length transaction. It is not immediately apparent that arm's-length markets are more prone to irreversible capital mobility. Escaping state regulation may be facilitated by the ease with which internalized transactions can be concealed. Moreover mobilizing an evasive response to state regulation is likely to be facilitated by the coordinating capacity of the bank or firm hierarchy. Nevertheless it is possible that the inertia of the bureacratic structure within which bank intermediation and transfer pricing occurs may give state authorities greater purchase for imposing regulations.

This difference should not be overstated however. Currency markets are not as atomized and fluid as they are sometimes portrayed. Foreign-exchange trading is migrating to interbank sites and away from arm's-length markets such as the Chicago Mercantile Exchange because of the greater capacity of the former to handle large trades (Nusbaum, 1995). There is increasing concentration among these banks: the proportion of forex business in London accounted for by the top-ten institutions increased from 37 per cent in 1989 to 44 per cent in 1992 (Crowe, 1995). Derivatives trading, which would include swaps and forward contracts in foreign exchange, remains surprisingly concentrated as well: the world's top-ten banks are likely to account for well over half of all transactions.[8] Settlement of foreign-exchange trading has traditionally relied on bilateral arrangements between banks but in 1994 a clearinghouse, called Multinet, was set up by eight US and Canadian banks.[9] In short, foreign-exchange trading relies on a set of easily identifiable institutions that could provide a basis for state regulation as do banks and MNCs for loans and transfer pricing.

It is often overlooked as well that foreign-exchange transactions are not completely unregulated. The UK, for instance, recently upgraded its 'loose collection of basic principles and extra-statutory concessions' regarding the taxation of gains and losses from foreign-exchange transactions to a much more specific law that will affect both domestic and foreign firms (Penney and Moncrieff, 1995; Boneham, 1995). In a recent decision, the British Securities and Futures Authority fined Morgan Stanley $348 000 for inadequate supervision of foreign-exchange trading that lost its clients $28 million (Truell, 1995, p. D1). Similarly, the impact of foreign-exchange trades are incorporated into firms' balance sheets according to well-defined practices and have implications for the taxation of profits (Bishop and Dixon, 1992, chapter 14).[10] Controls on money-laundering, which could provide a model for closer regulation of foreign-exchange trading, have also been strengthened in recent years.[11]

The third factor which differentiates the three cases is simply the length of time which states have had to learn how to regulate the relevant financial flows. The Basle Committee has now had more than two decades with which to devise more effective bank regulations. As noted above, the recognition by state authorities of transfer pricing as a potential problem dates back to the League of Nations; by contrast, interest in a foreign-exchange tax has only become significant in the past few years.

Taken together, these three factors, none of which has been associated with the structure of capital mobility, suggest that states can take successful initiatives to control international financial flows but that it takes time for states to learn about and construct appropriate institutions upon which regulation can be based. This requires negotiation and, as in other issue areas, an auspicious convergence of regulatory and political concerns (such as a Japanese economic challenge) for the most prominent actor – the USA – is also relevant.

Conclusion

This essay has argued that the notion of a *structure* of capital mobility, while usefully highlighting the influence on policy-making of capital markets, can also be misleading. If the term *structure* (as opposed to *constraint*) is to be meaningful it needs to connote a high degree of persistence and irreversibility – and imply that it lies beneath or beyond the practices of states. Moreover, current uses of the notion of structure treat it as an attribute of the system as a whole. The differences between successful state initiatives to enhance control of banking and transfer pricing, on the one hand, and unsuccessful initiatives to control foreign-exchange trading on the other, indicate that the qualities of capital mobility that are implied by the notion of structure are not present.[12]

This conclusion highlights the need to continue to analyse the concrete practices of states and firms and to not rely too heavily on notions of deep or systemic structures. States continue to be surprisingly creative in their initiatives to control capital flows. Excessive emphasis on structural constraint can contribute to foreclosing consideration of potentially useful policy options.

Notes

1 For information on the Concordat and its implementation see various issues of *Report on International Developments in Banking Supervision* published by the Basle Committee, and Porter (1993).

2 Because capital – most of which is equity – is more expensive than deposits as a source of funds, capital standards restrained the strategy of rapid growth and high volume that had been followed by most international banks.

3 This and other comments in this paragraph are based on Basle Committee, 1994, chapter IX; IMF, 1995 especially the background paper on 'Capital Adequacy and Internal Risk Management', pp. 135–49; and 'Central Bankers Agree'.

4 For a more extensive discussion of the FET see Porter (1996), from which this section draws extensively.

5 These paragraphs are based on the following sources: Langmore (1995); Felix (1995c and 1995a); various *Financial Post* articles on the G-7 Summit available at the G-7 web site, University of Toronto; from a personal communication with a senior Finance Department official; and from Crossette (1995, p. 4).

6 After noting its advantages and practical drawbacks the Commission (1995, p. 219) commented of the Tobin tax: 'We urge the UN and the Bretton Woods institutions to explore the feasibility of such a system in consultation with the regulatory authorities of the leading financial markets'.

7 The possibility that existing efforts could be expanded is confirmed by the way in which money-laundering was added to the Basle Committee's agenda. As one of its officials (Freeland, 1994, pp. 237–8) noted:

> a few years ago, it would have been difficult to conceive that the Basle Committee, which deals with concerns about the prudential soundness of banks, would have become involved in this topic at all. However, the Committee's higher profile became a target for the U.S. Congress, who directed the U.S. members of the Committee to bring the matter to our table. Initially there was some reluctance to deal with it, because there were questions of legal competence for at least some of the Committee member institutions...there was some debate as to whether the text should rule on the ethics of soliciting nonresident deposits that contravene civil but not criminal law, such as tax or exchange control regulations. However, it was decided that this was outside the scope of the Statement.

8 This figure is based on 'Big Boys in a Big Business', *Fortune*, 7 March 1994, p. 49 in which the notional value of the top ten is $15.3 trillion. This compares to a worldwide total of about $16 trillion. The first total includes double counting however (counting of both parties to a single transaction). My reduction for this double counting is conservative as many (perhaps most) of the top ten's transactions would have counterparties from outside the top ten.

9 It is not clear, however, how successful this arrangement will be. Some of the largest banks declined to join and there was no European participation (Lipin, 1994).

10 Significantly, the second and third of the US's Advance Pricing Agreements were established in 1992 between US and UK tax authorities for Sumitomo and Barclay's banks. They cover income allocations for interest rate and cross-currency swaps and constitute 'a very important development in the taxation of international financial markets' (Pagan and Wilkie, 1993, p. 194). The OECD (1984) has issued transfer-pricing-related guidelines for the taxation of multinational banking enterprises.

11 Key documents are the Basle Committee's Statement of Principles on Money Laundering of 1989 and an international Financial Action Task Force report which has made 40 recommendations to governments. The OECD's 1987 Report *International Tax Avoidance and Evasion* is also relevant.

12 It should be noted that it does not make sense to measure the strength of the structure of capital mobility by the difficulty that states have in regulating it as this would make explanations of state policies based on structure tautological.

9
Financial Globalization and Social Response? A Polanyian View*

Eric Helleiner

Karl Polanyi's 1944 book *The Great Transformation* has long been considered a classic within the field of international political economy (IPE). Interest in his work, however, has experienced a considerable revival in recent years among IPE scholars studying economic globalization. While conventional wisdom holds that the current globalization of market forces is something fundamentally new, Polanyi's book is seen to be useful in reminding us of an important historical precedent: the spread of the 'self-regulating' market on an increasingly global basis in the nineteenth century.

The two central arguments in Polanyi's work have attracted particular attention. First, Polanyi challenged the notion popular among economic liberals of his day that the nineteenth-century market economy had emerged as a result of inevitable or 'natural' economic forces. He argued an opposite case: 'There was nothing natural about *laissez-faire*; free markets could never have come into being merely by allowing things to take their course... *laissez-faire* itself was enforced by the state' (1944, p. 139). In the contemporary age, this argument has been used to challenge the view – again held most strongly within economic liberal circles – that economic globalization is an inevitable product of technological and market developments. Like Polanyi, many IPE scholars have sought to demonstrate the extent to which today's integrated

* Some portions of this chapter have appeared before (1995a) and the chapter as a whole was published previously (2000), and is reprinted here with permission. I am grateful for permission to reprint *Studies in Political Economy* to Black Rose Press and the Karl Polanyi Institute. For useful comments on earlier drafts I am indebted to Greg Albo, Barry Buzan, Leo Panitch, Bent Sofus-Tranoy, Helge Hveem, Robert Wolfe and each of the contributors to this volume.

global economy has in fact been actively 'made' by state decisions and political choices.

Second, Polanyi questioned the economic liberal assumption that the nineteenth-century market-based economic order had been a socially sustainable order. He argued that the economic liberalism had been a hopelessly 'utopian' ideology based on the unrealistic assumption that society could tolerate the instabilities and upheavals of the 'self-regulating market'. From Polanyi's perspective, the breakdown of the nineteenth-century liberal international economic order had been inevitable as these instabilities and upheavals provoked spontaneous social 'countermovements' that reasserted social control over markets beginning in the late nineteenth century and culminating in the 1930s. Those who draw on Polanyi's work today cite this second argument to question the liberal case that the contemporary globalization of market forces is irreversible. From a modern Polanyian perspective, the current globalization trend will provoke a social response similar to that which Polanyi analysed.

It is hardly surprising that *The Great Transformation* has received special notice from those studying the financial dimensions of globalization in the current age (Cerny, 1993; Hawley, 1984; Pauly 1988; Underhill, 1991; Notermans, 1993; Eichengreen, 1996). One of the more interesting aspects of Polanyi's book is his analysis of the central position of a globally-integrated financial system in the nineteenth-century world economy. Of Polanyi's two central arguments, the first has so far attracted more attention than the second among financial specialists. His ideas have been cited prominently by those who have made the case that financial globalization is a product not just of technological and market developments, but also of active state decisions and political choices (Pauly, 1988; Underhill, 1991). Specifically, today's globalized financial order is shown to have been actively 'made' by political decisions during the last two decades to liberalize capital controls that had existed in most countries since the 1930s.[1]

Less attention has been given to the potential relevance of Polanyi's ideas in analysing the future of the contemporary global financial marketplace. To be sure, like Polanyi, many have highlighted the social upheavals caused by the contemporary global financial order, both in terms of exchange-rate and trade instability and in terms of the declining policy autonomy of the Keynesian welfare state. But Polanyi's argument that these instabilities will induce social 'countermovements' that successfully rule global financial markets under a degree of social control has had few supporters. The dominant view – even among many sympathetic to Polanyi's argument – is that the new liberal global financial order is here to stay, especially given the difficulties involved in regulating the new global markets.

In this chapter I suggest that the second argument in Polanyi's work may in fact be just as relevant as the first in analysing the contemporary world of 'haute finance'. Drawing on his analysis of the pre-1939 period, I advance several reasons why we might question the assumption that today's liberal global financial order is a sustainable one. Indeed, I argue that the financial globalization trend has already begun to induce various social responses of the kind that Polanyi analyzed in the pre-Second World War period. My argument is not that history is simply repeating itself; as I show, the strategies of contemporary 'countermovements' for reining finance back under a form of social control differ considerably from those pursued in that earlier era. Despite these differences, these social responses to financial globalization do suggest to me that there is considerable evidence to support Polanyi's second thesis in the current era.

Social responses at the global level

The first piece of evidence to support Polanyi's case comes from what may at first seem an unusual source: the activities of the world's leading central bankers. Since the mid-1970s, these central bankers – rather than populist social forces – have been at the forefront of an initiative to reregulate the emerging globalized financial order. Working within the Bank for International Settlements, the G-10 central bankers have quietly succeeded in creating an increasingly elaborate regime that facilitates the regulation and supervision of the world's leading international financial markets in a cooperative fashion. In addition to its growing sophistication, this regime has also extended its geographical reach well-beyond the G-10 countries to include the various 'offshore' financial centres which are often said to be impossible to regulate (Porter, 1993; Kapstein, 1994a).

Although central bankers may seem unlikely leaders of a Polanyian-style 'countermovement', it is important to recall that Polanyi's analysis gave them a central role in the late nineteenth century. He noted that the first form of countermovement in the monetary sphere in that era was led by élite groups who demanded that central banks actively intervene in the unregulated financial order to protect businesses from unstable, fluctuating business conditions and financial crises. In Polanyi's (1944, p. 202) words, the emergence of active central banking marked the first form of 'monetary protectionism' from the liberal financial order. The activities of the G-10 central bankers have been driven by a similar concern. Without some form of limited regulation and supervision, they have worried that the new global financial marketplace would be prone to extremely destabilizing financial crises.

In Polanyi's analysis, the behaviour of central banks in the late nineteenth century was important not just in and of itself in reducing socially disruptive financial instability. It was also significant in setting the scene for a second, more interventionist form of countermovement in the financial sphere. By highlighting the fact that financial issues were issues of public policy, the rise of central banking in that era opened a political space for other more populist social groups to demand that money and finance be regulated in more significant ways to serve broader social goals. The new central banking mechanisms not only showed that such regulation was possible, but also provided institutional frameworks which could be used to pursue such regulation.

Again, one can see certain parallels in the current era. The BIS regulatory and supervisory regime has already acted as a kind of limited form of countermovement that has lessened instability and reduced the risk of socially-disruptive financial crises. At the same time, the regime may also be creating a political and institutional space for more extensive forms of intervention in the global financial order. This is most apparent if one looks at the debates surrounding the 'Tobin tax' proposal.

The Tobin tax proposal represents the most prominent initiative today to respond to financial globalization in a way that is in keeping with the financial objectives of the 1944 Bretton Woods conference. As John Ruggie (1982) has pointed out, the Bretton Woods negotiators drew many of the same lessons from the prewar experience as did Polanyi about the social unsustainability of a liberal international financial order. In Ruggie's words, the negotiators were guided by an 'embedded liberal' ideology that sought to build a modified liberal order that was more compatible with social stability and less 'disembedded' from society than the nineteenth-century liberal order that Polanyi described. The key way that they sought to 'embed' international finance in society was by giving each national government the right to use capital controls to prevent financial movements that were deemed socially disruptive. Particularly worrisome to the architects of Bretton Woods were 'speculative' and 'disequilibrating' capital movements that might pose a threat to the policy autonomy of the new

Keynesian welfare state as well as to stable exchange rates and trade patterns (Helleiner, 1944, ch. 2). This 'embedded liberal' financial vision has been threatened with the dramatic elimination of national capital controls over the last two decades. The 'Tobin tax' proposal, however, represents an important initiative to revive it.

First put forward in the 1970s by the economist James Tobin, the proposal is to introduce a very small transaction tax (perhaps 0.25 per cent) on all spot foreign-exchange transactions. In quite Polanyian terms, Tobin has argued that the tax would discourage short-term, speculative cross-border financial movements that are causing socially-disruptive adjustments to trade patterns and exchange rates as well as a reduction in the policy autonomy of governments.[2] At the same time, the tax would not prevent more desirable long-term productive capital movements since its level would be quite insignificant as a cost item. Tobin's ideas are thus very much in keeping with the kind of 'embedded liberal' framework of thought that was dominant at Bretton Woods. International financial markets are not to be discouraged entirely; rather, they are simply to be regulated in ways that are more compatible with social stability than the fully liberal order that has emerged today. In Tobin's (1978, p. 158) famous phrase, the objective is simply to 'throw some sand in the well-greased wheels' of international financial markets.

What many find so attractive about the proposal is that it appears to provide a much more effective mechanism for realizing those embedded liberal goals than the mechanism put forward at Bretton Woods. Instead of cumbersome capital controls, Tobin's proposal substitutes a very minor tax (at a level insignificant to businesses outside the financial sector) and leaves it to market actors to decide which financial movements are worth pursuing in this context. A further key benefit of the tax, according to its proponents, is that it would provide considerable revenue which might be used domestically to fund social programmes or internationally to address global inequities or common global problems.

Opponents of the Tobin tax have been quick to dismiss it on the pragmatic grounds that it could never be implemented in an effective fashion. Unless the tax is introduced in all financial centres at once, they argue that market actors will simply move their footloose financial activities to financial centres where it is not applied. The prospects of the tax ever being implemented are thus said to be next to zero given the difficulties of getting all states to implement it. In particular, opponents of the tax anticipate collective problems that would plague cooperative initiatives in this area since individual states – particularly the small offshore centres – would find it tempting to keep their markets free of the tax while others implemented it.[3]

These arguments, however, overstate the political difficulties involved in its implementation. To begin with, Tobin-tax advocates have pointed out that the existence of the BIS regulatory and supervisory regime demonstrates the possibility of achieving a level of cooperation necessary to impose a standard form of regulatory practices on financial actors around the world (Langmore, 1995, p. 192; Greider, 1988, pp. 609–11). As noted above, this regime covers not just the leading financial centres but also the various offshore financial centres that critics argue would be unlikely to go along with a global reregulatory initiative. The BIS regime has thus been helpful to Tobin-tax advocates in exactly the way that Polanyi predicted: it has demonstrated that international financial regulation is politically possible and that it is thus a legitimate subject of public policy debates. Also in keeping with Polanyi's predictions, some Tobin-tax advocates have suggested that the specific institutional frameworks that have been constructed through the BIS regime could even be directly useful in implementing the tax (Greider, 1988; Felix, 1995a, p. 207).[4]

Critics of the Tobin tax have also exaggerated the number of countries that would need to be involved in implementing the Tobin tax. Foreign-exchange trading is, after all, highly concentrated in a few financial-centres of the world at the moment: seven financial centre countries account for 80 per cent of the trading (Felix, 1995b, p. 43).[5] The trading is concentrated in this way for good reasons; it relies on dense networks of informational, accountancy and legal services that only such centres can provide in a concentrated and reliable form (Thrift, 1994). The likelihood of foreign-exchange-trading business fleeing in massive quantities to lightly regulated offshore financial centres is thus overstated (Felix, 1995b, pp. 43–4; Kenen, 1996). Moreover, as Richard Cooper points out, even if this threat were to arise, the leading financial centres could threaten to withdraw key services from jurisdictions that did not abide by the tax. He concludes:

> it would not be necessary to get universal agreement on the tax. It would suffice to stipulate that disputes arising over foreign-exchange transactions could not be adjudicated in countries of the leading financial centres unless the tax had been paid. Since it takes years to establish a reputation for fair and impartial dispute settlements, a small tax would be unlikely to drive transactions to tax-free countries without such reputations.[6]

If cooperation in implementing the tax is required just between the leading financial centres, the collective action problems would seem to be no worse than those associated with macroeconomic coordination (a possible alternative way of restoring a degree of public control over the markets favoured by many economic liberals). Indeed, they would seem to be easier to resolve since the Tobin tax requires a level of coordination of policies that is much simpler than the far-reaching and complex changes to domestic fiscal and monetary policy that are required for effective macroeconomic coordination. And yet, while the G-7 have been prepared to expend considerable efforts fostering the latter, they have so far declared initiatives to implement the Tobin tax proposal to be futile.

The collective-action problems associated with implementing the Tobin tax would also seem to be easier to manage than those associated with macroeconomic coordination because of the potential leadership role of the USA and Britain. If the Tobin tax is to be successfully implemented, it is particularly important that it be supported by Britain and the United States because they house the most important foreign-exchange markets in the world. This position not only ensures that their cooperation is essential for the tax to be effective; it also gives them a form of 'structural power' that could be used to encourage all foreign governments to introduce the tax (Strange, 1986). The potential effectiveness of this structural power was demonstrated in the negotiations leading up to the 1988 capital-adequacy agreement when Britain and the USA threatened to block access to their financial markets to any banks whose governments had not agreed to the new regulations. Given the centrality of these markets to any major bank in the world, the threat was enormously effective in encouraging foreign governments to agree to the British and American proposal (Kapstein, 1994a, ch. 5). The US government also used the same weapon to encourage foreign governments to agree to its new reporting requirements relating to drug money after 1988 (Helleiner, 1999b). In each of these episodes, the USA and Britain have thus shown that leadership can play a key role in overcoming the collective-action problems which exist in initiatives to regulate international financial markets.

Whether these two countries might use their power to support the Tobin tax is, of course, difficult to predict. Such a move would represent a reversal of the leadership role they have each played in supporting financial liberalization over the last two decades. Still, the possibility should not be ruled out, especially as the structural position of these countries changes in the global political economy. In the USA, a support for the proposal already exists[7] and one can imagine it growing if there were a crisis of confidence in the dollar (a crisis that could easily be provoked by many developments in the coming years, including the creation of the European common currency). The dollar crisis in 1978–79, for example, led to considerable discussion in the US government about the need to reduce the country's vulnerability to speculative international financial movements (Helleiner, 1994, pp. 131–9). A similar crisis today could be expected to lead to a stronger regulatory response from the US government given the new political prominence of isolationist sentiments and attacks on the liberal world economy in US political circles in the post-Cold War era.

The British government might also be more inclined to accept regulations on its financial markets as London's financial status shifts from bring primarily an offshore eurodollar market centre to more of a regional financial centre within Europe. As European cooperation accelerates, Britain may also find itself increasingly on the receiving end of unwelcome Europe-wide regulatory proposals in finance. Indeed, this possibility has already been raised by Brussels' proposals in 1989 for a Europe-wide withholding tax, the reciprocity provision in the second banking directive, and German statements about the need for the future European central bank to impose Europe-wide reserve requirements (Helleiner, 1996a).

A Polanyian analysis would predict, however, that the most important development generating support for the Tobin tax in the USA, Britain and elsewhere should be the social instability and upheavals that Tobin and others argue are produced by the new global financial order itself. Certainly, social responses to declining policy autonomy of governments in the face of global financial markets are visible, most recently and perhaps most dramatically in the nation-wide strikes in France in late 1995. Journalist Erik Izraelewicz summed up a common interpretation of the strikes at the time: 'For the first time in a rich country, we are having a strike against globalization, a massive and collective reaction against financial globalization and its consequences' (*The Globe and Mail*, 7 December 1995, p. A18). At the 1996 Davos Forum, the world's élite also were treated to a lecture from the Forum's founders – Klaus Schwab and Claude Smadja – insisting that they 'start taking the backlash against globalization seriously'. They noted (perhaps too melodramatically): '[t]he mood in these [industrial] democracies is one of hopelessness and anxiety. This can easily turn into revolt, as December's unrest in France showed' (Friedman, 1996).

Analyses such as these should obviously be viewed somewhat cautiously; often the social protests described are reacting to developments that are unrelated to financial globalization. As economic liberals are increasingly keen to point out, the negative consequences of financial globalization are frequently exaggerated, especially the consequences in terms of the lost policy autonomy of governments (Woodall, 1995). But even if recent social movements have sometimes misdirected their anger, the increased focus on 'financial globalization' as a target against which to protest is worthy of note at a political level. Indeed, it is this very development that presumably has encouraged economic liberals to begin to emphasize that the declined power of the state in a globalized financial world has been overstated. Ironically, the prime sources of these overstatements in the past were economic liberals themselves keen to invoke the 'myth of the powerless state' (Woodall, 1995) to justify their preference for a limited state role in the economy.

Although 'financial globalization' has increasingly become a target of criticism in political circles, this development has not as yet translated into massive public campaigns for the implementation of the Tobin tax. No doubt the existence of the welfare state in the contemporary era has lessened social protest against financial liberalism by reducing the kinds of social costs experienced in the period analysed by Polanyi. The distribution of the costs and benefits of financial liberalism would also seem to work against efforts to generate widescale support for the Tobin tax. The costs associated with financial openness – the loss of policy autonomy, growing exchange-rate instability – are, after all, quite dispersed in their impact and relatively abstract from the standpoint of domestic social groups. By contrast, some of the benefits are highly visible and concentrated in their impact, such as the freedom provided to businesses to operate at the international level without cumbersome capital controls or the attraction of financial capital to domestic markets. Initiatives to promote the Tobin tax, thus, have tended to encounter enormous opposition from the financial community, without at the same generating large-scale countervailing interest and enthusiasm from the general public.

There is, however, one circumstance in which these political dynamics associated with international financial regulation seem to be altered: during and in the wake of foreign-exchange crises. Such crises have the effect of raising the political profile of international financial issues and, more specifically, highlighting the costs associated with financial liberalism. The 1929–31 international financial crisis demonstrated this in a particularly dramatic way. More recently, the European exchange-rate crisis of 1992–3 and the Mexican financial crisis of late 1994 generated widespread public debate on the drawbacks of financial liberalism. The Tobin tax proposal attracted considerable attention and a growing number of prominent supporters in the wake of these crises. His ideas began to be actively discussed in leading media outlets as well as in multilateral fora such as the UNDP, UNCTAD, the UN Social Summit and the preparatory discussions for the 1995 G-7 summit. Interest in the proposal also began to be expressed by a number of governments, such as those in Canada, France and Australia (Langmore, 1995; Helleiner, 1996a; McQuaig, 1998). Undoubtedly, the revenue benefits of the tax only enhanced the attractiveness of the proposal from the standpoint of these governments, since each are managing considerable fiscal deficits.[8]

If foreign-exchange crises generate Polanyian-style countermovements against unfettered financial liberalism, one can anticipate that reregulatory initiatives such as the Tobin tax are likely to attract growing support in the coming years. For as the volume of foreign-exchange trading expands, states are finding it more and more difficult to contain such crises. As the IMF reported in the wake of the European exchange-rate crisis, the volume of foreign-exchange trading now dwarfs the intervention capacities of the world's leading central banks. The trend towards increased cross-border investing by pension funds and other institutional investors also looks likely only to accelerate the volume of trading (Helleiner, 1996a). This provides yet one more reason to anticipate that the political momentum behind the Tobin tax initiative is unlikely to dissipate.

The multi-level nature of social responses

If the BIS regime and the Tobin tax initiative represent two examples of nascent countermovements at the global level, other developments below the global level would also seem to fit Polanyi's predictions. One of these is the formation of regional financial zones, of which the European Monetary System (EMS) is the most well-developed. A central rationale for the formation of the EMS in 1979 was a kind of Polanyian one: that of establishing a regional 'zone of monetary stability' in the increasingly volatile global financial environment. Like the BIS regime, this initiative represents only a relatively limited form of countermovement in that it has not sought to inhibit capital mobility. Indeed, European financial politics have moved in a decidedly liberal direction since the formation of the EMS. Not only have EC countries fully liberalized capital movements under the Single European Act, but the Economic and Monetary Union (EMU) initiative also embodies a conception of the position of money in society that is very much in keeping with economic liberal tradition. At the same time, however, many of the supporters of EMU also see it as a way for individual national governments to regain a degree of influence and power *vis-à-vis* the increasingly powerful global financial markets. Moreover, following Polanyi's analysis, European monetary and financial cooperation can be seen to be creating regional financial structures that might be used for a more interventionist form of countermovement over the longer term. In particular, the prospect has been raised – most recently by Jacques Delors at the end of the 1992–3 exchange rate crisis – of the introduction of region-wide exchange controls *vis-à-vis* the rest of the world, an initiative that would have been difficult to consider seriously not very long ago (Barber, 1993).

In addition to global and regional developments, there are also forms of Polanyian countermovement against financial globalization that are increasingly evident at the local level. Perhaps the most prominent involves the growing popularity of 'local-currency' experiments. Since the early 1980s, hundreds of these local currencies have been created across the world in countries ranging from Australia to Sweden. These local monetary experiments have involved the creation of currencies which are usually denominated in the national currency but are not convertible into it; they serve simply as a means of exchange within a clearly defined local community network. According to their proponents, these forms of money not only help reduce the vulnerability of local communities to the global financial 'casino', but also act as a kind of local form of 'capital control' since money is encouraged to remain within the local community. By facilitating economic transactions in poor communities that are starved of cash, local currencies also provide a primitive 'macroeconomic stimulus' to such communities.

Interestingly, many local-currency advocates draw directly on Polanyi's thought to support their monetary initiative. They argue that these forms of money are restoring a sense of social 'embeddedness' to the functioning of money, a characteristic that national currencies appear to have increasingly lost in the contemporary global financial environment (Rotstein and Duncan, 1991; Dobson, 1993). Instead of 'embedding' money in society through the mechanism of the state regulation of money, however, local-currency supporters prefer to pursue this goal through voluntarist community initiatives. Here again Polanyi's work is cited, particularly his endorsement of Robert Owen's community-oriented 'labour notes' in the early nineteenth century (Ekins, 1986). The preference for voluntarist non-state initiatives among local-currency advocates is no longer motivated by quite the same 'utopian socialist' goals as Owen, however. Instead, it often reflects a 'green' critique of the nation-state, a critique that suggests that the nation-state was never terribly responsive to the democratic aspirations and true needs of local communities (Helleiner, 1996c). The non-statist orientation of the local-currency advocates also often simply reflects a defeatist view that the state no longer has the power to regulate money effectively in this age of globalization.[9]

A final type of countermovement within the contemporary global financial order is represented by the growth of nationalist groups who attack the new globalized financial markets for undermining national sovereignty and policy autonomy.[10] These groups appear to want to reimpose capital controls at the national level in order to restore the kind of world that existed in the middle decades of this century. In some instances, the politics of these groups is quite right of centre (for example Jean Marie Le Pen in France or Pat Buchanan in the USA) and their rhetoric can be reminiscent of critiques of the power of 'haute finance' from the interwar period. Indeed, the broader political messages of nationalist groups from the right often bears a considerable resemblance to the right-wing forms of countermovement that Polanyi analysed in that earlier era.

Their emergence may provide some evidence to confirm Susan Strange's (1986, p. 192) predictions that political movements arousing 'strong and violent nationalist emotions' similar to those in the 1930s are likely to result from the 'casino-like' atmosphere of risk and uncertainty that she argues exists in this age of global finance. Indeed, the parallels between Strange's analysis and Polanyi's in this respect are worth noting. A central objective of Polanyi's book was to explain the rise of fascism in central Europe during the interwar period. In particular, he sought to critique the liberal argument (well outlined in Friedrich Hayek's *The Road to Serfdom* that was published in the same year as Polanyi's work) that the rise of fascism had been a product of collectivist thinking and the decline of liberal values. According to Polanyi, it was in fact liberals themselves that were partly to blame for the rise of fascism since their 'utopian' project of disembedding the economy from society had induced an inevitable social response, of which the fascist movement was one strand. As Polanyi (1944, p. 30) put it: 'In order to understand German fascism, we must revert to Ricardian England.'[11]

It is interesting to note that nationalist movements calling for capital controls – whether of a left (Panitch, 1994; Glyn, 1986) or right-wing variety – are the only type of 'countermovement' today that appears to be pursuing a form of politics that is focused on the unilateral behaviour of a single nation-state. The building of the BIS regime, for example, has involved complex forms of international cooperation. Advocates of the Tobin tax are also involved in transnational forms of political activism because of their recognition that all states must be encouraged to introduce the tax at the same time. Similarly, the initiatives in the European Community have involved innovative forms of supranational political cooperation at the regional level. The local currency movement is also reasserting the importance of sub-national political and economic spaces in a context when the nation-state no longer appears capable to preserving social stability.

This multi-levelled feature of contemporary countermovements contrasts with the period analysed by Polanyi when countermovements focused most of their energies on a national form of politics. For the left and right alike in that earlier era, social control over money and finance was to be achieved primarily through the unilateral activities of each individual nation-state. Not until the Bretton Woods meeting was there a serious initiative to move these activities to a different level, and, even then, many of the Bretton Woods financial provisions simply sought international legitimation and support for the inward-looking national interventionist initiatives of individual states.[12]

The difference between the two periods appears to reflect a recognition of the large hurdles to be overcome in building political support for unilateral nationally-based responses to financial globalization. The high degree of economic interdependence ensures that the costs associated with the implementation of tight effective national capital controls would be considerable. Given the transnationalization of business over the past two decades, unilateral national capital controls will be opposed strongly by large and powerful segments of the business community and such controls will also be more easily evaded by firms operating transnationally (Goodman and Pauly, 1993). Technological change has also made unilateral nationally-based reregulatory strategies more difficult. This is not necessarily because the technical capacity of states to monitor financial cross-border financial transactions has necessarily decreased in an age of information technology. Indeed, electronic money transfers are channelled through centralized payments systems and they leave electronic traces, both of which make them potentially easier to track by state authorities than traditional money flows (Helleiner, 1998). Rather, the importance of technological change may be that the new mobility of financial capital in a world of global telecommunications has ensured that unilateral regulatory initiatives will be strongly opposed on the grounds that they will place domestic financial markets at a competitive disadvantage *vis-à-vis* foreign financial markets (Cerny, 1994).

More broadly, many of those involved in countermovements have recognized that the nation-state as a political-economic entity has been challenged in a more serious way by those constructing the contemporary world market economy than was the case in the nineteenth century. The liberal international economic order of the previous century was in fact constructed at the same time that economic liberals were *strengthening* the nation-state by building nationally-consolidated markets and national legal-bureaucratic institutions to support these markets. In the monetary and financial sphere, for example, the international gold standard was monetary order built solidly on the foundation of new national currency structures and national central banks that liberals constructed during the nineteenth century (Helleiner, 1997). During that era, the world market economy was an 'inter-national' economic order created clearly on the foundation of strong territorially-bound nation-states.

By contrast, economic liberals in the last third of the twentieth century have shown less commitment to the nation-state as a political-economic institution in their drive to build a global market order. They have embraced political-economic innovations such as the 'offshore' eurocurrency markets and regional integration initiatives which have undermined the power and economic territoriality of the nation-state. They have also sought to weaken national institutions that served to 'embed' markets and bind the state and the national citizen under an ideology of 'welfare-nationalism' (Cox, 1987) from the late nineteenth century onwards. Indeed, in the monetary and financial sector, economic liberals such as Hayek (1976) have increasingly even called into question the need for the very national currencies and national central banks that their liberal counterparts in the nineteenth and early twentieth centuries built. The result, as John Ruggie (1993) and Eric Hobsbawm (1990, pp. 25,182) have noted, has been the emergence of a global economy with a different, more deterritorialized structure than its nineteenth-century counterpart.

In this context, a countermovement that seeks to reestablish social controls over the market with a unilateral nationalist project encounters additional barriers to the ones already mentioned. In the financial realm, unilateral national capital controls will not easily prevent speculation against the national currency in offshore eurocurrency markets. In contexts such as Western Europe or North America, such controls will probably also challenge commitments associated with regional integration initiatives. A countermovement relying on political appeals to concepts such as sovereignty and nationalism may also generate less enthusiasm and resonate less effectively than in the era Polanyi studied because these concepts are being challenged in broader ways.

To summarize, then, Polanyi's prediction that countermovements will emerge in an effort to protect society from the instability of the 'self-regulating market' appears to be beginning to be borne out in the contemporary global financial realm. The countermovements are also as varied in their social base as they were in the period analysed by Polanyi. In addition to these similarities between the two eras, however, there is also an important difference: many of the contemporary movements are less attracted to unilateral nationalist strategies for pursuing 'monetary protectionism'. They seek to re-embed the market via activities at the local, regional and global levels as well.

The obvious difficulty facing many of these contemporary countermovements is that, in seeking alternative levels at which to pursue their Polanyian goals, they are also counting on alternative senses of 'society' to emerge in reaction against the self-regulating market. In the pre-1945 period, the 'nation' was both the agent of the Polanyian countermovement as well as the designated 'society' to be protected. Today, many contemporary countermovements are suggesting that 'societies' also exist at a global, regional and local level that are not only deserving of protection but also capable of responding in the ways they hope. Indeed, much of their activity seems devoted to efforts to cultivate these alternative senses of society. How successful this kind of political project can be remains a open question.[13]

One final point must be made about the prospects for the contemporary liberal global financial order. As Polanyi points out, the international gold standard in the pre-1939 era did not collapse as a direct result of the activities of the countermovements he analysed. Rather, the immediate cause of its collapse was the momentous market crisis of 1929–31. Any analysis of the future of the contemporary global financial order must thus also allow for the possibility of such a momentous crisis. In Charles Kindleberger's (1978) words, financial markets are, after all, particularly prone to 'panics, manias, and crashes'. Although the BIS regime provides a greater insurance against such a crisis in the contemporary era, its existence does not rule out the possibility.

Indeed, were he alive today, Polanyi would likely argue that the probability of such a crisis will increase the more that various countermovements are successful in their efforts to subject money and finance to forms of social control. According to his analysis, the emergence of countermovements from the late nineteenth century onwards increasingly impaired the self-regulating character of global markets in ways that encouraged greater and greater market instability. The collapse of the international gold standard in the interwar period, for example, was accelerated by the growing demands of critics of liberalism for more active political control over monetary and financial policy. As Barry Eichengreen (1992, 1996) has recently shown, not only did these demands render more difficult the efforts of central banks to cooperate autonomously in containing international financial crises, they also prompted increasingly disruptive speculative financial movements as the 'credibility' and predictability of government financial policy came into question. A similar set of developments might be provoked if some contemporary countermovements – especially the nationalist variants and those seeking regional closure in Europe – were to gain in political strength.

Conclusion

A Polanyian analysis presents an alternative perspective on the historical origins and future prospects of the contemporary global financial order from that offered by economic liberals. As other writers have noted, Polanyi prompts us to recognize that the contemporary global financial order has been consciously 'made' by states rather than having simply been the product of inevitable market and technological pressures. At the same time, I have suggested that Polanyi's work is also useful in calling into question the future durability of the new liberal global financial order. Specifically, he encourages us to look for the emergence of various social countermovements that might be seeking – some with more success than others – to restore a degree of social control over the global financial realm.

To apply Polanyi's ideas to the contemporary context is not to suggest that history is simply repeating itself. As I have noted, a central difference between the pre-1939 period and the contemporary era is the role of the nation-state in both the creation of a global market order and the reaction to it. In the period described by Polanyi, both the liberal project and the rise of the countermovements it induced were intricately connected with the growth and consolidation of the nation-state. In the contemporary period, the globalization trend as well as the reactions to it appear to be playing a role in undermining the nation-state's strength and legitimacy as a political-economic unit.

This is not to suggest that states are vanishing as powerful actors in the current era. Since states have authored the globalization trend, it is difficult to conclude that it is a process somehow out of their control. Indeed, as Stephen Krasner and Janice Thomson (1989) suggest, states have often acquired greater powers in the process of constructing and enforcing the rules on which the new global economy operates. What *is* being challenged, however, is a specific historical form of state – the nation-state – which was organized around a particular notion of economic territoriality, state–citizen relations, and political identity (Helleiner, 1997). In drawing this distinction, I find a way to agree with the arguments put forward by both John Ruggie (1993) and Ethan Kapstein (1993) in their debate about the implications of financial globalization for the nature of world order. Ruggie's argument that the trend is encouraging radically new forms of economic space and territoriality is certainly borne out by developments such as the emergence of the euromarket. At the same time, Kapstein is also correct to point out that states retain a position of primacy in global financial markets including the 'offshore' euromarkets. To my mind, their debate is less a debate than a discussion in which they are talking at cross-purposes. Their two positions can be reconciled by simply acknowledging that it is only a certain historical form of state – rather than the state itself – that is being eroded by financial globalization (Helleiner, 1999a).

If the Polanyian interpretation of financial globalization presented in this chapter is helpful in resolving this theoretical conundrum, it is also useful in questioning economic liberal views on the origins and future of the globalized financial order. But what label best describes the perspective from which Polanyi's challenge is derived? This is a difficult question to answer since his work seems to appeal equally to a number of the different 'schools' within the field of IPE. Realists, for example, have been attracted to his emphasis on the centrality of the state in creating and sustaining markets (Gilpin, 1987), while those on the left cite his work to back their argument that a society built on market principles is not socially sustainable (Gill, 1995). As I have noted elsewhere (Helleiner, 1996c), many contemporary greens are also attracted to his critique of the large-scale nature of political and economic life in the industrial age; and liberals from a more 'embedded liberal' tradition have also found elements of his critique of unfettered markets useful (Ruggie, 1982).

The current resurgence of interest in Polanyi's work is presumably linked to this very fact. In an age when economic liberalism is in ascendence, Polanyi offers a interesting critique of its ideas that appeals equally to various schools of thought that feel uneasy about this turn of events. If his perspective is hard to pin down, the target of his criticism is certainly clear from the footnotes in the text of *The Great Transformation*: the 'Austrian school' of economic liberals led by Hayek and Ludwig von Mises which provided the intellectual backing for the revival of economic liberalism in the last third of this century. Polanyi encountered this school during his intellectually formative years in Vienna before the Second World War and his 1944 book stands as one of the first sustained critiques of the school. It is perhaps for this reason above all that his book is attracting renewed interest in an era when the influence of this school has become increasingly substantial and global in scope.

Notes

1 Interestingly, these decisions can also been seen to be driven by some similar political pressures as those which Polanyi identified as significant in creating the nineteenth century world market order (Helleiner, 1995a).

2 As Tobin (1978, p. 154) puts it: 'National economies and national governments are not capable of adjusting to massive movements of funds across the foreign exchanges, without real hardship and without significant sacrifice of the objectives of national economic policy with respect to employment, output, and inflation.'

3 Some critics also predict large-scale evasion via the use or creation of financial instruments that are not covered by the tax but which could serve a similar function as spot foreign-exchange transactions. For a critique of this view, see the comments of James Tobin, Barry Eichengreen and Charles Wyplosz in their respective contributions to Ul Haq *et al.* (1996, pp. xv, 31, 278).

4 In a similar vein, Akyuz and Cornford (1994) discuss the potential usefulness of the BIS regime for an initiative that would apply capital charges to banks' open positions in foreign exchange as a possible alternative to Tobin's specific tax proposal.

5 These countries are: the UK, the USA, Japan, Singapore, Switzerland, Hong Kong and Germany.

6 Cooper (1994, p. 141). Kenen (1996) also suggests that authorities could tax foreign-exchange transactions with financial centres that were not implementing the tax at a very high rate.

7 Langmore (1995, p. 192) cites a US opinion survey showing that roughly two-thirds of respondents supported the introduction of the tax. He also notes interest in the proposals among prominent White House officials such as Larry Summers (the US Under-Secretary of the Treasury for International Affairs) and Joseph Stiglitz (a member of the President's Council of Economic Advisors).

8 As Felix (1995a, p. 205) notes, in this age of anti-tax populism, governments such as these are searching for sources of tax revenue that are not 'politically suicidal'. In his words, '[a] tax on foreign exchange speculation may meet this specification, since in US political jargon, it's a tax on "Wall Street" not "Main Street".'

9 It is worth noting that local currencies have proliferated at various moments in history when the state's capacity to manage money effectively was eroded. During the early 1930s, for example, local currencies were used extensively in the USA and in countries across Europe (Weishaar and Parrish, 1933).

10 Pauly (1995, p. 384) also sees these groups as representing the kind of 'defensive impulse' that Polanyi predicts. See also Loriaux (1991, p. 307).

11 Strange's entire book in fact has interesting parallels with Polanyi's thought. Her critique of the existing financial order is that it encourages a degree of social upheaval and instability that is unsustainable and also 'politically unacceptable to a free society' (p. 191). This was also the key concern for Polanyi.

12 Indeed, this was exactly the kind of international activity that Polanyi also advocated at the end of *The Great Transformation* (1994, pp. 253–4).

13 For a sceptical view, see Panitch (1994). For a more optimistic view, see Held (1995). For a discussion of how Held's ideas might apply to the financial sector, see Helleiner (1995b).

References

Akyuz, Y. and A. Cornford (1994) 'Regimes for International Capital Movements and Some Proposals for Reform', mimeo (Paris: UNCTAD, May).

Andrews, D. M. (1992) 'From Ad Hoc to Institutionalized Coordination and Beyond: Twenty Years of European Monetary Integration', in *Findings* (Cambridge, MA: Centre for International Studies, MIT).

——(1993) 'The Global Origins of the Maastrich Treaty on EMU: Closing the Window of Opportunity', in A. W. Cafruny and G. G. Rosenthal (eds), *The State of the European Community, Vol. 2: The Maastricht Debates and Beyond* (Boulder, CO: Lynne Rienner).

——(1994) 'Capital Mobility and the State Autonomy: Toward a Structural Theory of International Monetary Relations', *International Studies Quarterly*, 38(2), June, pp. 193–218.

——(1997) 'Bargaining Power and Policy Interdependence: Monetary Diplomacy in the Postwar International System', paper delivered at the 93rd Annual Meeting of the American Political Science Association, 28–31 August, Washington, DC.

——and T. D. Willett (1997) 'Financial Interdependence and the State: International Monetary Relations at Century's End', *International Organization*, 51 (3), pp. 479–511.

Aronson, J. D. (1977) *Money and Power: Banks and the World Monetary System* (Beverly Hills, CA: Sage).

Arrow, K. J. and M. Kurz (1970) *Public Investment, the Rate of Return, and Optimal Fiscal Policy* (Baltimore: Johns Hopkins University Press).

Ashley, R. K. (1986) 'The Poverty of Neorealism', chapter 9 in R. O. Keohane (ed.), *Neorealism and Its Critics* (New York: Columbia University Press).

'A Who's Who on the BIS' (1992) *International Economy*, Nov./Dec., pp. 11–27.

Bailey, F. (1991) *The Junk Bond Revolution: Michael Milken, Wall Street and the Roaring Eighties* (London: Fourth Estate).

Bakker, A. F. P. (1996) *The Liberalization of Capital Movements in Europe: The Monetary Committee and Financial Integration, 1958–1994* (London: Kluwer Academic Publishers).

Ball, M. (1994) 'The Great Rating Debate', *Corporate Finance*, April, pp. 18–21.

Ball, T. (1985) 'The Incoherence of Inter-generational Justice', *Inquiry*, 28, pp. 321–37.

Bannock, G., R. E. Baxter and E. Davis (1987) *Dictionary of Economics* (London: *The Economist* Books/Hutchinson).

Barber, B. R. (1995) *Jihad vs. McWorld: How Globalism and Tribalism are Reshaping the World* (New York: Ballantine).

Barber, L. (1993) 'Delors pushes for monetary "fortress Europe"' *Financial Times*, 18 September.

Barro, R. J. (1974) 'Are Government Bonds Net Wealth?', *Journal of Political Economy*, 82, pp. 1095–1117.

Barry, B. (1978) 'Circumstances of Justice and Future Generations', in R. I. Sikora and B. Barry (eds), *Obligations to Future Generations* Philadelphia: Temple University Press, pp. 204–248.

Basle Committee on Banking Supervision, *Report on International Developments in Banking Supervision*, various years.

Bauchard, P. (1986) *La Guerre des Deux Roses* (Paris: Spasset).

Berger, S. and R. Dore (eds) (1996) *National Diversity and Global Capitalism* (Ithaca, NY: Cornell University Press).

Berry, J. M. and C. Chandler (1995) 'Fast Currency Trades Feed Fears of a Crisis', *Washington Post*, 17 April, pp. A1, A13.

Birnkrant, H. J. and J. E. Crocker, Jr. (1994a) 'Despite Improvements, Transfer Pricing Regs. Still Carry a Risk of Double Taxation', *Journal of Taxation*, 81(6), December.

——— (1994b) 'Transfer Pricing Final Regs. Increase Flexibility, but not Certainty, in Choice of Method', *Journal of Taxation*, 81(6), November.

Bischel, J. E. (1990) 'The Section 482 White Paper and Superroyalties: Existing and Proposed Transfer Pricing Methods,' *Bulletin for International Fiscal Documentation*, 44(2), February.

Bishop, P. and D. Dixon (1992) *Foreign Exchange Handbook* (New York: McGraw-Hill Inc).

Blanchard, O. J. and S. Fischer (1989) *Lectures on Macroeconomics* (Cambridge: MIT Press).

Bloomberg (1994) 'Standards of Japanese Credit Ratings Questioned,' *Bloomberg Business News*, (Online service) 8 April.

Boidman, N. (1992) 'The Effect of the APA and Other US Transfer-Pricing Initiatives in Canada and Other Countries', *The Tax Executive*, 44(4), July–August, pp. 254–61.

—— (1995) 'Can an Efficient Transfer Pricing Strategy be Developed under Canadian Law?', *The Tax Executive*, 47(4), July–August, pp. 290–6.

Boneham, D. (1995) 'Forex and FI: The New Regime for the Taxation of Foreign Exchange Gains and Losses and Financial Instruments has Begun,' *Accountancy*, April, p. 157.

Bonifiglio, J. D. (1995) 'Tax Planning Strategies for Multinationals Under the New Transfer Pricing Regulations,' *The International Tax Journal*, 21(4), Fall, pp. 1–15.

Boskin, M. J. and C. E. McLure Jr. (eds) (1990) *World Tax Reform* (San Francisco: ICS Press).

Bryant, R. (1986) 'International Financial Intermediation: Underlying Trends and Implications for Government Policies', in Y. Suzuki and H. Yomo (eds), *Financial Innovation and Monetary Policy* (Tokyo: University of Tokyo Press).

—— (1987) *International Financial Intermediation* (Washington, DC: Brookings Institution).

Buerkle, T. (1993) 'In Search of an EC Money Policy', *International Herald Tribune* 25 October.

Business International Corporation and Ernst and Young (1991) *International Transfer Pricing* (New York: Business International).

Cameron, S. (1993) 'How the Gravy Train Went Off the Rails', *The Globe and Mail*, 6 February, p. D1.

Canada, Government of (1972) *Foreign Direct Investment in Canada* (the Gray Report) (Ottawa: Information Canada).

Cargill T. and S. Ryama (1988) *The Transition of Finance in Japan and the United States: A Comparative Perspective* (Stanford, CA: Hoover Institution Press).
'Central Bankers Agree on Plan to Cover Risks' (1995) *The Wall Street Journal*, 13 April, p. A4.
Cerny, P. G. (1990) *The Changing Architecture of Politics: Structure, Agency, and the Future of the State* (London: Sage).
——(ed.) (1993) *Finance and World Politics* (Aldershot: Elgar).
——(1994) 'The Dynamics of Financial Globalization: Technology, Market Structure and Policy Response', *Policy Sciences*, 27, pp. 57–89.
Clark, W. R. (1998) 'Agents and Structures: Two Views of Preferences, Two Views of Institutions', *International Studies Quarterly* 42, June, pp. 245–70.
Cohen, B. J. (1993) 'The Triad and the Unholy Trinity: Lessons for the Pacific Region', in R. Higgot, R. Leaver, and J. Ravenhill (eds), *Pacific Economic Relations in the 1990s: Cooperation and Conflict?* (London: Allen & Unwin).
——(1996) 'Phoenix Risen: The Resurrection of Global Finance', *World Politics*, p. 48.
——(1998) *The Geography of Money* (Ithaca, NY: Cornell University Press).
Cole, R. T. (1991) 'New Competent Authority Procedure Allows for Increased Flexibility', *The Journal of Taxation*, 74(6) (June 1991), pp. 380–5.
——(1995) 'Advance Pricing Agreement Practice Under the New Rules', *Journal of Taxation*, 83(4), October, pp. 215–22.
——and G. W. Rubloff (1992) 'Proposed Transfer Pricing Regulations Under Section 482 of the Internal Revenue Code', *Bulletin for International Fiscal Documentation*, 46(6), June, pp. 292–8.
Coleman, J. (1990) *Foundations of Social Theory* (Cambridge: Harvard University Press).
Coleman, W. and T. Porter (1994) 'Regulating International Banking and Securities: Emerging Co-operation Among National Authorities', in R. Stubbs and G. Underhill (eds), *Political Economy and the Changing Global Order* (New York: St Martin's Press).
Collier, D. (1993) 'The Comparative Method', in A. W. Finifter, ed, *Political Science: The State of the Discipline II* (Washington, DC: The American Political Science Association).
Commission on Global Governance (1995) *Our Global Neighbourhood* (Oxford: Oxford University Press).
Conlan, T. J., M. T. Wrightson, and D. R. Beam (1990) *Taxing Choices: The Politics of Tax Reform* (Washington, DC: Congressional Quarterly Press).
Cooper, R. (1994) 'What Future for the International Monetary System?', in Pierre Siklos (ed.), *Varieties of Monetary Reforms* (London: Kluwer Academic Publishers).
Coopers and Lybrand (1993) *International Transfer Pricing Strategy* (Bicester: CCH Editions).
Cowles, M. G. (1995) 'Setting the Agenda for a New Europe: The ERT and EC 1992', *Journal of Common Market Studies*, 33, December, pp. 501–26.
Cowling, K. and R. Sugden (1987) *Transnational Monopoly Capitalism* (Brighton: Wheatsheaf).
Cox, R. W. (1986) 'Social Forces, States and World Orders: Beyond International Relations Theory', in R. O. Keohane (ed.), *Neorealism and Its Critics* (New York: Columbia University Press).

——(1987) *Production, Power and World Order: Social Forces in the Making of History* (New York: Columbia University Press).
——with T. J. Sinclair (1996) *Approaches to World Order* (Cambridge: Cambridge University Press).
Crane, D. (1993) 'Fighting Deficit: Massive Changes Loom for Canada', *The Toronto Star*, 25 September, p. 1.
Crosette, B. (1995) 'As World Leaders Confer on Poverty, Mitterand Urges New Tax', *The New York Times*, 12 March, p. 4.
Crowe, C. (1995) 'Forex Shake-Out Creates a Super-League', *Euromoney*, January, pp. 103–4.
Cutler, A. C., V. Haufler, T. Porter (eds) (1999) *Private Authority and International Affairs* (Albany, N. Y.: State University of New York).
Dale, R. (1984) *The Regulation of International Banking* (Cambridge: Woodhead-Faulkner).
Dobbin, F. (1992) 'The Origins of Private Social Insurance – Public Policy and Fringe Benefits in America, 1920–1950,' *American Journal of Sociology*, 97(5), pp. 1416–1445.
Dobson, R. (1993) *Bringing the Economy Home from the Market* (Montreal: Black Rose).
Dornbusch, R. (1980) *Open Economy Macroeconomics* (New York: Basic Books).
——and S. Fischer (1994) *Macroeconomics*, 6th edn (New York: McGraw Hill).
Drake, W. J. and K. Nicolaïdis (1992) 'Ideas, Interests, and Institutionalization: "Trade in Services" and the Uruguay Round', *International Organization*, 46(1), Winter, pp. 37–100.
Dunning, J. H. (1988) *Explaining International Production* (London: Unwin Hyman).
——(1993) *The Globalization of Business: The Challenge of the 1990s* (London and New York: Routledge).
Dwyer, J. H. (1997) *Restructuring the Market – Restructuring the State: The Dynamics of Financial Market Reform in Japan*, PhD dissertation (Ann Arbor, MI: University Microfilms International).
Eckstein, H. (1975) 'Case Study and Theory in Political Science', in F. I. Greenstein and N. W. Polsby (eds), *Handbook of Political Science. Vol. 7: Strategies of Inquiry* Reading, MA: Addison-Wesley, pp. 79–137.
Economist, The (1992) 'New Maps of Policy', 19 September, pp. 24–30.
Economist, The (1993) 'New Tricks to Learn: A Survey of International Banking.' April 10.
Economist, The (1993) 'Canada's Worrying Bond Spree', 28 August, p. 76.
Economist, The (1994) 'Auf Wiedersehen, M3,' 28 May, p. 84.
Eichengreen, B. (1991) 'Relaxing the External Constraint: Europe in the 1930s', in G. Alogoskoufis, L. Papademos and R. Portes (eds), *External Constraints on Macroeconomic Policy: The European Experience* (Cambridge: Cambridge University Press).
——(1992) *Golden Fetters* (Oxford: Oxford University Press).
——(1993) 'European Monetary Unification,' *Journal of Economic Literature* 31, September, pp. 1321–57.
——(1996) *Globalizing Capital: A History of the International Monetary System* (Princeton, NJ: Princeton University Press).

Eisner, R. (1994) *The Misunderstood Economy: What Counts and How to Count It* (Boston: Harvard Business School Press).
Ekins, P. (1986) 'Local Currency', in P. Ekins (ed.), *The Living Economy* (London: Routledge & Kegan Paul).
Engelen, K. (1994) 'A European Nightmare: Unchecked American Rating Agencies Become Continent's New Boss-Men', *The International Economy*, 7(6), November/December, pp. 46–50.
Epstein, G. A. (1996) 'International Capital Mobility and the Scope for National Economic Management', in R. Boyer and D. Drache (eds), *States Against Markets: The Limits of Globalization* (London: Routledge).
—— and H. Gintis. (1995) 'International Capital Markets and National Economic Policy.' *Review of International Political Economy*, 2(4), Autumn, pp. 693–718.
Ernst and Young, Inc. (1990) *A Strategy for the ECU* (London: Kogan Page).
Ernst and Young, Inc. (1996) 'Transfer Pricing Monitor', Internet Edition @ www.ey.com/us/press/transur.htm.
Far Eastern Economic Review (1998) 'Moody's Swings', 13 August, p. 13.
Feldman, R. (1986) *Japanese Financial Markets: Deficits, Dilemmas, and Deregulation* (Cambridge, MA: MIT Press).
Feldstein, M. and C. Horioka (1980) 'Domestic Savings and International Capital Flows', *The Economic Journal*. 90: pp. 314–29.
Felix, D. (1995a) 'The Tobin Tax Proposal', *Futures*, 27, pp. 195–208.
—— (1995b) 'Financial Globalization versus Free Trade: The Case for the Tobin Tax,' mimeo, November.
Felix, David (1995c), 'Financial Globalization and the Tobin Tax,' *Challenge*, May/June, pp. 56–9.
Fisher, I. (1933) 'The Debt-Deflation Theory of Great Depressions', *Econometrica*, 1, 1933, pp. 337–357.
Fleming, J. M. (1962) *Domestic Financial Policies Under Fixed and Floating Exchange Rates* (Washington, DC: International Monetary Fund).
Frankel, J. A. (1990) 'Quantifying International Capital Mobility in the 1980s', in D. Das (ed.), *Current Issues in International Trade and International Finance* (London: Oxford University Press).
Frankel, J. (1991) 'Quantifying International Capital Mobility in the 1980's', in D. Bernheim and J. Shonen (eds), *National Savings and Economic Performance* (Chicago: University of Chicago Press).
—— (1992) 'Measuring International Capital Mobility: A Review', AEA Papers and Proceedings. May.
Frankel, Jeffrey (1996) 'How Well do Foreign Exchange Markets Work? Might a Tobin Tax Help?', in Mahbub ul Haq, Inge Kaul and Isabelle Grunberg, eds, *The Tobin Tax: Coping with Financial Volatility* New York: Oxford University Press, pp. 41–81.
Franko, L., M. Patton, J. Wheeler, and C. S. Triplett (1994) 'The International Tax Showdown', *Journal of International Taxation*, 20(3), Summer.
Fratianni, M., J. von Hagen and C. Waller (1992) *The Maastricht Way to EMU*, Princeton University: Essays in International Finance 187, June.
Freeland, Charles (1994) 'The Work of the Basle Committee', in Robert C. Effros, ed., *Current Legal Issues Affecting Central Banks* Washington, DC: International Monetary Fund, pp. 231–40.

Freeman, J. R. (1989) *Democracy and Markets* (Ithaca, NY: Cornell University Press).

French, K. R. and J. M. Poterba (1990) 'Japanese and US Cross-Border Common Stock Investments.' *Journal of Japanese and International Economies*. Vol. 4, December 1990, pp. 476–93.

Frenkel, J., A. Razin, and E. Sadka (1991) *International Taxation in an Integrated World* (Cambridge, MA: MIT Press).

Frieden, J. A. (1991a) 'Invested Interests: The Politics of National Economic Policies in a World of Global Finance', *International Organization*, 45(4), pp. 425–51.

——(1991b) *Debt, Development and Democracy: Modern Political Economy and Latin America, 1965–1985* (Princeton: Princeton University Press).

Frieden, J. and R. Rogowski (1996) 'The Impact of the International Economy on National Policies: An Analytical Overview', in R. Keohane and H. Milner (eds), *Internationalization and Domestic Politics* (Cambridge: Cambridge University Press).

Friedman, T. (1996) 'Beware Traders, We All Have Our Zyuganovs', *International Herald Tribune*. February 8.

Garrett, G. (1995) 'Capital Mobility, Trade, and the Domestic Politics of Economic Policy', *International Organization*, 49(4), Autumn, pp. 657–87.

——(1998) *Partisan Politics in the Global Economy* (Cambridge: Cambridge University Press).

——and P. Lange (1991) 'Political Responses to Interdependence: What's "Left" for the Left?' *International Organization* 45(4), Autumn: pp. 539–64.

——and P. Lange (1996) 'Internationalization, Institutions, and Political Change', in R. O. Keohane and H. V. Milner, *Internationalization and Domestic Politics* (Cambridge: Cambridge University Press).

General Accounting Office (1981) *IRS Could Better Protect U. S. Tax Interests in Determining the Income of Multinational Corporations*, GAO report no. GGD-81–81 Washington, DC: GAO, 30 September.

General Accounting Office (1992) *International Taxation: Problems Persist in Determining Tax Effects of Intercompany Prices*, GAO report no. GAO/GGD-92–98 Washington, DC: GAO, 15 June.

General Accounting Office (1994) *Tax Administration: Information on IRS' International Tax Compliance Activities*, GAO report no. GAO/GGD-94–96FS Washington, DC: GAO, 27 June.

General Accounting Office (1995) *Transfer Pricing and Information on Nonpayment of Tax*, GAO report no. GAO/GGD-95–101 Washington, DC: GAO, 13 April.

General Accounting Office (1997) *Taxpayer Compliance: Analyzing the Nature of the Income Tax Gap*, GAO report no. GAO/T-GGD-97–35 Washington, DC: GAO, 9 January.

George, A. L., and T. J. McKeown (1985) 'Case Studies and Theories of Organizational Decision Making', in *Advances in Information Processing in Organizations*, Vol. 2 (Santa Barbara, CA: JAI Press).

Giavazi, F. and A. Giovannini (1989) *Limiting Exchange Rate Flexibility: The European Monetary System* (Cambridge, MA: MIT Press).

Giddens, A. (1984) *The Constitution of Society: Outline of the Theory of Structuration* (Cambridge: Polity Press).

Gill, S. (1992) 'Economic Globalization and the Internationalization of Authority: Limits and Contradictions.' *Geoforum*. 23(3), pp. 269–83.
——(1995) 'Theorizing the Interregnum', in B.Hettne (ed.), *International Political Economy* (London: Zed Books).
——and D. Law (1988) *The Global Political Economy: Perspectives, Problems, and Policies* (Baltimore: Johns Hopkins University Press).
——and D. Law (1989) 'Global Hegemony and the Structural Power of Capital', *International Studies Quarterly*, 33(4), December, pp. 475–499.
Gilpin, R. (1975) *U. S. Power and the Multinational Corporation* (New York: Basic Books).
——(1987) *The Political Economy of International Relations* (Princeton, NJ: Princeton University Press).
Giovannini, A. (1992) 'Economic and Monetary Union: What Happened? Exploring the Political Dimension of Optimum Currency Areas', in *The Monetary Future of Europe*, Report of a conference organized by the Centre for Economic Policy Research in La Coruña, Spain, December.
Glyn, A. (1986) 'Capital Flight and Exchange Controls' *New Left Review*. 155: pp. 37–49.
Goldstein, J. and R. O. Keohane, eds.(1993) *Ideas and Foreign Policy: Beliefs, Institutions and Political Change* (Ithaca, NY: Cornell University Press).
Goodman, J. B. (1992) *Monetary Sovereignty: The Politics of Central Banking in Western Europe* (Ithaca, NY: Cornell University Press).
——and L. W. Pauly (1993) 'The Obsolescence of Capital Controls? Economic Management in an Age of Global Markets', *World Politics*, 46, pp. 50–82.
Gordon, R. H., and J. K. MacKie-Mason (1995) 'Why is there Corporate Taxation in a Small Open Economy? The Role of Transfer Pricing and Income Shifting', in M. Feldstein, J. R. Hines Jr., and R. G. Hubbard, *The Effects of Taxation on Multinational Corporations* Chicago, IL., University of Chicago Press, pp. 67–94.
Gourevitch, P. (1986) *Politics in Hard Times: Comparative Responses to International Economic Crises* (Ithaca, NY: Cornell University Press).
Gowa, J. (1983) *Closing the Gold Window* (Ithaca, NY: Cornell University Press).
——(1988) 'Public Goods and Political Institutions: Trade and Monetary Policy Processes in the United States', *International Organization* 42, Winter: pp. 15–32.
Granwell, A. W. *et al.* (1992) 'Proposed Section 482 Regulations: Compatibility of Use of the Comparable Profit Interval with International Norms', *Bulletin for International Fiscal Documentation*, 46(6), June, pp. 287–91.
Greenhouse, S. (1993) 'Central-Bank Gripes About a New World,' *The New York Times*, 23 August.
Greenwood J. and M. Aspinwall(1998) *Collective Action in the European Union: Interests and the New Politics of Associability* (London: Routledge).
Greider, W. (1988) 'The Money Question' *World Policy Journal*, p. 5.
Grieco, J. M. (1984) *Between Autonomy and Dependency: India's Experience with the International Computer Industry* (Berkeley: University of California Press).
Grogan-Green, L. (1993) 'Moody's Analyst Says Deficit Threat "Exaggerated"', *The Financial Post*. October 29, p. 28.
Gros, D. and N. Thygesen (1992) *European Monetary Integration* (London: Longman).
Grubert, H., T. Goodspeed, and D. Swenson (1993) 'Explaining the Low Taxable Income of Foreign-Controlled Companies in the United States', in

A. Giovannini, R. G. Hubbard, and J. Slemrod (eds), *Studies in International Taxation* (Chicago: University of Chicago Press).

Haas, E. (1958) *The Uniting of Europe* (Stanford, CA: Stanford University Press).

——(1964) *Beyond the Nation State* (Stanford, CA: Stanford University Press).

——(1971) 'The study of regional integration: Reflections on the joy and anguish of pre-theorizing', in L. Lindberg and A. Sheingold (eds), *Regional Integration: Theory and Research* (Cambridge, MA: Harvard University Press).

——(1975) *The Obsolescence of Regional Integration Theory* (Berkeley: Institute of International Studies, University of California).

Halimi, S. *Sisyphus is Tired: The French Left and the Exercise of Power, 1924–1986* (Ph. D. dissertation, Berkeley, CA: University of California at Berkeley).

Hall, P. (1987) 'The Evolution of Economic Policy under Mitterrand', in S. Hoffmann, G. Ross, and S. Malzacher (eds), *The Mitterrand Experiment: Continuity and Change in Modern France* New York: Oxford University Press, pp. 54–72.

——(1993) 'Policy Paradigms, Social Learning, and the State,' *Comparative Politics* April.

——and R. Franzese (1997) 'Mixed Signals: Central Bank Independence, Coordinated Wage Bargaining, and European Monetary Union,' draft manuscript, Harvard University, 22 December 1997.

Halliday, F. (1995) 'The End of the Cold War and International Relations: Some Analytic and Theoretical Conclusions', in K. Booth and S. Smith (eds), *International Relations Theory Today* (University Park: Pennsylvania State University Press).

Harper, L. (1994) 'New Tax Rules Expand Multinationals' Flexibility in Dealings with US Units', *The Wall Street Journal*, 6 July, A2.

Harvey, D. (1999) *The Limits to Capital*, 2nd edn (London and New York: Verso).

Hawley, J. (1984) 'Protecting Capital From Itself: US Attempts to Regulate the Eurocurrency System', *International Organization*, 38: pp. 131–65.

Hay, D., *et al.* (1994) 'Past and Present Work in the OECD on Transfer Pricing and Selected Issues', *Bulletin for International Fiscal Documentation*, 48(10), October.

Hayek, F. A. (1949) *Individualism and Economic Order* (London: Routledge & Kegan Paul).

——(1976) *The Denationalization of Money* (London: Institute for Economic Affairs).

Held, D. (1991) 'Democracy, the Nation-State and the Global System,' *Economy and Society* 20, 2: pp. 38–72.

——(ed.) (1995) *Cosmopolitan Democracy* (Cambridge: Polity Press).

——, A. McGrew, D. Goldblatt and J. Perraton (1999) *Global Transformations: Politics, Economics and Culture* (Stanford, CA: Stanford University Press).

Helleiner, E. (1994) *States and the Reemergence of Global Finance: From Bretton Woods to the 1990s* (Ithaca, NY: Cornell University Press).

——(ed.) (1994) 'The World of Money: The Political Economy of International Capital Mobility', special issue of *Policy Sciences*, 27(4).

——(1995a) 'Great Transformations: A Polanyian Perspective on the Contemporary Global Financial Order,' *Studies in Political Economy* 48: pp. 149–64.

——(1995b) 'Democratic Governance in an Era of Global Finance', in M. Cameron and M. Molot, (eds), *Canada Among Nations, 1994–95: Democracy and Foreign Policy* (Ottawa: Carleton University Press).

——(1995c) 'Explaining the Globalization of Financial Markets: Bringing States Back In', *Review of International Political Economy*, 2, pp. 315–41.
——(1996a) 'Post-Globalization: Is the Financial Liberalization Trend Likely to Be Reversed?' in R.Boyer and D.Drache, (eds), *States Against Markets: The Limits of Globalization* (New York: Routledge).
——(1996c) 'International Political Economy and the Greens', *New Political Economy* 1: pp. 59–78.
——(1997) 'One Money, One Nation: Territorial Currencies and the Nation-State', ARENA Working Paper (Oslo: University of Oslo).
——(1998) 'Electronic Money: A Challenge to the Sovereign State?', *Journal of International Affairs* 51: pp. 387–409.
——(1999a) 'Sovereignty, Territoriality and the Globalization of Finance', in D. Smith, D. Solinger and S. Topic (eds), *The State and Sovereignty in the World Economy* (London: Routledge).
——(1999b) 'Liberalism, State Power and the Regulation of Illicit Activity in Global Finance', in R. Friman and P. Andreas (eds), *The Illicit Global Economy and State Power* (New York: Rowman & Littlefield).
——(2000) 'Globalization and Haute Finance: Deja vu?', in K. McRobbie and Kari Polanyi Levitt, (eds), *Karl Polanyi in Vienna: The Contemporary Significance of the Great Transformation* (Montreal: Black Rose Books, 2000), pp. 12–31.
Henning, C. R. (1994) *Currencies and Politics in the United States, Germany, and Japan* (Washington, DC: Institute for International Economics).
Hewson, M. and T. J. Sinclair (eds) (1999) *Approaches to Global Governance Theory* (Albany, NY: State University of New York).
Hirschman, A. (1970) *Exit, Voice, and Loyalty* (Cambridge, Mass: Harvard University Press).
Hirst, P. and G. Thompson (1996) *Globalization in Question* (Cambridge: Blackwell).
Hobsbawm, E. (1990) *Nations and Nationalism Since 1780* (Cambridge: Cambridge University Press).
Horiuchi, A. (1980) *Nihon no Kiny Seisaku* (Tokyo: University of Tokyo Press).
Horne, J. (1985) *Japan's Financial Markets: Conflict and Consensus in Policymaking* (London: George Allen & Unwin).
Huber, E. and J. D. Stephens (1993) 'The Swedish Welfare State at the Crossroads', *Current Sweden*, p. 394.
Humphreys, B. (1994) 'International Transfer Pricing: More Important than Ever Before!' *CMA Magazine*, May, pp. 24–6.
——and A. McCrodan (1995) 'Transfer Reactions,' *CA Magazine*, September, pp. 32–4, 52.
Hymer, S. H. (1960) 'The International Operations of National Firms, A Study of Foreign Direct Investment.' PhD dissertation, Massachusetts Institute of Technology.
International Monetary Fund (1992) *Developments in International Exchange and Payments Systems* (Washington, DC: International Monetary Fund).
International Monetary Fund (1995) 'Are World Savings Adequate?' *IMF Survey* 3 July, pp. 201–09.
International Monetary Fund (1995) *International Capital Markets: Developments, Prospects, and Policy Issues* Washington, DC: IMF, August.

Iversen, T. and N. Thygesen (1998) 'Denmark: From External to Internal Adjustment', in E. Jones, J. Frieden and F. Torres (eds) *Joining Europe's Monetary Club* (New York: St Martin's Press).

Jenkins, B. (1992) *The Paradox of Continental Production: National Investment Policies in North America* (Ithaca, NY: Cornell University Press).

Barry Jones, R. J. (1995) *Globalisation and Interdependence in the International Political Economy* (London: Pinter).

Kane, E. (1981) 'Accelerating Inflation, Technological Innovation, and the Decreasing Effectiveness of Banking Regulation', *Journal of Finance*, 36, May: pp. 355–67.

——(1987) 'Competitive Financial Reregulation: An International Perspective', in R. Portes and A. Swoboda (eds), *Threats to International Stability* (Cambridge: Cambridge University Press).

——(1988) 'How Market Forces Influence the Strucure of Financial Regulation', in W. Haraf and R. Kishmeider (eds), *Restructuring Banking and Financial Services in America* (Washington, DC: American Enterprise Institute).

Kapstein, E. B. (1993) 'Territoriality and Who is "US"' *International Organization* 47, pp. 501–3.

——(1994a) *Governing the Global Economy: International Finance and the State* (Cambridge, MA: Harvard University Press).

——(1994b), 'Governing Global Finance', *The Washington Quarterly*, 17(2), Spring, pp. 77–87.

Kemp, L. (1984) *The Wardley Guide to World Money and Securities Markets* (London: Euromoney Publications).

Kenen, P. (1996) 'The Feasibility of Taxing Foreign-Exchange Transactions', in M.Ul Haq, I.Kaul and I.Grunberg (eds), *The Tobin Tax* (Oxford: Oxford University Press).

Keohane R. O. and Milner, H. V. (1996) 'Internationalization and Domestic Politics: A Conclusion', in R. O. Keohane and H. V. Milner (eds), *Internationalization and Domestic Politics* (Cambridge: Cambridge University Press).

Keynes, J. M. (1971 [1923]) *A Tract on Monetary Reform*, Volume IV from the *Collected Writings of John Maynard Keynes* (London and New York: Macmillan and St Martin's Press).

Kindleberger, C. P. (1969) *American Business Abroad* (New Haven, CN: Yale University Press).

Kindleberger, C. P. (1978) *Manias, Panics and Crashes* (London: Macmillan – now Palgrave).

Kobrin, S. J. (1987) 'Testing the Bargaining Hypothesis in the Manufacturing Sector of Developing Countries.' *International Organization*, 41 (4), Autumn: pp. 609–38.

Kral, Ken, Jack Serota, Carmen Johnson, and Price Waterhouse LLP International Tax Services (1995) 'Complying with Global Transfer Pricing Rules.' *Journal of Accountancy*, September, pp. 28–9.

Krasner, S. D. (1978a) 'United States Commercial and Monetary Policy: Unravelling the Paradox of External Strength and Internal Weakness', in P. Katzenstein, ed., *Between Power and Plenty* (Madison: University of Wisconsin Press).

——(1978b) *Defending the National Interest* (Princeton: Princeton University Press, 1978).

Krugman, P. (1993) 'What Do We Need to Know about the International Monetary System?' *Princeton Essays in International Finance* (No. 190, Princeton: Department of Economics, July).

Kurzer, P. (1993) *Business and Banking: Political Change and Economic Integration in Western Europe* (Ithaca, NY: Cornell University Press).

Langbein, S. I., 1986, 'The Unitary Method and the Myth of Arm's Length', *Tax Notes*, 17 February, 1986.

Langmore, J. (1995) 'Restructuring Economic and Financial Power' *Futures* pp. 27.

Lawrence, H. (1996) 'Regulatory Competition and the Politics of Financial Market Reform in Britain and the Japan', *Governance*, 9 (3): pp. 311–41.

Lee, D., and R. McKenzie (1989) 'The International Political Economy of Declining Tax Rates', *National Tax Journal*, 42(1) (March) pp. 79–83.

Leibfried, S. and P. Pierson (1995) 'Semisovereign Welfare States: Social Policy in a Multitiered Europe', in *European Social Policy*, edited by S. Leibfried and P. Pierson (Washington: Brookings Institution).

Leiderman, L. and M. Blejer (1988) 'Modeling and Testing Ricardian Equivalence: A Survey,' *IMF Staff Papers* March.

Lindbeck, A., P. Molander, T. Persson, O. Petersson, A. Sandmo, B. Svedenborg and N. Thygesen (1994) *Turning Sweden Around* (Cambridge: MIT Press).

Lindberg, L. and S. Scheingold, (1970) *Europe's Would-Be Polity* (Englewood Cliffs, NJ: Prentice-Hall).

Lindblom, C. (1977) *Politics and Markets: The Worlds' Political-Economic Systems* (New York: Basic Books).

Lipin, S. (1994) 'Eight Banks form Clearinghouse to Cut Cost of Foreign-Exchange Transactions.' *The Wall Street Journal*, 1 August, p. A2.

Lipschutz, R. D. (1992) 'Reconstructing World Politics: The Emergence of Global Civil Society', *Millennium: Journal of International Studies*, 21(3) Winter, pp. 389–420.

Litan, R. E. (1992) 'Nightmare in Basle: The 'Politically Incorrect Case for How the BIS Capital Standards Smothered Global Growth', *International Economy*, Nov./Dec., pp. 7–10.

Loriaux, M. (1991) *France after Hegemony: International Change and Financial Reform* (Ithaca, NY: Cornell University Press).

Louis, J.-V. (1988) 'Monetary Capacity in the Single European Act', *Common Market Law Review*, 25, pp. 9–34.

Ludlow, P. (1982) *The Making of the European Monetary System* (London: Butterworth).

Lukes, S. (1974) *Power: A Radical View* (London: Macmillan – now Palgrave).

Lyons, J. T. (1996), 'The Struggle Against International Fiscal Fraud: Tax Avoidance and Tax Evasion', *Bulletin for International Fiscal Documentation*, 50(3) (March 1996), pp. 100–4.

Machlup, F. (1965) 'Adjustment, Compensatory Correction, and Financing of Imbalances in International Payments', in R. E. Baldwin *et al*, *Trade, Growth, and the Balance of Payments: Essays in Honor of Gottfried Haberler* (Chicago: Rand McNally & Company), pp. 185–213.

Malnes, R. (1990) *The environment and duties to future generations: an elaboration of 'sustainable development'* (Oslo: The Fridjof Nansen Institute).

Mansfield, E. D. and H. V. Milner (eds) (1997) *The Political Economy of Regionalism* (New York: Columbia University Press).

Martin, R. (1994) 'Stateless Monies, Global Financial Integration and National Economic Autonomy: the End of Geography?' in *Money, Power and Space*, edited by S. Corbridge, N. Thrift and R. Martin (Oxford: Basil Blackwell).
Matthews, K. (1992) 'Could the U. S. Really Raise $45 Billion from Foreign Firms?' *Tax Notes*, 2 November, pp. 577–9.
Mauroy, P. (1982) *C'est Ici le Chemin* (Paris: Flammarion).
McCarthy, S. (1993) 'Canada's Debt', *The Toronto Star*, 21 March, p. B1.
McKenzie, C. (1992) 'Recent Developments in Japan's Financial Markets', in C. McKenzie and M. Stutchbury (eds), *Japanese Financial Markets and the Role of the Yen* (Sydney: Allen & Unwin).
McKenzie, R. and D. Lee (1991) *Quicksilver Capital* (New York: Free Press).
McNamara, K. R. (1998) *The Currency of Ideas: Monetary Politics in the European Union* (Ithaca, NY: Cornell University Press).
McNamara, K. and E. Jones (1996) 'The Clash of Institutions: Germany in European Monetary Affairs', *German Politics and Society*, 14, Fall, pp. 5–30.
McQuaig, L. (1998) *The Cult of Impotence: Selling the Myth of Powerlessness in the Global Economy* (Toronto: Viking).
Milner, H. (1988) *Resisting Protectionism* (Princeton: Princeton University Press).
Milner, H. V. and R. O. Keohane. (1996) 'Internationalization and Domestic Politics: A Conclusion.' *Internationalization and Domestic Politics*, edited by R. O. Keohane and H. V. Milner (Cambridge: Cambridge University Press).
Ministry of Finance, Banking Bureau (Kiny Seid Chsakai) and International Finance Bureau (Gaikoku Kawaseh Shingikai) (1987) 'Kiny Sakimono Torihiki no Seibe ni Tsuite' (Tokyo: Ministry of Finance).
Ministry of Finance, Financial System Research Council (1991) 'On the New Financial System', Final Subcommittee Report (Tokyo: Ministry of Finance).
Ministry of Finance, Securities Bureau, Securities and Exchange Council (1991) 'Shken Torihiki Shingikai Kihon Mondai Kenkykai Hkoku' (Tokyo: Ministry of Finance).
Ministry of Finance, Securities Bureau, Securities and Exchange Council (1987) 'Shken Sakimono Shij no Seibi ni Tsuite' (Tokyo: Ministry of Finance).
Moody's Investors Service (1992) 'Pennsylvania Turnpike Commission', *Moody's Municipal Credit Report* (New York: Moody's Investors Service), 12 August.
Moran, M. (1991) *The Politics of the Financial Services Revolution: The USA, UK and Japan* (London: Macmillan – and now Palgrave).
Moran, T. (1974) *Multinational Corporations and the Politics of Dependence: Copper in Chile* (Princeton, NJ: Princeton University Press).
Moravcsik, A. (1991) 'Negotiating the Single European Act: National Interests and Conventional Statecraft in the European Community', *International Organization*, 45 (1), Winter, pp. 19–56.
——'Why the European Community Strengthens the State: Domestic Politics and International Cooperation', *Working Paper Series #52* (Cambridge, MA: Centre for European Studies, Harvard University).
Moses, J. W. (1994) 'Abdication from National Policy Autonomy: What's Left to Leave?', *Politics and Society*, 22, pp. 125–48.
——(1995a) 'The Fiscal Constraints on Social Democracy', *Nordic Journal of Political Economy*, 22, pp. 49–68.
——(1995b) 'The Social Democratic Predicament in the Emerging European Union: A Capital Dilemma', *Journal of European Public Policy*, 2, pp. 407–26.

——(1997) 'Trojan Horses: Putnam, ECU Linkage, and the EU Ambitions of Nordic Elites', *Review of International Political Economy* 4, Summer, pp. 382–415.

——and B. S. Tranøy (1995) 'Norge i den nye verdensokonomien', in T. L. Knutsen G. Sørbø and S. Gjerdåker (eds), *Norges Utenrikspolitikk* Oslo: Cappelen, pp. 106–123.

Mundell, R. A. (1968) *International Economics* (New York: Macmillan – now Palgrave).

Mussa, M. and M. Goldstein (1993) 'The Integration of World Capital Markets', in *Changing Capital Markets: Implications for Monetary Policy* (Kansas City, KS: Federal Reserve Bank of Kansas City, 1993).

Nakaishi, A. (1991) 'The Foreign Exchange Market', in Foundation for Advanced Information and Research (ed.), *Japan's Financial Markets* (Tokyo: FAIR).

North, D. (1990) *Institutions, Institutional Change and Economic Performance* (Cambridge: Cambridge University Press).

Notermans, T. (1993) 'The Abdication from National Policy Autonomy: Why the Macroeconomic Policy Regime Has Become so Unfavourable to Labor', *Politics and Society* 21: pp. 133–67.

Nusbaum, D. (1995) 'Trading the Wide World of Foreign Exchange', *Futures*, April, pp. 62–6.

Oatley, T. H. (1997) *Exchange Rate Cooperation in the European Union* (Ann Arbor: University of Michigan Press).

O'Brien, R. (1992) *Global Financial Integration: The End of Geography* (London: The Royal Institute of International Affairs/Pinter).

Odell, J. (1982) *U. S. International Monetary Policy* (Princeton: Princeton University Press).

——(1988) 'From London to Bretton Woods; Sources of Change in Bargaining Strategies and Outcomes', *Journal of Public Policy*, 8, July–December, pp. 287–316.

O'Driscoll Jr., G. P. (1977) 'The Ricardian Nonequivalence Theorem', *Journal of Political Economy*, 85, pp. 207–211.

Organization for Economic Cooperation and Development (1963) *Draft Convention on Double Taxation of Income and Capital* (Paris: OECD).

Organization for Economic Cooperation and Development (1979) *Transfer Pricing and Multinational Enterprises* (Paris: OECD).

Organization for Economic Cooperation and Development (1984) *Transfer Pricing and Multinational Enterprises: Three Taxation Issues* (Paris: OECD).

Organization for Economic Cooperation and Development (1987) *International Tax Avoidance and Evasion* (Paris: OECD).

Organization for Economic Cooperation and Development (1996) *Model Tax Convention on Income and Capital: Condensed Version* (Paris: OECD).

Organization for Economic Cooperation and Development (1989) *Competition in Banking*, by G. Bröker (Paris: OECD).

Organization for Economic Cooperation and Development (1995) *Transfer Pricing Guidelines for Multinational Enterprises and Tax Administrations* (Paris: OECD).

Organization for Economic Cooperation and Development (1993) *Aspects of Transfer Pricing Within Multinational Enterprise:The United States Proposed Regulations*, A Report by the Fiscal Committee on the Proposed Regulations Under Section 482 IRC (Paris: OECD).

Offe, K. and Wiesenthal, H. (1980) 'Two Logics of Collective Action: Theoretical Notes on Social Class and Organizational Forms', in M. Zeitlin (ed.) *Political Power and Social Theory*, 1, pp. 67–116.

Olson, M. (1965) *The Logic of Collective Action* (Cambridge: Harvard University Press).

Oye, K. (1986) 'The Sterling-Dollar-Franc Triangle: Monetary Diplomacy 1929–1937', in K. Oye, ed., *Cooperation Under Anarchy* (Princeton: Princeton University Press).

Padoa-Schoppa, T. (1985) 'Squaring the Circle, or the Conundrum of International Monetary Reform', *Catalyst, A Journal of Policy Debate*, 1 Spring, pp. 63–72.

Padoa-Schioppa, T. (1987) *Equity, Efficiency, and Growth* (Brussels: Commission of the European Communities).

Pagan, J. C. (1993) 'Indications fo Future Policy in the Latest OECD Task Force Report', *Bulletin for International Fiscal Documentation*, 47(4), April.

——and J. S. Wilkie (1992) 'Transfer Pricing in the 1990s: Do the Latest US Developments Relate to a Global Economy?', *Bulletin for International Fiscal Documentation*, 46(6), June, pp. 299–306.

Pagan, Jill C. and J. Scott Wilkie (1993) *Transfer Pricing Strategy in a Global Economy* (Amsterdam: IBFD Publications).

Panitch, Leo (1994) 'Globalisation and the State', in R. Miliband and L.Panitch, (eds), *Socialist Register 1994*. (London: Merlin Press).

Pauly, L. W. (1988) *Opening Financial Markets* (Ithaca, NY: Cornell University Press).

——(1994) 'National Financial Structures, Capital Mobility, and International Economic Rules: The Normative Consequences of East Asian, European, and American Distinctiveness', *Policy Sciences*, 27(4), pp. 343–63.

——(1995) 'Capital Mobility, State Autonomy, and Political Legitimacy', *Journal of International Affairs* 48: pp. 369–388.

——(1997) *Who Elected the Bankers? Surveillance and Control in the World Economy* (Ithaca, NY: Cornell University Press).

Pechman, J. (1987) 'Introduction: Recent Developments', *Comparative Tax Systems: Europe*, pp. 1–32.

Penney, M. and R. Moncrieff (1995) 'UK Forex Rules: What Do the Changes Mean for U. S. Multinationals?' *International Taxation Journal*, 21(4), Fall, pp. 46–59.

Peters, B. G. (1991) *The Politics of Taxation: A Comparative Perspective* (Cambridge: Basil Blackwell).

Petit, P. (1989) 'Expansionary Policies in a Restrictive World', in P. Guerrieri and P. C. Padoan (eds), *The Political Economy of European Integration: States, Markets, and Institutions* (Herfordshire, UK: Harvester Wheatsheaf).

Pfister, T. (1985) *La Vie Quotidienne à Matignon du Temps de Pierre Mauroy* (Paris: Hachette).

Picciotto, Sol (1989) 'Slicing a Shadow: Business Taxation in an International Framework', in Leigh Hancher and Michael Moran *Capitalism, Culture and Economic Regulation* (Oxford: Clarendon Press), pp. 11–48.

Picciotto, S. (1992) *International Business Taxation: A Study in the Internationalization of Business Regulation* (New York: Quorum Books).

Pierson, P. (1996) 'The Path to European Integration: a historical institutionalist analysis', *Comparative Political Studies*, 29 (2), 123–63.

——(1994) 'The New Politics of the Welfare State,' paper presented at the Conference of Europeanists, Chicago.
——(1995) *Dismantling the Welfare State* (Cambridge: Cambridge University Press).
Polanyi, K. (1944) *The Great Transformation: The Political and Economic Origins of Our Time* (Beacon: Boston).
Pollins, B. (1993) 'Global Capital: Two Financial Booms Compared', unpublished paper.
Porter, T. (1993) *States, Markets and Regimes in Global Finance* (London: Macmillan – now Palgrave).
Porter, Tony (1996) 'Capital Mobility and Currency Markets: Can they be Tamed?', *International Journal.*
Poterba J. and L. Summers (1987) 'Finite Lifetimes and the Savings Effects of Budget Deficits', *Journal of Monetary Economics*, September.
Przeworski, A., and M. Wallerstein (1988) 'Structural Dependence of the State on Capital', *American Political Science Review*, 82(1) March, 11–30.
Quigley, M. B. (1992) 'A Commentary on How the Proposed Regulations Affect the General Principles of Section 482 . . .', *Bulletin for International Fiscal Documentation*, 46(6), June, 281–6.
Reed, Stanley, L. Holyoke and Douglas Harb (1994) 'Here Comes the Great Global Tax War', *Business Week* 30 May, pp. 55–6.
Ricardo, D. (1951) *The Works and Correspondence of David Ricardo*, edited by Piero Sraffa (Cambridge: Cambridge University Press).
Riksgäldskontoret (1994) *Statistisk Årsbok* (Stockholm: Riksgäldskontoret).
——(1997) *Statistisk Årsbok* (Stockholm: Riksgäldskontoret).
Rogowski, R. (1989) *Commerce and Coalitions* (Princeton: Princeton University Press).
Rose, R. (1986) 'Maximizing Tax Revenue While Minimizing Political Costs', *Journal of Public Policy*, 5(3), pp. 289–320.
Rosenbluth, F. (1989) *Financial Politics in Contemporary Japan* (Ithaca, NY: Cornell University Press).
Rothschild, L. W., Jr., and P. L. Rae (1989) 'Highlights of the Section 482 White Paper', *Bulletin for International Fiscal Documentation*, 43(4), April.
Rotstein, A. and C. Duncan (1991) 'For a Second Economy', in Daniel Drache and Meric Gertler (eds), *The New Era of Global Competition* (Kingston: McGill-Queen's University Press).
Rubenstein, J. M. (1992) *The Changing US Auto Industry: A Geographical Analysis.* (London and New York: Routledge).
Ruchelman, S. C. (1993) 'Transfer Pricing Regulations Issued in the United States', *Bulletin for International Fiscal Documentation*, 47(4), April, pp. 188–95.
Ruchelman, Stanley C. (1996) 'US Taxation of International Operations: Trends and New Developments.' *International Tax Journal*, 22(1), Winter, pp. 1–43.
Ruggie, J. G. (1982) 'International Regimes, Transactions and Change: Embedded Liberalism in the Postwar Economic Order', *International Organization* 36: pp. 379–415.
——(1983) 'International Regimes, Transactions and Change: Embedded Liberalism in the Postwar Economic Order', in S. Krasner (ed.), *International Regimes* (Ithaca: Cornell University Press), pp. 196–232.

Ruggie, John Gerard (1986) 'Continuity and Transformation in the World Polity: Toward a Neorealist Synthesis', in Robert O. Keohane (ed.), *Neorealism and its Critics* (New York: Columbia University Press).

Ruggie, J. G. (1993) 'Territoriality and Beyond' *International Organization*, 47, pp. 139–74.

Sandholtz, W. (1993) 'Choosing Union: Monetary Politics and Maastricht,' *International Organization*, 47, Winter, pp. 1–39.

——and J. Zysman (1989) '1992: Recasting the European Bargain,' *World Politics*, 42, October, pp. 95–128.

Sandrino, Gloria L. (1994) 'The NAFTA Investment Chapter and Foreign Direct Investment in Mexico: A Third World Perspective', *The Vanderbilt Journal of Transnational Law*, 27(2), May, pp. 259–327.

Sargent, T. (1987) *Dynamic Macroeconomic Theory* (Cambridge: Harvard University Press).

SCB [Statistiska Centralbyrån] (1995) *Statistisk Årsbok '95* (Stockholm: SCB).

Schwartz, F. (1991) *Advice and Consent: The Politics of Consultation in Japan*, PhD Dissertation., Harvard University, 1991.

Semkow, B. (1985) 'Japanese Banking Law: Current Deregulation and Liberalization of Domestic and External Financial Transactions', *Law and Policy in International Business*, 17, pp. 81–155.

——(1993) 'Japan's Financial System Reform Act', *Butterworths Journal of International Banking and Financial Law*. October: pp. 435–46.

Shirreff, D. (1993) 'Can Anyone Tame the Currency Market?', *Euromoney*, September, pp. 60–9.

——(1999) 'If it Moves, Rate it', *Euromoney*, no. 367, November, pp. 77–8.

Sinclair, T. J. (1994a) 'Passing Judgement: Credit Rating Processes as Regulatory Mechanisms of Governance in the Emerging World Order', *Review of International Political Economy*, 1, Spring, pp. 133–159.

——(1994b) 'Between State and Market: Hegemony and Institutions of Collective Action Under Conditions of International Capital Mobility', *Policy Sciences*, 27(4), pp. 447–66.

——(1995) 'Guarding the Gates of Capital: Credit Rating Processes and the Global Political Economy', PhD dissertation (Toronto: York University).

——(1999) 'Bond-Rating Agencies and Coordination in the Global Political Economy', in A. C. Cutler, V. Haufler and T. Porter (eds), *Private Authority and International Affairs* (Albany, NY: State University of New York Press).

——(2000a) 'Reinventing Authority: Embeddded Knowledge Networks and the New Global Finance', *Environment and Planning C: Government and Policy*, 18(4), August.

——(2000b) 'Deficit Discourse: The Social Construction of Fiscal Rectitude', in R. D. Germain (ed.), *Globalization and Its Critics: Perspectives from Political Economy* (London and New York: Macmillan–now Palgrave).

Smith, G. V. and R. L. Parr (1989) *Valuation of Intellectual Property and Intangible Assets* (New York: John Wiley & Sons).

Spulber, D. (1989) *Regulation and Markets* (Cambridge, MA: MIT Press).

Steinmo, S. (1993) *Taxation and Democracy* (New Haven, CN: Yale University Press).

——(1994) 'The End of Redistribution? International Pressures and Domestic Tax Policy Choices', *Challenge*, November–December.

Stephens, J. D. (1994) 'The Scandinavian Welfare States: Development and Crisis', paper presented at the International Sociological Association Meetings, Bielefeld, Germany, July.

—— E. Huber and L. Ray (1994) 'The Welfare State in Hard Times', paper prepared for delivery at the conference on the 'Politics and Political Economy of Contemporary Capitalism', University of North Carolina, Chapel Hill, 9–11 September.

Stern, G. H. (1987) 'The Federal Budget's Effects on Inter-generational Equity: Undone or Not Undone?', *Quarterly Review*, Federal Reserve Bank of Minneapolis, Winter, pp. 2–6.

Stewart, M. (1983) *The Age of Interdependence* (Cambridge, MA: MIT Press).

Stokey, N. L. and R. E. Lucas (1989) *Recursive Methods in Economic Dynamics* (Cambridge, MA: Harvard University Press).

Strange, S. (1986) *Casino Capitalism*. (Oxford: Blackwell).

—— (1988) *States and Markets* (London: Pinter).

—— (1990) 'Finance, Information and Power', *Review of International Studies*, 16(3), July, pp. 259–74.

—— (1996) *The Retreat of the State: The Diffusion of Power in the World Economy*. (Cambridge: Cambridge University Press).

Tanzi, V. (1995) *Taxation in an Integrating World* (Washington, DC: Brookings Institution).

Thelen, K. and S. Steinmo (1992) 'Historical Institutionalism in Comparative Politics', in S. Steinmo, K. Thelen, and F. Longstreth (eds), *Structuring Politics: Historical Institutionalism in Comparative Analysis* (New York: Cambridge University Press).

Thomas, K. P. (1995) 'Auto Bargaining in Canada', in S Chan (ed.), *Foreign Direct Investment in a Changing Global Political Economy* (London: Macmillan – now Palgrave).

—— (1996) 'EU Regulation of State Aid to Industry: Lessons for North America', in C. C. Paraskevopoulos, R. Grinspun and G. Eaton (eds), *Economic Integration in the Americas* (Aldershot: Edward Elgar).

—— (1997) *Capital Beyond Borders: States and Firms in the Auto Industry, 1960–94* (New York: St Martin's Press).

—— (2000) *Competing for Capital: Europe and North America in a Global Era* (Washington: Georgetown University Press).

Thomson J. and S. Krasner (1989) 'Global Transactions and the Consolidation of Sovereignty', in E. Czempiel and J. Rosenau (eds), *Global Changes and Theoretical Challenges* (Lexington, MA: Lexington Books).

Thrift, N. (1994) 'On the Social and Cultural Determinants of International Financial Centres', in S. Corbridge, N. Thrift and R.Martin (eds), *Money, Power and Space*. (Oxford: Blackwell).

—— (1996) *Spatial Formations* (London and Thousand Oaks, CA: Sage).

Tobin, J. (1978) 'A Proposal for International Monetary Reform', *The Eastern Economic Journal*, 4, pp. 153–59.

Tobin, J. (1987) 'A Proposal for International Monetary Reform', In J. Tobin, *Essays in Economics: Theory and Policy* (Cambridge and London: MIT Press), pp. 488–94.

—— (1996) 'Prologue', in Mahbub ul Haq, Inge Kaul and Isabelle Grunberg (eds), *The Tobin Tax: Coping with Financial Volatility* New York: Oxford University Press, pp. ix–xviii.

Tower E. and T. D. Willett (1976) 'The Theory of Optimum Currency Areas and Exchange Rate Flexibility', *Special Papers in International Economics* (11 Princeton, NJ: International Finance Section, Department of Economics, Princeton University).

Trentmann, F. (1998) 'Political Culture and Political Economy: interest, ideology, and free trade,' *Review of International Political Economy* 5, 2, Summer, pp. 217–251.

Truell, P. (1995) 'Britain Fines Wall St. Firm in Client Deals', *The New York Times*, May 31, p. D1.

Tsoukalis, L. (1977) *The Politics and Economics of European Monetary Integration* (London: Allen & Unwin).

Turro, J. (1993) 'Treasury's Mogle Offers Insights on New Transfer Pricing Regs', *Tax Notes*, 58(6), 8 February, pp. 683–4.

——(1992) 'Treasury Works Against the Clock on Transfer Pricing Regulations', *Tax Notes*, 57(13), 21 December, pp. 1621–2.

ul Huq, M. I. Kaul and I. Grunberg (eds) (1996) *The Tobin Tax: Coping with Financial Volatility* (Oxford: Oxford University Press).

Underhill, G. R.D. (1991) 'Markets Beyond Politics? The State and the Internationalization of Financial Markets', *European Journal of Political Research*, 19, pp. 197–225.

——(1995) 'Global Capital Markets and EU Financial Integration', Paper presented to the annual workshop of the International Political Economy Group, British International Studies Association, Political Economy Research Centre, University of Sheffield, Sheffield, England, March 31.

United Nations Centre on Transnational Corporations (1988) *Transnational Corporations in World Development: Trends and Prospects* (New York: United Nations).

United States Treasury and Internal Revenue Service (1988) *A Study of Intercompany Pricing*, Discussion Draft (18 October 1988).

Verdun, A. (1996) 'EMU-The Product of Policy Learning and Consensus Among Monetary Experts', *The European Policy Process, Occasional Paper #7* (Colchester, UK: Human Capital Mobility Network, University of Essex).

Verlage, H. C. (1975) *Transfer Pricing for Multinational Enterprises* (Rotterdam: Rotterdam University Press).

Vernon, R. (1971) *Sovereignty at Bay: The Multinational Spread of US Enterprises* (New York: Basic Books).

Vogel, S. (1996) *Freer Markets, More Rules: Regulatory Reform in Advanced Industrial Countries* (Ithaca, NY: Cornell University Press).

——(1997) 'Can Japan Disengage? Winner and Losers in Japan's Political Economy, and the Ties That Bind Them', *Berkeley Roundtable on the International Economy Working Paper* 111, December.

——(1999) 'When Interests are not Preferences: the Cautionary Tale of Japanese Consumers', *Comparative Politics*, 31(2), January, pp. 187–207.

Walkom, T. (1993) 'Debt Crisis? What Debt Crisis?', *The Toronto Star*, March 27, p. D4.

Wallerstein, M., and A. Przeworski (1995) 'Capital Taxation with Open Borders', *Review of International Political Economy*, 2(3), Summer, pp. 425–45.

Waltz, K. N. (1979) *Theory of International Politics* (Reading, MA: Addison-Wesley).

Waters, R. (1992) 'The Awesome Power of a Triple-A.' *Financial Times*. May 14, p. 21.

Watson, M. (1999) 'Rethinking Capital Mobility, Re-regulating Financial Markets', *New Political Economy*, 4(1), March.
Webb, M. C. (1991) 'International Economic Structures, Government Interests, and International Coordination of Macroeconomic Adjustment Policies', *International Organization*, 45, 3, Summer, pp. 309–342.
——(1994) 'Capital Mobility and the Possibilities for International Policy Coordination', *Policy Sciences*, 27: pp. 395–423.
——(1995a) *The Political Economy of Policy Coordination: International Macroeconomic Adjustment Since 1945* (Ithaca, New York: Cornell University Press).
——(1995b) 'International Cooperation and the Taxation of TNCs: Character and Historical Origins', paper presented at the 1995 Annual Convention of the International Studies Association, Chicago, Illinois, February.
——(1996) 'International Cooperation and the Taxation of Transnational Business: The OECD and the EU,' Paper presentated to the Annual Meeting of the American Political Science Association. San Francisco, CA, 29 August–1 September.
Weishaar, W and W. Parrish (1933), *Men Without Money* (New York, Putnam's).
Wendt, A. (1987) 'The Agent-Structure Problem in International Relations Theory', *International Organization*, 41(3), Summer, pp. 335–70.
——(1992) 'Anarchy is What States Make of It,' *International Organization* 46, Spring, pp. 391–425.
Willett, T. and C. Wihlborg (1990) 'International Capital Flows, the Dollar, and U. S. Financial Policies', in W. Haraf and T. Willett (eds), *Monetary Policy for a Volatile Global Economy* (Washington: American Enterprise Institute).
Williams, D. (1991) *Trends in International Taxation* (Amsterdam: International Bureau of Fiscal Documentation).
Williamson, J. (1977) *The Failure of World Monetary Reform* (New York: New York University Press).
Williamson, O. E. (1985) *The Economic Institutions of Capitalism: Firms, Markets, Relational Contracting* (New York: Free Press).
Winters, J. A. (1994) 'Power and the Control of Capital', *World Politics*, 46, April, pp. 419–52.
——(1996) *Power in Motion: Capital Mobility and the Indonesian State* (Ithaca, NY: Cornell University Press).
Woodall, P. (1995) 'The Myth of the Powerless State', *The Economist* 7 October.
World Commission on Environment and Development (1987) *From One Earth to One World: An Overview*, Gro Harlem Brundtland, Commission chair (Oxford: Oxford University Press).
Wriston, W. B. (1992) *The Twilight of Sovereighty: How the Information Revolution is Transforming Our World.* (New York: Charles Scribner's Sons).
Zysman, J. (1983) *Governments, Markets, and Growth: Financial Systems and the Politics of Industrial Change* (Ithaca, NY: Cornell University Press).

Index